Friends

Teacher's Book 3

Patricia Mugglestone
Ela Leśnikowska
Kasia Niedźwiecka

Longman

Contents

Introduction

Welcome to *Friends*. This introduction:
- describes how the course functions for students and teachers;
- outlines the principles on which the material was developed;
- describes the course and its components.

We hope you will find it useful and enjoy working with *Friends*!

Friends for Students

Friends is a four-level English course for upper primary and lower secondary school children, taking young learners from zero beginner to a pre-intermediate level of English competency. Students in this age range are in the transitional period between childhood and their teenage years. They are still developing intellectually and emotionally and at their own individual pace. Each level of *Friends* addresses the learning needs and interests of such students and has been specifically written for their cognitive level.

Friends Starter takes into consideration that children between the ages of nine and ten are very receptive to visual, auditory and kinaesthetic cues. They need to be offered a wide variety of exercises and activities in order to maintain their interest and motivation. It is also easier for them to learn sentences and phrases rather than complicated grammar rules. All these aspects have been reflected in the way *Friends Starter* has been designed. Language is introduced in small chunks which are easy to remember. There are many songs and games, which help students acquire grammar rules unconsciously.

Friends 1 recognises that the students are one year older and have some command of English already. Language is not presented in chunks any more but introduced step by step, which makes it easier for students to understand and remember. Songs and games help students to practise grammar in a fun way and ensure that they will not get bored during their English lessons. Students are also made aware of their learning processes in Skills boxes, which in *Friends 1* focus mainly on retaining new vocabulary.

Friends 2 and 3 acknowledge the fact that students' cognitive skills are developing and thus grammar is presented more explicitly throughout, although the fun element of songs and games is still present in the books. Students are also encouraged to take more responsibility for monitoring their learning process – Skills boxes offer useful tips on how to tackle various listening, writing, reading and speaking tasks.

The levels 'grow' with students also in terms of the topics exploited. The amount of cultural information and extra reading material is increased from four units in *Friends Starter* and *Friends 1* to eight units in *Friends 2* and *Friends 3*. Students have a chance to increase their knowledge about English speaking countries and they're provided with extra reading material to complement the lessons.

Friends for Teachers

Friends has been designed with busy teachers in mind.

Lesson preparation

The format of units in the Students' Book guarantees successful lessons. Clear headings and predictable exercise sequences make *Friends* very easy to teach with little preparation by the teacher. Extension ideas and photocopiable activities in the Teacher's Resource Book and the Activity Book offer a flexibility to the basic pattern of the lesson. Culture and Reading Corners provide extra material, which can be used as a break during grammar based lessons.

The Activity Book offers further exercises for homework. As the exercises strongly reflect themes and language from the Students' Book input, teachers don't need to spend too much time on explaining the homework tasks to their students.

Evaluation and assessment

Teachers are now expected to monitor students' progress and make regular assessments, which has greatly increased an already heavy workload. *Friends* provides support for assessment in each Teacher's Resource Book, which contains photocopiable tests. Yet more tests are available in the Test Books. The Test Books offer extra help with assessment by supplying ready-to-use charts for keeping records of students' grades.

Dealing with mixed-ability classes

One of the most difficult issues teachers are faced with are mixed-level classes. *Friends* offers support with this problem. For very able students, more challenging exercises are included in the Activity Books in the Use Your English section. For the best students there are extra activities in the Tests Books. Weaker students will benefit from the substantial amount of revision throughout *Friends*, the Check Yourself tests and the initially slow pace of the course. Projects and the play will allow all students to contribute to the class, irrespective of their abilities. Even the weakest students can participate and enjoy a sense of real success.

Friends has been designed for varied teaching situations. Students will range from zero beginners to pupils who have had up to five years of English in primary school. For this reason *Friends* offers two possible entry points. Students can either follow a slower and less demanding path by starting with *Friends Starter,* or a steeper path starting with *Friends 1*.

Friends Starter entry is suitable for complete beginners or students who have had a small amount of exposure to English, perhaps through oral work or songs. *Friends 1* is a suitable entry point for students who have experienced a minimum of two years of primary English. While these students are still very young, they can now cope with the more difficult aspects of *Friends 1* due to their previous exposure to the language. The first half of *Friends 1* covers the same grammatical items as *Friends Starter*, but with a wider scope of knowledge and lexis; the second half introduces new language. *Friends 2* and *3* also start from a thorough revision of the previous level. This system helps weaker students become more confident learners, and more talented students have a chance to become fluent.

We hope you will find it useful and enjoy working with *Friends*!

Principles behind the course

1 Motivating students

Memorable materials

Language is made memorable through interesting and motivating materials. For this reason great care has been taken in *Friends* to present language items in distinct thematic unit types. There are three such unit types in *Friends Starter*, and four thematic unit types in the other books in the series. In this introduction, the different thematic units are called 'strands'. The four strands in *Friends 3* are:

- **The Londoners**   The first strand follows the lives of a group of school friends living in London. Students can identify with the Londoners, who are of the same age as them. Through this strand students learn the language they need for everyday situations. Students also learn about life in Great Britain.
- **Crazy Reporters**   In the second strand, two cartoon characters interview a succession of eccentric characters, allowing language items to be presented in a humorous context. Students always enjoy humour and the language is made memorable to them through funny situations, songs and jokes.
- **Friends' Club**   The third strand is a magazine for friends around the world. The magazine is run by two editors and features letters and interviews from children all over the world. Students can expand their knowledge about the world as well as identify with the lives of other children at a similar age.
- **Story Time**   In the fourth strand, four fiction stories are used to introduce new language items. Each story is written in a different style. There is a 'teen romance', a magical story in an everyday setting, a dramatic tale set in Viking times and the story of a rock band's road to riches. As the students become involved in the stories, the new language items are imprinted on their minds for easy recall.

Fun in *Friends*

In addition to the four strands which make the book very varied, *Friends* is bursting with new ideas, activities and exercises which are so interesting that students will be tempted to read the book and do the exercises in advance! The book has songs, chants, games, puzzles, projects, quizzes and a play to perform. The very high quality of photos, illustrations and audio material will add to students' motivation and desire to learn. These factors make *Friends* lively and inspiring, and in such a rich context language is easier to remember.

2 The three-step methodology

Each input unit is divided into three steps – *Presentation*, *Comprehension* and *Practice*. These clear headings make the teaching sequence very easy to follow. The type of *Presentation* differs according to strand. It is either a photo story, a cartoon, a magazine with letters and interviews or an episode of a story. *Comprehension* tasks are varied and include matching, multiple-choice exercises, true/false sentences and answering questions. *Practice* sections progress from guided exercises to freer activities towards the end of the lesson as students become more confident with the new language they are learning. Activities exploit listening, reading, writing and speaking, and thus as well as practising the new function or grammar item, they also practise the four skills.

3 A strong grammatical syllabus

While *Friends* is a multi-syllabus course, covering communication, vocabulary and skills, special emphasis has been placed on the grammar syllabus. Grammar is introduced methodologically and gradually. It is always followed by thorough practice exercises. This approach organises the framework of the language in the minds of the students.

The Activity Book units offer the unique feature of a Language Diary, which complements the Students' Book units. This is where students can check their understanding of grammar and reinforce it.

Finally, attention is also paid to exceptions to grammar rules and common mistakes for young learners. *Be careful* boxes highlight potential grammatical errors. Subsequent activities then help eradicate such mistakes in students' work.

4 Teaching vocabulary

Vocabulary is taught in a highly controlled manner. New words are presented in the Presentation sections. No new words are introduced in the Activity Book or in the Revision sections. The very few new words used in the Culture and Reading Corners are introduced in the context of illustrations. Numerous exercises in the input units, Revisions and the Activity Book help students to retain the new words.

New words are presented and practised in lexical sets; this makes it easier for students to remember them. In the Activity Book these sets of words are listed in the Language Diaries. In this way students are encouraged to record vocabulary systematically and meaningfully.

5 An emphasis on skills

The four skills of listening, speaking, reading and writing are all systematically treated throughout the input units, but there are also special sections in the Students' Book (Culture Corners and Reading Corners) and in the Activity Book (Skills Corners) where the four skills are consolidated. No new grammar items are presented in these units, so students can focus on the skills themselves. For the same reason, the vocabulary in the Culture, Reading and Skills Corners is carefully controlled.

In addition, there are ten 'skills boxes' throughout the Students' Book which focus on particular skills: listening, speaking, reading, writing and dictionary use. They contain practical and useful tips on how to improve skills such as listening for detail, guessing words from context, linking ideas, etc. Each box is followed by an exercise to practise that specific skill.

For further exposure to the spoken and written language outside the classroom, plenty of reading and writing is provided in *Friends* to consolidate oral work.

6 *Friends* Reading Programme

Although all four skills are thoroughly developed in *Friends*, there is special emphasis on reading. Reading is an especially important skill as it enables students to become independent learners. Through reading, students learn new vocabulary and spelling, recycle grammar and learn how to structure written texts. The Reading Programme in *Friends 3* has been developed in recognition of the importance of reading, and it consists of:

- Story Time strand – four captivating stories introduce students to fiction;
- four Reading Corners – introduce students to Penguin Readers;
- eight Skills Corners in the Activity Book focus on reading.

The interest in the stories in the course encourages students to have a positive attitude to reading outside the classroom.

7 Communication Programme

Speaking is the most difficult skill to teach and it requires a lot of practice. *Friends* offers step-by-step speaking development, from very controlled exercises which practise the language to less guided activities and games. A photocopiable speaking activity is included for each unit, there are games in the Revision sections and there are projects in the Culture and Reading Corners. In addition to all of these components there is a play which is designed in such a way that all students in the class can participate. All of these activities require pair work or group work. They develop speaking as well as communication skills. They create an environment for co-operation and friendship in the classroom.

8 Exposure to the culture of English-speaking countries

There are two Culture Corners in *Friends Starter* and *Friends 1* and four Culture Corners in *Friends 2* and *Friends 3*. They introduce students to the idea of English being spoken in many countries, not just Great Britain. By introducing children from these countries, students become familiar with the lifestyle of their friends around the world.

9 Testing system

Frequent testing and evaluation gives students a sense of achievement and prepares them for difficult exams in the future. It is also a source of information for teachers as to whether remedial teaching is necessary. The *Friends* testing system comprises:

- Check Yourself tests in the Activity Book;
- Check Tests in the Teacher's Resource Book;
- A and B Language Tests in the Test Book;
- A and B Skills Tests in the Test Book.

Check Yourself tests and Check Tests test the same material and are a short and quick way of assessing progress.

Tests in the Test Book have an UCLES exams orientation. In addition to Language tests, which cover every module, there are Skills Tests after every two modules.

The grading chart which is included in the Test Book introduction offers a way of evaluating students that shows how they do separately in every skill and in grammar and vocabulary. Using the chart, teachers can easily find out about their students' strong and weak points and can be more constructive in their feedback.

10 Building confidence

Building confidence has also been given special consideration in *Friends*, as it is a very important factor for young students who are just starting to learn a language.

The input units all follow the same pattern so that students can quickly recognise and learn what is expected of them. Activities are as simple as possible to set up and rubrics are clear and short. This helps students to feel in control of their learning and therefore confident.

Most importantly, the expectations of the *Friends* course are realistic for students of this age. The objectives of each lesson are achievable and the exercises are manageable. The number of new words introduced is controlled to make them manageable. Nothing seems too difficult to understand to the students and their confidence is reinforced for successful learning.

The components of the course

The components at each level are:
- a Students' Book;
- an Activity Book;
- a Teacher's Resource Book;
- a set of class cassettes;
- a Test Book with a cassette.

They have been very carefully planned to create a coherent system of materials catering to all of a teacher's and a student's needs. The chart *How does Friends work?*, on page 6, shows the links between the components of *Friends 3*.

How does Friends work?

Students' Book

Activity Book

Teacher's Resource Book

Test Booklet

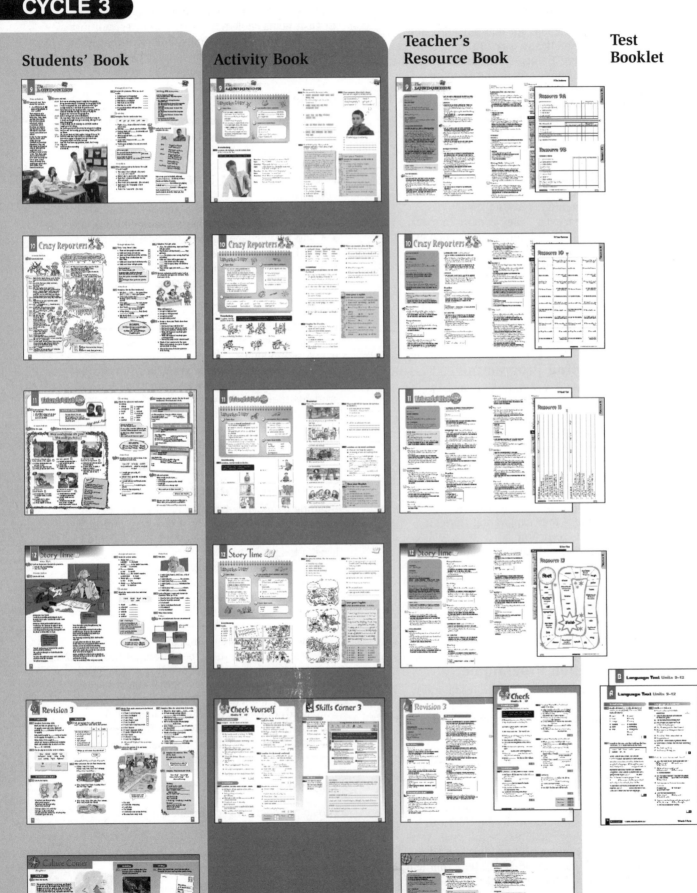

Students' Book

Activity Book

Teacher's Resource Book

Test Booklet

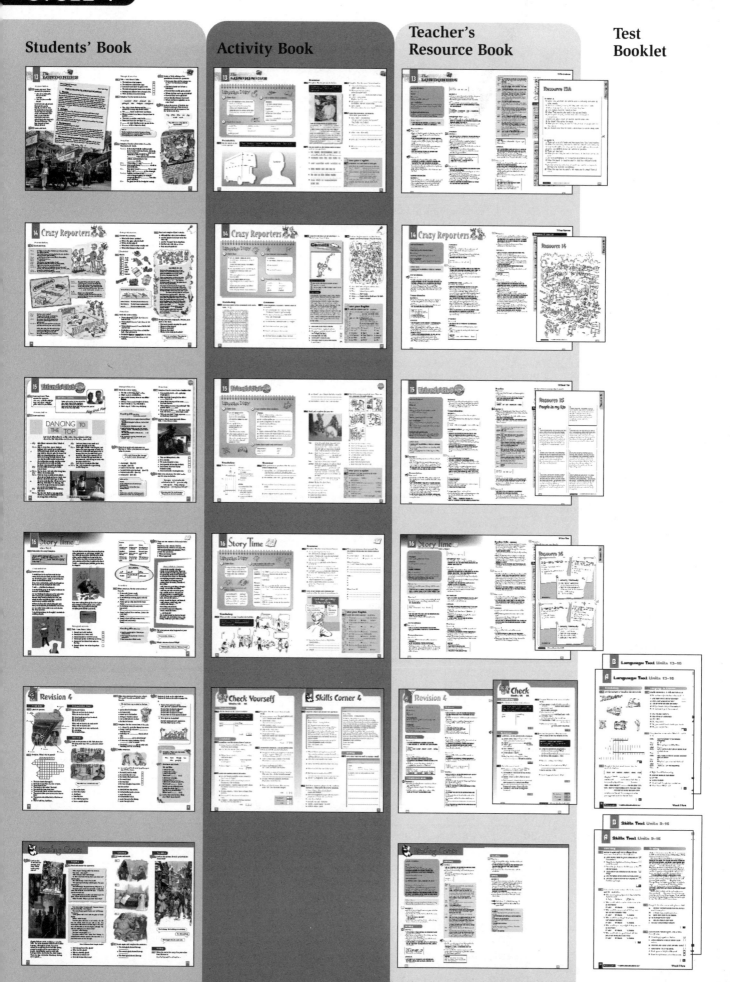

Students' Book contents

Components

The Students' Book

The *Friends 3* Students' Book contains eight modules. Each module consists of four input units where language items are introduced and practised. Each of the four input units is part of a distinct strand. **The Londoners** follows the everyday life of four school friends from London. The **Crazy Reporters** interview a succession of eccentric characters in humorous situations. **Friends' Club** presents letters and interviews with children all over the world. **Story Time** includes four stories: *Summer Meeting*, *Make a Wish*, *The Story of Magnus*, and *The Streetboys*.

Every module is followed by a **Revision** unit, which recycles material from the module. Revision units are divided into Vocabulary, Pronunciation chant, Grammar and Fun Time or Song Time sections.

Every Revision is followed by a **Reading Corner** or **Culture Corner** – an integrated skills lesson in which all four skills are systematically exploited.

In addition to the above, the Students' Book contains:
- **Play** for the end of the year school performance;
- **Word list** – organised unit by unit and covering all the vocabulary of *Friends 3*;
- **Irregular verbs** – a table with the Infinitive, Past Simple and Past Participle forms of all irregular verbs occurring in the Students' Book.

1 Specific features of the Students' Book input units

Warm up

Most units in *Friends 3* begin with a warm-up activity, which introduces the main topic of the unit to the students. In The Londoners it's often an informative text about London or the Londoners' lifestyles; in Friends' Club it is an Editors' Letter introducing the main topic of the unit; and in Story Time it's Remember the Story!, which summarises previous episodes of the story.

Presentation

The four thematic 'strands' expose students to a variety of text types. Target language is presented in a meaningful and interesting context, making learning a pleasurable experience. The dialogues or texts are always recorded and can be presented in a variety of ways. You may decide that students should listen to them first with their books closed or that they should follow the text in the books. It is advisable to play the recording twice or make students repeat the phrases of the dialogues so that they can read or act them out fluently.

Comprehension

Every input text is followed by a comprehension exercise, which develops understanding. It is a very important step, which helps teachers to see if students understood the text or dialogue and whether some words or phrases still need to be explained. There are several types of comprehension exercise – questions, true/false sentences, multiple-choice and matching tasks.

Vocabulary

New words are presented and practised in lexical sets; this makes it easier for students to remember them. Each cycle presents at least two new sets of vocabulary. In the Activity Book these sets of words are listed in the Language Diaries. In this way students are encouraged to record vocabulary systematically and meaningfully.

Language boxes

Language boxes serve to focus on new language items introduced in the presentation texts and dialogues. Language boxes usually follow the comprehension exercises. However, in some cycles of the Students' Book, there are examples of Language boxes preceding comprehension exercises because students will need the new structure in order to answer the comprehension questions. In some units there are two Language boxes.

Be careful boxes

These boxes highlight special difficulties in order to help students avoid certain language errors.

Skills boxes

These boxes help students with specific skills (listening, reading, writing and speaking) as well as dictionary use. There are ten such boxes throughout the Students' Book. They contain practical and useful tips on how to improve skills such as listening for detail, guessing words from context, linking ideas, etc. Each box is followed by an exercise to practise that specific skill.

Practice

All Language or Be Careful boxes are followed by practice exercises. Grammar exercises consolidate the target structure. They also enable the teacher to see if students are able to manipulate the target language. They start from very controlled practice, which is a comprehension of the box, and move on to freer exercises at the end of the lesson. The Practice exercises are varied and are listening, speaking and writing exercises. They can be done individually, in pairs or in groups.

Listening exercises

Listening exercises play an important role in **Friends**. As well as helping students to develop strategies to understand spoken discourse, they also help students to expand their knowledge and experience of the sound system, rhythm, intonation and stress of English. There is a variety of listening exercises in **Friends**, some of which check the general comprehension of the text and some of which train students to listen for specific information.

Speaking exercises

These exercises are designed so that students will be able to practise words and structures that they have just met. More able students will also be able to express themselves more freely.

As students' linguistic resources develop and their confidence increases, the emphasis of speaking exercises gradually changes from practice of the underlying grammar or structure to freer oral expression in communicative contexts.

In addition to the speaking exercises in the Students' Book, in the Teacher's Resource Book there is a photocopiable communication activity to go with each input unit. The activity gives yet another opportunity to recycle the vocabulary and grammar introduced in the unit and build students' confidence in speaking.

Writing exercises

Students practise and consolidate vocabulary and structures from the lesson in these exercises. Clear examples are given and tasks are carefully controlled, but there is also scope for more able students to express themselves more freely. It is very likely that the written tasks will be used for homework but it is useful to do some writing exercises in class so that you can monitor and help students while they work.

Songs

The songs focus on, or consolidate, new language items. They are often used for listening activities but they can also be sung and chanted by the students. The songs and chants in the input unit are linked to the content or topic of the particular unit in which they occur, so they can be a meaningful and enjoyable part of the lesson for the students.

2 Specific features of the Students' Book Revision units

Revising material very often is very important at this young age. Revision sections are after every four input units in *Friends 3*.

Vocabulary revision

Vocabulary exercises in Revision sections consolidate vocabulary from the whole module. By using various types of exercise (organising words into sets according to topic, dealing with synonyms and antonyms, selecting odd words, matching words and definitions, labelling pictures, word searches, completing texts with the missing words, crosswords) they help students to remember the vocabulary better.

Pronunciation

Pronunciation exercises are worthwhile activities because clear, intelligible pronunciation can be achieved by young learners. In *Friends 3* the emphasis is on intonation and stress. In every Revision unit there is a recorded chant for the students to learn. These chants are designed to be fun, so that the students can enjoy themselves while practising their pronunciation. They provide an important change of pace for the lesson and a chance to relax.

Grammar revision

Grammar sections consolidate the language from the input units. The exercises are very varied and very often practise language through games and activities.

Fun Time & Song Time

In every Revision unit there is a song or a game. Each song is followed by its 'karaoke' version, recorded so that the students can sing along to the background music. As for the karaoke versions of the play songs, at the end of the play there is only the karaoke version of the last song, 'Baby, baby'. The karaoke versions of the first three songs are recorded in the Revision sections: song 1, 'I used to be sad …' (see Revision 4); song 2, 'If I could make a wish …' (see Revision 3); song 3, 'I was walking down the street …' (see Revision 1).

At the end of each Revision unit, after completing the relevant section in the Activity Book and Check Yourself test, teachers may wish to set one of the relevant photocopiable tests from the Teacher's Resource Book.

3 Specific features of the Students' Book Culture and Reading Corners

Both Culture and Reading Corners are a vehicle for skills practice. The four skills are practised thoroughly. Grammar structures and vocabulary from previous input units are recycled and new lexical items are controlled to enable students to focus on skills development and increasing fluency.

Culture Corners allow students to learn about and engage in cultural topics through the medium of English.

Reading Corners introduce short stories to show students that they can read and understand quite long and complicated texts at their level.

Projects

Some Reading and Culture Corners contain projects. These provide students with opportunities to work individually, in pairs or in groups on a piece of work which incorporates their own ideas. All of the students' projects, not just the best ones, should be displayed, so as to encourage less able students.

Students' Book cassettes

The class cassettes contain all the recorded material from the Students' Book. This includes all presentation texts, listening comprehension exercises, pronunciation exercises, songs and chants.

Activity Book

The Activity Book exercises are intended to be used for homework. However, if time allows, they can be done in class and treated as an additional revision of the unit. Certain parts of the Activity Book, such as Skills Corners, require the teacher's guidance, particularly when they are done for the first time. They may contain exercise types that have not been introduced in the Students' Book.

Friends 3 Activity Book contains the following sections:

Input units

The input units in the Students' Book have corresponding double page units in the Activity Book. Each unit in the Activity Book opens with a **Language Diary**, which is a summary of the lesson. If possible, the teacher should read through the Language Diary with the students before they work on it alone. The Language Diary comprises the following sections:

• **I know that ...** A brief explanation of the grammar points, with clear examples.

• **I can ...** Grammar boxes or sentences to complete, or a place for students to write their own examples. Students should be able to complete these boxes without referring to the Students' Book. However, there is always the Students' Book to check in case of doubt.

• **I know these words ...** New vocabulary for students to remember from the unit. They can translate these words into their first language.

The Language Diary should be treated as a personal section, which helps students to better remember new language. Students might be allowed to do the exercises in the Language Diary on their own, or alternatively teachers might want to ask students to do these during a lesson as a preparation for homework. It is also meant to help them do the exercises that follow.

The Language Diary is then followed by the exercises organised in **Vocabulary** and **Grammar** sections, which reflect the Students' Book Revisions.

There is a **Use your English** exercise at the end of each unit. This is an exam-oriented type of exercise, which is also quite difficult and could be treated as an extra activity for better students.

Check Yourself tests

Every cycle of four units is followed by a one-page self-assessment test. Through these regular tests teachers can encourage students to evaluate their own progress and understand what they need to review. On completion of the test, students evaluate themselves using the key from the back of the Activity Book.

Please note that there are corresponding tests in this Teacher's Resource Book. The Check Yourself tests and the Teacher's Resource Book Check tests are A and B versions of the same test. The tests in the Activity Book should be treated as practice before the 'real' test.

Skills Corners

Every Check Yourself page is followed by a Skills Corner page. Its aim is to practise reading and writing skills. No new vocabulary is introduced in these pages; the aim is to consolidate language from the previous units and to present and practise known language in different contexts.

Friends 3 Game

The game at the back of the Activity Book is a summary of material from the Students' Book. Students ask each other questions about information acquired during the course. The questions are based on the different strands, and students are referred to the appropriate units (if necessary), for example: *How old is Stonehenge?* (The Londoners), *Where is the Channel?* (Crazy Reporters), *Who founded Microsoft?* (Friends' Club), *What kind of film was made in 'Summer Meeting'?* (Story Time).

Test Book

In addition to the tests in this Teacher's Resource Book, the Test Book offers additional Language Tests and Skills Tests. The task types are similar to the ones in UCLES exams, particularly at KET level. The tests allow teachers to keep a thorough and regular check on students' progress and to evaluate the need for remedial teaching. As they test skills as well as grammar and vocabulary, they provide an opportunity to assess students' progress in all areas of language learning, including listening.

Both the Skills Tests and Language Tests have two versions – A and B. These two versions can be used so that students sitting next to each other are not able to copy. Alternatively, Test A can be used first and Test B can be used to check improvement after remedial teaching.

The following sections are in the Test Book:
- **Introduction**, which offers help with grading students;
- **Language Tests** There are eight Tests A and eight Tests B. They revise each cycle of the Students' Book;
- **Skills Tests** There are four Tests A and four Tests B. They revise every two cycles of the Students' Book;
- **Extra tasks** There are eight extra tasks related to Language Tests and four extra tasks related to Skills Tests. These tasks are meant to help teachers deal with mixed-level classes. They can be given to the very talented students who complete the tests earlier than the rest of the class and would like to get top grades;
- **Tapescripts** and **key**.

Please note that the tests are accompanied by a cassette.

Key to symbols

    Exercise recorded on class cassette.

    Exercise recommended as pair work.

    Exercise recommended as group work.

Refer to another component.

The LONDONERS

Lesson objectives

Structures
Present Simple and Present Continuous
Present Continuous for temporary arrangements

Functions
Talking about favourite television programmes

Key vocabulary
TV programmes: *advertisement, cartoon, documentary, film, news, quiz, soap*

Background information
'BBC' stands for British Broadcasting Corporation. The other three main TV channels are ITV (Independent Television), Channel 4 and Channel 5. If you have a TV in your home, you must pay an annual TV licence fee to the government. Cable and satellite channels usually have a subscription system of payment.

Before class
- Make a copy of Resource 1A (page 120) for each S. Copy and cut up Resource 1B (page 121), so Ss have one information card each.
- Bring a short video clip of your favourite TV programme to show the class (Exercise 7 Extension).

Presentation

Exercise 1
- Ask Ss to read the two questions and see if they can guess how many main TV channels there are in Great Britain.
- Play the recording once for Ss to read and listen.
- Check Ss' answers to the first question and see how many of them guessed the correct answer.
- Ask the class how many TV channels there are in their country. Ask Ss to name the channels.

> **Answer**
> Five main TV channels in Great Britain

Extension
- Play the recording again for Ss to listen and read and answer these questions:
  What kind of programmes are on cable and satellite channels? (cartoons, news, documentaries, soaps)
  Which two channels do not have advertisements? (BBC1 and BBC2)

Exercise 2
- Ask Ss to look at the picture and talk about what they can see and what the young people are doing.
- Play the recording twice for Ss to listen and read. Ask Ss to name the people in the picture, e.g.

'Who is the boy?' (Mark) 'Who's sitting on the sofa?' (Kim) 'Who's got a glass of orange juice?' (Vicki)

Comprehension

Exercise 3
- Ask one of the Ss to read out the example in sentence 1.
- Tell Ss to refer back to the dialogue as they complete the sentences with the names.
- Check Ss' answers by asking individuals to read out the sentences.

> **Answers**
> 2 Kim   3 Mark   4 Rob   5 Kim   6 Mark

Vocabulary

Exercise 4
- Before doing the matching exercise, ask the class to repeat the words after you. Pay particular attention to word stress in the polysyllabic words. (1 ad*ver*tisement   2 car*toon*   3 docu*men*tary)
- Ss work in pairs, doing the matching exercise.

> **Answers**
> b 5   c 7   d 3   e 6   f 1   g 4

Language box   Present Simple and Present Continuous
- Read out the sentences in the Present Simple column to the class.
- Then, elicit more sentences from the class, using the Present Simple and the time expressions to talk about routines and general facts.
- Ask one of the Ss to read out the sentences and time expressions in the Present Continuous column.
- Then, elicit more sentences from the class, using the Present Continuous and the time expressions to talk about what is happening now and temporary arrangements.

Extension
- Ask Ss to close their books.
- Write on the board four of the time expressions, e.g. *always, sometimes, now, today*. In pairs, Ss write down four sentences using the time expressions. Go round and monitor the activity, checking that Ss use the correct verb tense.
- Each pair can then choose one of their sentences to read out to the class.

Be careful
- Read out the sentence to the class. Ask Ss if they can remember any other verbs that do not use the Present Continuous, e.g. *love, hate, know*.

Practice

Exercise 5

- Ask two Ss to read out the first two speeches of Kim and Vicki in the dialogue.
- Ss work individually, completing the dialogue with the correct forms of the verbs.
- Play the recording twice for Ss to listen and check their answers.

> **Answers**
> 2 know   5 records   8 are you looking
> 3 ask   6 Do you like   9 is he doing
> 4 are showing 7 is/are showing 10 is shouting
> (Numbers 4, 9 and 10 are also correct in the
> contracted form: 4 're showing 9 's he doing
> 10 's shouting)

Exercise 6

- Give Ss time to read through the sentences before you play the recording. Play the recording twice for Ss to complete the exercise.
- Check Ss' answers by playing the recording again, pausing after each answer.

> **Tapescript**
> **Mark:** Hello?
> **Rob:** Hi, is that Mark? It's Rob here.
> **Mark:** Yes, hello, Rob. What are you doing?
> **Rob:** Talking to you!
> **Mark:** Oh, ha, ha, ha. What are you doing apart from that?
> **Rob:** Well, I'm not really doing anything. We haven't got a television at the moment. We're waiting for a new one. It's awful. I'm really bored. Do you want to come round?
> **Mark:** I'd like to, Rob, but I'm watching *Star Trek*.
> **Rob:** Are you? Oh, no! That's my favourite programme! I always watch it!
> **Mark:** Actually they're showing advertisements right now. Why don't you come and watch the second half with me?
> **Rob:** Brilliant! Thanks, Mark. I'm coming right now.

> **Answers**
> 2 ✗ 3 ✗ 4 ✓ 5 ✓

Exercise 7

- Ask two of the Ss to read out the exchange.
- Elicit from the class suggestions for more questions to ask about TV programmes, e.g.: 'Which channel is it on?' 'When is it on?' 'Who is your favourite character?'
- Ss work in pairs, asking and answering questions about their favourite TV programmes. Go round and monitor the activity, paying particular attention to the correct use of the Present Simple and the Present Continuous.
- The class can then find out which TV programme the majority of them like best.

Extension

- The class could ask you questions about your favourite programme and then watch a short clip of that programme.

Resource 1 (pages 120–121)

Interaction: whole class
Exercise type: information gap
Aim: to practise Present Simple and Present Continuous, all forms
Language: Who lives at number 4? Where does Mr Brown live? What does Mr Waters usually do in his free time?

- Give each student a copy of Resource 1A and one information card from Resource 1B.
- Tell your Ss that the neighbours who live at Park Road usually do many interesting things but tonight they are all at home watching TV.
- The aim of the game is to find out who lives in each house (1–4), what they do in their free time and what TV programme they are watching now.
- Ss first write three pieces of information they have on their own card under the appropriate picture in Resource 1A (except for Emma and Tim Brown). The fourth piece will have to be discovered in the course of the game.
- Ss walk around the classroom asking questions, giving answers and completing Resource 1A. They mustn't look at each other's notes.
- Once Ss finish and are back at their desks, ask individual Ss to report to the class on what they learnt, e.g. 'Who lives at number 1?', 'Tell me about John.', etc.

> **Answers**
> House 1: John (F) – plays basketball, *cartoon*
>   Sally (I) – goes to the cinema, cartoon
> House 2: Mrs Waters (G) – goes for a walk, *documentary*
>   Mr Waters (B) – works in the garden, documentary
>   Chris Waters (D) – *listens to music, documentary*
> House 3: Emma (E) – *talks on the phone,* soap
> House 4: Mrs Brown (H) – *cooks dinner,* quiz
>   *Mr Brown* (C) – reads newspapers, quiz
>   Tim Brown (A) – reads books, quiz
>   Sue Brown (J) – does her homework, *quiz*

> **Activity Book Answers**
> **Language Diary**
> **2**
> general facts, now, temporary arrangements
> **Exercise 1**
> *across:* advertisement, documentary
> *down:* soap, quiz, news, film
> **Exercise 2**
> 2 are watching 3 visits 4 forgets 5 is staying
> 6 are/'re doing
> **Exercise 3**
> 2 doesn't live 3 is learning 4 is taking 5 lives
> 6 goes
> **Exercise 4**
> 2 are/'re watching 3 am/'m cooking 4 Do you like
> 5 Do you usually eat 6 usually sit 7 is finishing
> 8 don't want
> **Exercise 5**
> 2 Is 3 am 4 is 5 At 6 not

2 Crazy Reporters

Lesson objectives

Structure
Present Continuous for future arrangements

Functions
Talking about future arrangements

Key vocabulary
Going on holiday: *campsite, ferry, luggage, postcard, sightseeing, tent*

Background information
People can cross the English Channel by ferry, hovercraft or the channel tunnel (Eurotunnel). The channel tunnel between Folkestone and Sangatte (near Calais) was officially opened in May 1994. The trip takes about 35 minutes.

Before class
- Make a copy of Resource 2 (page 122) for each group.

Presentation
Exercise 1
- Ask the class to look at the pictures and describe the appearance of the characters and what they are doing. Ask Ss if they can predict what this unit is going to be about and why it is described as 'crazy'.
- Play the recording twice for Ss to listen and read the text.

Comprehension
Exercise 2
- Look at the example with the class. Ask Ss to look back at the dialogue in Exercise 1 and find and read out the sentences which tell us that George is not on holiday now but will be on holiday in the future ('Tomorrow morning he's going on a very crazy … holiday', 'Well, I'm going to France').
- Ss then continue the exercise.
- When checking Ss' answers, ask them to correct the false statements.

Answers
2 ✓   3 ✓   4 ✗   5 ✓   6 ✗

Vocabulary
Exercise 3
- Ask one of the Ss to read out the example.
- Ss complete the exercise working individually.
- Ss can compare answers in pairs before checking answers as a class. When checking answers, get the class to repeat the words after you.

Answers
2 ferry   3 campsite   4 sightseeing   5 luggage
6 postcard

Language box   Present Continuous for future arrangements
- Ask Ss if they can remember what functions of the Present Continuous they practised in Unit 1 (actions happening now and temporary arrangements). Explain that Unit 2 presents another function (talking about future arrangements) of the Present Continuous.
- Ask individual Ss to read out the sentences in the box.
- Ask the class to look back at the dialogue in Exercise 1 and find and read out other examples of the Present Continuous used for future arrangements, e.g. 'I'm going to France'.
- If appropriate for your class, compare these sentences with those using *will* (e.g. 'I'll go out and explore'). Remind Ss that we use the Present Continuous, not *will*, to say what somebody has already arranged or decided to do in the future. (Ss practise using *will* in Unit 9).

Practice
Exercise 4
- Give Ss time to read through the diary before you play the recording.
- Play the recording twice for Ss to listen and circle the correct arrangements.
- Check Ss' answers by playing the recording again, pausing after each answer.

Tapescript

Claire: When are you going to France, George?
George: I'm catching the ferry next Saturday.
Claire: Are you sleeping on the ferry?
George: No, I'm sleeping in a little French hotel. They've got a garden for Dobbin. Then on Sunday we're going to a campsite.
Claire: Is it in Paris?
George: No, but it is near Paris.
Claire: And Monday? Are you having a rest?
George: Oh, on Monday I'm exploring the countryside. Then on Tuesday I'm going to Paris.
Claire: Are you leaving Dobbin at the campsite?
George: No, I'm not. He likes big cities.
Claire: What are you doing on Wednesday?
George: I'm meeting some French friends. But we're not going to their house. They're coming to the campsite.
Claire: What's happening on Thursday? Are you sightseeing?
George: No, I'm going shopping. I want to buy some French cheese. Then on Friday we're going back home to England. We're just catching the ferry.
Claire: Well, have a great holiday, George. Send us a postcard!
George: OK, I'll do that.
Claire: Next week, we're finding out about a very strange and crazy sport. But that's all for now, so goodbye from Harry and me.
Harry: Bye!

Answers
Sunday/near   Monday/explore countryside
Tuesday/with   Wednesday/campsite
Thursday/go shopping   Friday/catch ferry

Exercise 5

● Ask one of the Ss to read out the first sentence of the text. Then, elicit suggestions from the class for the next sentence.
● Ss complete their paragraphs working individually.
● Check Ss' answers by asking two or three Ss to read out their paragraphs.

Suggested answers
They are sleeping in a hotel. On Sunday, they are going to a campsite near Paris. On Monday, George is exploring the countryside. On Tuesday, George is exploring Paris with Dobbin. On Wednesday, George is meeting some French friends at the campsite. On Thursday, George is going shopping. On Friday, they are catching the ferry home.

 ## Exercise 6

● Ask Ss to talk about what they can see in the pictures.
● Play the recording twice for Ss to listen and put the pictures in the correct order.
● Check Ss' answers by playing the recording again, pausing after each picture description.

Tapescript
Harry: I hope you liked our interview with George and Dobbin. Now we'd like to tell you about our plans for the next few weeks.
Claire: Next week we're finding out about a very strange bicycle race.
Harry: Yes, and then the week after that, we're presenting a TV quiz show. I'm very excited about that!
Claire: Then we're interviewing some twins with a good idea.
Harry: Well, a crazy idea!
Claire: Yes, well, and then the week after that we're talking to a schoolgirl about her new website.
Harry: Then we're talking to a lady called Claris. She has made a lot of very crazy things. That'll be an interesting interview.
Claire: After that we're interviewing a man in a tree.
Harry: That's right. And finally we're talking about food.
Claire: Good. That'll be the best one. I like food.
Harry: Hmm, let's wait and see.

Answers
2 d   3 g   4 e   5 a   6 f   7 c

 ## Extension

● In pairs, Ss choose one of the pictures and guess what could be crazy about the person or the situation.
● The pairs then report back to the class and see how many different ideas they have thought of. As Ss work through the course, they can find out if any of their ideas are correct.

 ## Exercise 7

● Read out the instructions and the example diary entry to the class. Check that Ss understand that they have to write two crazy entries in their own diaries. Elicit some suggestions for crazy diary entries from the class so that all the Ss have some ideas to work from.
● Ss write their diaries for the next week.
● Then, in pairs, Ss ask each other about their arrangements for the next week and try to spot their partner's crazy things. Go round and monitor the activity.

Resource 2 (page 122)

Interaction: whole class or groups of seven
Exercise type: information gap
Aim: to practise the Present Continuous for future arrangements – all forms
Language: What is Harry doing on Tuesday?
● Give each S a copy of a page from Harry's diary. Ss will complete his diary for this week.
● Ss walk around the classroom asking questions, giving answers and making notes. Make sure that Ss don't look at each other's notes.
● Once Ss complete the missing information and are back at their desks, ask comprehension questions, e.g. 'What are Harry's plans for the weekend?', 'What is he doing on Tuesday?'

Answers
Monday: Basketball training.
Tuesday: Meet Claire and write an article for 'Crazy Reporters'.
Wednesday: No school! Trip to the Natural History Museum.
Thursday: Visit grandparents.
Friday: Cinema with Dan, film 'Billy Elliot'.
Saturday: Help Mum with shopping/tidy up my room.
Sunday: Dad's birthday – big garden party at home.

Activity Book Answers
Language Diary
2
Students' own answers
Exercise 1
2 luggage   3 tent   4 ferry   5 campsite
keyword: sightseeing
Exercise 2
2 How is he going round Paris? He is/'s going round Paris by tourist bus.
3 Is he having lunch in the Eiffel Tower? No, he is/'s having lunch on the River Seine.
4 Who is he meeting at half past two? He is/'s meeting (his) friends.
5 Where is he going at four? He is/'s going to/visiting the Louvre museum.
6 How is he going back to the campsite? He is/'s catching the train back to the campsite.
Exercise 3
2 are/'re going   3 are/'re making   4 are/'re working
5 are/'re buying   6 Are we staying
Exercise 4
Students' own answers
Exercise 5
2 best   3 campsite   4 sailing   5 reporter
6 shopping

3 Friends' Club

Before class
- Copy and cut up Resource 3 (page 123) for each group of Ss.
- Tell Ss they are going to write about a famous person they admire in this unit. Ask Ss to bring in a picture of the famous person they choose (Exercise 9).

Exercise 1
- Read the instruction to the class.
- Ss then listen to the recording and read the text.
- Encourage the class to say what they know about Linda McCartney, Nelson Mandela and Bill Gates.

Presentation

Exercise 2
- Play the recording twice for Ss to listen as they look at the pictures and read the text. Then ask Ss to talk about what they can see in the pictures.

Comprehension
Exercise 3
- Ss work individually, referring back to the text and writing down the answers to the questions.
- Check Ss' answers by asking pairs of Ss to read out each question and answer.

> **Answers**
> 1 He formed his own company, Microsoft.
> 2 Because it made personal home computers possible.
> 3 1998
> 4 ninety-seven million dollars
> 5 He gives it to charity.

Vocabulary
Exercise 4
- Ask Ss to look at sentences 1–6 and to repeat the adjectives after you.
- Ss can do the exercise working in pairs.

> **Answers**
> 2 e 3 b 4 f 5 a 6 c

Language box Past Simple
- Ask individual Ss to read out the positive, negative and question sentences in the box.
- Read through the time expressions with the class and then ask Ss to make sentences using some of the time expressions, e.g. 'My sister left university a year ago.'

Extension
- Write some verbs that have irregular Past Simple forms on the board and ask Ss to make sentences using these verbs in the Past Simple: *make, go, buy, eat, drink, come, write.*

Practice
Exercise 5
- Ask one of the Ss to read out the first two sentences of the text. Elicit from the class the answer to item 2. (became)
- Ss then complete the exercise working individually.
- Check Ss' answers by asking individuals to read out the complete sentences of the text.

> **Answers**
> 2 became 3 took 4 met 5 didn't like 6 weren't
> 7 got 8 learned/learnt 9 formed 10 did 11 wrote

Exercise 6
- Ask one of the Ss to read out the example.
- Ss work individually, writing out the questions.
- Check that the questions are correct before Ss work in pairs, asking and answering the questions.

> **Answers**
> 2 What was her first job? She was a (professional) photographer.
> 3 When did she meet Paul? She met him in 1967.
> 4 Which musical instrument did Linda play? She played the keyboard.
> 5 What did they call their band? They called their band 'Wings'.
> 6 What other interests did she have? She was interested in animal charities and cooking.

Listening Skills: predicting
- Read out the tips in the Listening Skills box.
- Ask Ss to look back at the pictures on page 8 and the questions in Exercise 3 in this unit. Encourage Ss to say what they predicted from the pictures and what facts they needed in order to answer the questions (and what information they didn't need).

Exercise 7

- Work through the three questions with the class.
- For question 1, encourage Ss to pool their knowledge about Nelson Mandela.
- For question 2, Ss can work in pairs, brainstorming vocabulary to describe the picture.
- For question 3, ask one of the Ss to read out the example question and answer. Encourage the class to guess the answers to the remaining questions.

Exercise 8

- Play the recording twice for Ss to listen and answer the questions.
- Check Ss' answers by asking pairs of Ss to ask and answer each question.

> **Tapescript**
> **Ally:** Jake, why did you choose Nelson Mandela?
> **Jake:** I live in South Africa, and Nelson Mandela is my hero.
> **Ally:** Why is he your hero? Please tell us about him.
> **Jake:** Well, he was born in 1918, in a small village near my home town. In those days, South Africans with black skin did not have very much freedom. They were usually poor and their children often didn't go to school. This situation made some people very angry, and Mandela became the leader of this group of people.
> **Ally:** Was his family poor?
> **Jake:** No, he didn't come from a poor family. He was lucky, because he went to school and university. But a lot of important people didn't like him and he went to prison many times. The last time, he stayed there for 28 years. Imagine that! 28 years in prison! When he finally came out of prison, in 1990, he quickly became a leader again. This time, people listened to him. Four years later he became the president of my country, at the age of 76. He was president for five years and in that time he travelled all over the world. He always taught that people must learn to live together. These days, life is very different for black people in my country, because Nelson Mandela was so brave all those years ago.

> **Suggested answers**
> 2 They didn't have much freedom. They were usually poor. The children often didn't go to school.
> 3 No. ('he didn't come from a poor family', but we don't know how rich his family were)
> 4 He went to prison.
> 5 He became president.

Extension

- Play the recording again and ask Ss to listen for extra information, e.g. When was Nelson Mandela born? Was he born in a city?
- After Ss have listened to the recording, ask them to say what else they remember about Nelson Mandela.

Exercise 9

- In pairs, ask Ss to show their pictures of famous people and describe them for a few minutes.
- Tell Ss they can write about a famous living or dead person. Advise them to refer back to Sally's letter in Exercise 5 for useful expressions to use in their own paragraph, e.g. *I really admire*, *He/She was born*, *At first*, *In* (1967), etc.

Resource 3 (page 123)

Interaction: group work
Exercise type: responding to text clues; guessing
Aim: to practise the Past Simple – all forms
Language: Is it a man or a woman? When was he/she born? What nationality was he/she? Did he/she discover something? Was he/she a politician/actor/writer?

- Before the activity make sure that your Ss know all the words which describe the people on the cards (e.g. *mathematician, radioactivity, scientist, inventor, explorer, sailor, radium, prototype*).
- Divide the class into groups of three Ss.
- Give each group a set of cards from Resource 3. Make sure that the cards are face down.
- *Option 1:* Ss draw cards from the set one by one and describe the person without giving his/her name away. The others in the group guess who it is.
- *Option 2:* Ss draw cards from the set one by one. The other Ss ask ten questions trying to guess who the person on the card is.

Extension

- Ask your Ss to prepare their own sets of cards. They can use the blank cards which are at the bottom of Resource 3. Encourage Ss to find interesting clues about the lives of famous people.

> **Activity Book Answers**
> **Language Diary**
> **2**
> Students' own answers
> **Exercise 1**
> 2 famous 3 talented 4 generous 5 fantastic
> 6 fascinating
> **Exercise 2**
> 2 a 3 e 4 f 5 c 6 d
> **Exercise 3**
> 2 loved 3 didn't join 4 wanted 5 didn't want
> 6 joined 7 played 8 became 9 married
> **Exercise 4**
> 2 was he in prison
> 3 did he leave prison
> 4 did he become President of South Africa
> 5 was he
> 6 did he get married for the third time
> **Exercise 5**
> Students' own answers
> **Exercise 6**
> 2 when 3 did 4 did 5 ago 6 last

Lesson objectives

Structures
Past Simple and Past Continuous

Function
Setting a scene

Key vocabulary
Verbs: *blush, continue, giggle, hurry, jump, laugh, notice, shout, throw*

Background information
'Summer Meeting' is a two-part story about a group of young people in the summer holidays. It deals with a situation experienced by many young people – being a newcomer and wanting to make friends with an established group. The main characters are Harriet (who has just moved into the seaside town with her parents), Scott (a friendly, popular boy) and Jilly (one of Scott's friends, who fancies him). In the first episode, the group of friends see Harriet on the beach. Scott is the only one who is friendly towards Harriet and introduces himself. However, the next day Harriet overhears Scott talking to his friends and saying that she was 'nobody special'.

Before class
- Depending on the option, copy and cut up Resource 4 (page 124) for each pair or group of three Ss.
- Ask Ss to bring a copy of a picture or photo from a magazine that could illustrate the opening scene of a story. Show them an example of what you have in mind and bring some pictures/photos yourself in case some of the Ss' pictures are not suitable (Exercise 6 Extension).

 Exercise 1
- Remind Ss of the predicting skills they practised in Unit 3 (page 9).
- In pairs, Ss predict what this story is about by using clues from the title and the picture. Tell Ss they can find out if their predictions are correct in the next exercise.

Presentation
 Exercise 2
- Give Ss more practice in using predicting skills by asking them to read through the sentences in Exercise 3 so that they know what information they need before they listen to the recording.
- Then play the recording twice for Ss to listen and follow the text in Exercise 2.

Comprehension
Exercise 3
- Advise Ss to refer back to the text in Exercise 2 to help them decide which words to circle.
- Check Ss' answers by asking individuals to read out the complete sentences.

> **Answers**
> 2 watching   3 Scott   4 Scott's   5 reading a book
> 6 heard

Extension
- Give the class one minute to study the text in Exercise 2 again.
- Ss then close their books and take turns to give more facts about the first day of the story and the following day, e.g. 'The sun was shining. Scott and his friends were playing volleyball. Harriet and Scott felt terrible at the end of the second day.'

Language box Past Simple and Past Continuous
- Ask individual Ss to read out the sentences in the box.
- Ss may find it helpful to understand the difference between continuous and completed actions if you draw timelines on the board to illustrate the sentences, e.g.:

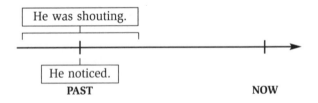

Exercise 4
- Read out the first sentence to the class.
- Ss complete the exercise working individually.
- They can compare answers in pairs before checking answers as a class.
- If any of the Ss have problems with the answers, tell them to refer to the Language box to help them.

> **Answers**
> 2 was telling a funny story
> 3 were listening and laughing
> 4 was reading a book/sitting on the sand

Practice

Exercise 5

- Advise Ss to quickly read through the text before they start completing it with the verbs.
- Ss do the exercise working individually.
- Check Ss' answers by asking individuals to read out the complete sentences.

Answers	
2 looked	7 was listening
3 was raining	8 was buying
4 didn't go	9 saw
5 went	10 didn't say
6 was looking	11 walked

 ### Exercise 6

- Ask one of the Ss to read out the first three sentences of the text, including sentence d.
- Advise Ss to quickly read through the text before they start completing it with sentences a–f.
- Ss can compare answers in pairs before listening to the recording and checking their answers.

Answers
2 b   3 c   4 f   5 e   6 a

Extension

- If you and/or the Ss have brought in pictures or photos to illustrate the opening scene of a story, put Ss in pairs or groups of three and ask each group to choose one picture/photo.
- Ss may find it helpful if you demonstrate the activity yourself. Hold up one of the pictures and narrate the start of a story to match the picture.
- Each pair or group works together writing the opening scene to match their picture. Go round and monitor the activity, helping with vocabulary where necessary and pointing out any serious errors that need correcting.
- Then display all the pictures for the class to see. Each group reads out their paragraph and the rest of the class guesses the picture to match the story.

Resource 4 (page 124)

Interaction: pair work or group work
Exercise type: ordering events in a story
Aim: to practise the Past Simple, the Past Continuous and narration

- Before the activity, make sure that your Ss understand all the words in the story, e.g. *knock, policy, lie, kitten.*
- Tell the Ss that they are going to reconstruct a story that is in 18 parts which aren't in order.
- Divide the class into pairs or groups of three. Give a set of cards to each pair or group. Together they have to put the story into its correct order. This can be done as a race to see which pair or group can complete the exercise first. The correct order of the story is shown in Resource 4, reading left to right.

Activity Book Answers
Language Diary
2
2 c   3 a   4 b
Exercise 1
2 b   3 d   4 a   5 e   6 f
Exercise 2
1 were swimming   2 was watching, noticed
3 were talking, shouted   4 said, left
5 was telling, saw   6 were talking, was standing
Exercise 3
2 was riding   3 saw   4 was talking   5 looked
6 turned   7 ran
Exercise 4
1 ... were playing volleyball.
2 Jilly was reading on the beach when she heard her name.
3 She looked up.
4 Some friends were calling her.
5 Jilly put down her book.
6 Then she jumped up and ran towards the group.
Exercise 5
Students' own answers
Exercise 6
2 was resting   3 Did you catch   4 bought
5 was shining   6 was doing

Revision 1

Vocabulary

Exercise 1
- Ask Ss to look at the picture and guess the man's age, nationality and occupation.
- Ss work individually, finding five more adjectives in the word snake.
- Ss can compare answers in pairs before checking answers as a class.
- After checking Ss' answers, ask Ss to make sentences using the adjectives, e.g. *My aunt is very generous. She gives me some money every time she sees me.*

Answers
famous   fascinating   generous   successful   talented

Exercise 2
- Read out the example sentence to the class.
- Ss work in pairs, giving an example of each type of TV programme.
- The pairs then report back to the class and see how many different programmes they have thought of in each category.

Exercise 3
- Ask the class to look at the picture while one S reads out the example in sentence 1.
- Advise Ss to read through the whole text before starting to complete it. Ss do the exercise working individually.
- Check Ss' answers by asking individuals to read out the sentences and spell the missing words.

Answers
2 tent   3 postcard   4 luggage   5 ferry

Pronunciation chant

Exercise 4
- Ask Ss to look at the picture and say what they can see in the suitcase.
- Explain that the syllables in bold type in the chant are the stressed syllables. Play the recording and ask Ss to listen carefully to the stress and rhythm of the sentences.
- Then play the recording again for Ss to listen and repeat the chant. If Ss have problems with the pronunciation of any sounds or words, ask them to say those sounds or words after you.

Extension
- Divide Ss into teams of three or four.
- Give Ss a few minutes to practise the chant in their groups, before presenting it to the class to see which group is the best.

Grammar

Exercise 5
- Ask one of the Ss to read out the example in sentence 1. Remind them that we use the Present Simple to describe habits and routines.
- Ss complete the exercise working individually.
- Check Ss' answers by asking individuals to read out the sentences.
- After checking Ss' answers, remind them of the pronunciation practice in Exercise 4 and ask them to work out the stress patterns in sentences 3, 7 and 8. Some of the Ss then say these sentences again using the correct stress patterns.

Answers
2 are you laughing   3 does he come from
4 do you have   5 's raining   6 Are you going
7 don't go   8 am staying

Exercise 6
- Read out the instructions to the class and ask two Ss to read out the example question and answer. Remind Ss to use the Present Continuous for future arrangements in their diaries.
- Ss work in pairs, Student A reading the diary on page 13 and Student B reading the diary on page 104. If you have an odd number of Ss in the class, have a group of three Ss and let the weaker pair share the part of Student A.
- Go round and monitor the activity, paying particular attention to the use of the Present Continuous.
- Some of the pairs say their dialogues for the class to hear. Ss can find out if they all chose the same time to meet.

Exercise 7

- Ask two Ss to read out the example item and complete the answer.
- Ss complete the exercise working individually.
- Check Ss' answers by asking individuals to read out the sentences.

Answers
1 got up
2 phoned, didn't answer, were you doing
3 was doing, remembered
4 went, did you buy
5 saw, were you wearing
6 were waiting, came

Exercise 8

- Advise Ss to read through each mini-dialogue before they start completing it.
- If you wish, Ss can do the exercise in pairs and practise reading the dialogues aloud in their pairs.
- Check Ss' answers by asking some of the pairs to read out the dialogues.

Answers

2 am/'m doing	8 saw
3 Do you usually do	9 was sitting
4 are coming	10 Did you speak
5 did you go	11 was standing
6 Did you go	12 saw
7 were flying	13 didn't notice

 Song Time

- Elicit when the action in the song takes place (the past) and what tenses could be used (Past Continuous and Past Simple).
- Ask Ss, in groups of four or five, to think of appropriate collocations to complete the gaps in the song. Go round and monitor. If you wish, ask some groups to tell the class their alternatives.
- Play the recording twice, so Ss can compare their ideas with the song and complete the gaps.

Answers
1 was walking   2 saw   3 was driving   4 when

 Extension

- Ask Ss to write another verse for the song in groups of four or five.
- Ss then swap groups and tell their new group their verse. The class can vote on the best one.

 Check Yourself Units 1–4 – Activity Book page 10

 Check Units 1–4 – Teacher's Book page 111

 Language Tests A/B Units 1–4 – Test Book pages 6–9

Culture Corner

Scotland

Lesson objectives

Skills

To practise reading for factual information
To guess the meaning of unknown vocabulary from contextual clues
To practise listening for main facts in a story
To write a story

Key vocabulary

Scotland: *bagpipes, Ben Nevis, Gaelic, Hogmanay, island, kilt, legend, loch, Nessie, tartan, tattoo, thistle*
Robert Bruce: *cave, spider, web*

Background information

Robert Bruce (1274–1329) became King Robert I of Scotland in 1306. The battle referred to in the text is the Battle of Bannockburn (1314).

Before class

If you have any pictures/postcards or objects (e.g. a piece of tartan) from Scotland bring them to the lesson to show the class (Exercise 1).

Reading

 ### Exercise 1

- Ask Ss to look at the map and photographs and say what they know about Scotland. If you have any pictures or objects from Scotland, show these to the Ss and talk about them.
- Use the pictures in the book to revise or present vocabulary, e.g. *loch, castle, mountain*.
- Play the recording, pausing after each section of text, for Ss to listen and read the text. After each section of text, ask one or two comprehension questions, e.g.:
  Section 1: 'What is Nessie?' 'How high is Ben Nevis?'
  Section 2: 'Is a kilt a pair of trousers?' 'Who wears kilts?'
  Section 3: 'Does everyone in Scotland speak Gaelic?' 'What are two Gaelic words?'
  Section 4: 'Where is the festival in Scotland?' 'What is New Year's Eve in Scottish?'
- Play the recording again without pausing between the sections.

Exercise 2

- Ask Ss to say the words (a–g) after you to practise pronunciation.
- Look at the example item with the class.
- Ss complete the exercise working in pairs. Tell them to refer back to the text in Exercise 1, if they wish.

Answers

2 f   3 a   4 g   5 e   6 b   7 d

Speaking

 ### Exercise 3

- Check that Ss understand the meaning of *legend* by asking them to give examples of legends in their own country.
- Ask Ss to look at the pictures and repeat the words (*cave, spider, web*) after you.
- Ask Ss to look at the picture of the man. Tell them his name is Robert. Ss describe his appearance and guess how he is feeling. Ask Ss when they think this story happened.
- In pairs, Ss read the four questions and discuss possible answers.
- The pairs then exchange ideas as a whole class. At this stage don't tell Ss if their ideas are correct or not.

Listening

 ### Exercise 4

- Give Ss time to read through the questions before you play the recording.
- Play the recording twice for Ss to listen and answer the questions.
- Check Ss' answers by playing the recording again, pausing after each answer.

Tapescript

The story of Robert Bruce.
England and Scotland weren't always friends. In the old days, they had different kings and queens and the Scots hated the English and the English hated the Scots. Well, Robert Bruce was the king of Scotland, about 800 years ago, and he was fighting the English. The English soldiers were winning, and Robert Bruce hid from them in a cave. He stayed there for three months. He was sad and frightened and he wanted to run away from Scotland. Then he noticed a spider in the cave. It was building a huge web. The spider fell down many, many times, but it tried again and again. After a long time it finished the web. Robert Bruce said, 'I will try again too!' He went back to his men and said, 'Be strong! We can do it!' After that, they won an important battle against the English.

Answers

1 The king of Scotland   2 the English   3 no
4 in a cave   5 to run away from Scotland
6 a spider building a web
7 He went back to his men and won the battle.

- After checking Ss' answers, play the recording again and ask Ss to listen for extra information.
- Ss then tell the class what extra facts and information they can remember.

Writing

Exercise 5

- Read out the instructions and example sentences to the class. Point out that each paragraph uses some of the answers from Exercise 4.
- Ss work individually, writing out the story of Robert Bruce in three paragraphs. Go round and monitor the activity, pointing out any errors to be corrected.
- Ss then form pairs or groups of three and read each other's stories to see how different or similar they are.
- One or two individual Ss can then read out their stories to the class.

'Nessie' cartoon

- Ask Ss to look at the cartoon at the bottom of the page. Ask them:
  1: What does the photographer think he is seeing? (a monster)
  2: What is he really seeing? (a diver and his snorkel)
- Ask Ss if they have heard of any 'monsters' that are supposed to live in their country.
- Have they seen any photographs of monsters or ghosts? What do they think is the explanation?

 Skills Corner 1 – Activity Book page 11

> **Activity Book Answers for Skills Corner 1**
> **Exercise 1**
> A 5   B 2   C 4   D 1   E 3
> **Exercise 2**
> Students' own answers

5 The LONDONERS

Lesson objectives

Structures
Present Perfect and Past Simple

Functions
Asking and answering questions about things you have done in the past

Key vocabulary
Phrases with *get* and *have*: *get lost/ready, have a (great) time/lunch/a rest/a ride*

Background information
Leeds Castle in Kent has been called 'the loveliest castle in the world'. It has been a Norman stronghold, a royal residence of six of England's medieval queens and a palace of Henry VIII. Today, it is a popular tourist attraction and hosts events such as open-air concerts, banquets and weddings, balloon weekends, golf and conferences.
  More information about British castles can be found at www.castles-of-britain.com.

Before class
- Make a copy of Resource 5 (page 125) for each pair of Ss.
- Ask Ss to bring four or five pictures of places they have visited in their country or abroad, e.g. castles, churches, sports centres, seaside towns, cities, mountains (Exercise 5 Extension).

Presentation

Exercise 1
- Ask Ss to look at the pictures and talk about what they can see.
- Ask one of the Ss to read out the two questions.
- Play the recording for the class to listen and read the text.
- Ss then answer the first question (How old is Leeds Castle? About one thousand years old), and discuss the answer to the second question (Are there many castles in your country?).
- Check that Ss understand the meaning of *maze* before going on to Exercise 2.

Exercise 2
- Give Ss practice in using predicting skills by asking them to read through the true/false sentences in Exercise 3 so that they know what information they need before they listen to the recording.
- Then play the recording twice for Ss to listen and follow the text in Exercise 2.
- Ask Ss where the children are (in the centre of the maze).

Comprehension

Exercise 3
- Read out the example item to the class. Ask Ss to find and read out the part of the text that gives the answer (Vicki: 'I think this is the most fantastic place I've ever seen.').
- Ss complete the exercise working individually and referring back to the text to find the answers.
- When checking Ss' answers, ask them to correct the false statements and to read out the parts of the text that give the true statements.

> **Answers**
> 2 ✓ 3 ✗ 4 ✗ 5 ✓ 6 ✓

Vocabulary

Exercise 4
- Tell the class that this exercise practises the use of phrases with *have* and *get*. Ask one of the Ss to read out the example in sentence 1. Then elicit examples of other adjectives to go with the expression *I had a ... time* (e.g. *good/bad/ interesting/difficult/exciting*).
- Ss complete the exercise working individually.
- Check Ss' answers by asking individuals to read out the complete sentences.

> **Answers**
> 2 ride   3 ready   4 rest   5 lost   6 lunch

Extension
- Ss work in pairs, writing down different adjectives to complete the sentences. The pairs can then take turns reading out their sentences:
  1 I'm tired. I'm going to have ... (a sleep/a bath/ a shower).
  2 I'm hungry. Let's have ... (dinner/our picnic/ some sandwiches).
  3 Don't get ... (upset/angry/cross/impatient) again.

Language box Present Perfect and Past Simple
- Ask individual Ss to read out the two sets of sentences. Check that Ss remember that the Past Simple is used with a 'finished' time (e.g. *yesterday*) and to ask 'When?' or 'What time?' something happened. The Present Perfect is used when we talk about a time in the past until now (e.g. *Have you ever got lost?*).
- Ask Ss to look again at the sentence *I haven't seen so many balloons before* and to write the same sentence using *never*. (I've never seen so many balloons.)

Extension

- Ask Ss to look back at the text in Exercise 2 and to find and read out more sentences using the Past Simple (My mum *asked* for some information.) or the Present Perfect (I've never *been* in a maze before).

Practice

Exercise 5

- Advise Ss to read through each dialogue first before completing it. Ss do the exercise working individually.
- Check Ss' answers by having individuals read out the complete dialogues.

> **Answers**
> 2 have   3 did you go   4 went   5 have/'ve seen
> 6 did you see   7 saw   8 Did you like

- If appropriate, draw Ss attention to the short answer in question 2 and explain that it is also correct and natural to use this form, rather than repeating the whole phrase, *Yes, I have been to the USA*.

Extension

- Write on the board:
  Have you ever … ?   Yes, … ./No, … .
  When … ?   I … .
  What was it like?   It was … .
- Ss use the four or five pictures they have brought to class. They take turns to show their partner their pictures and ask and answer questions about the places. Go round and monitor the activity, paying particular attention to the correct use of the Past Simple and the Present Perfect.

Exercise 6

- Read out the instructions for Exercises 6, 7 and 8 to the class so that Ss are aware of the sequence of activities in these exercises.
- Read through the list of items in the 'Have you ever' column of the table in Exercise 6 and check that Ss understand them all.
- Ask two Ss to read out the example exchange.
- Ss work in pairs, taking turns to ask and answer the questions and to fill in the 'yes/no' column for their partner. Go round and monitor the activity.

Exercise 7

- Ask two Ss to read out the example dialogue. Elicit suggestions from the class for more questions and answers, e.g.:
  'What was it like?'
  'What was the best thing about it?'
  'Who did you go with?'
  'How long did you stay there?'
- Ss work in pairs, taking turns to ask their partner about all the 'yes' items in Exercise 6. Go round and monitor the activity.
- Some of the pairs can then say one of their dialogues for the class to hear.

Exercise 8

- Read out the instructions and example sentences to the class. Elicit suggestions for completing the second sentence.
- Ss work individually, writing about one of their partner's 'yes' answers and using the information they talked about in Exercise 7. Go round and monitor the activity, pointing out errors that need correcting.
- Each pair of Ss then forms a group of four with another pair. In turn, each S reads out their text to their group and their partner says if the information is correct.

Resource 5 (page 125)

Interaction: pair work
Exercise type: matching
Aim: to practise the Present Perfect and the Past Simple

- Tell the Ss that they are going to check whether they understand the difference between when the Present Perfect and the Past Simple tenses are used.
- Give a copy of Resource 5 to each pair of Ss. Their task is to match the verb forms (A or B) with the sentences provided. When they finish, each pair should present what they have decided and justify their choice.
- If you want to make the activity more competitive, give a point for each correct answer and see which pair is a winner.

> **Answers**
> 1B, 2A (yesterday)
> 3A (When), 4B (before)
> 5A (last week), 6B (ever)
> 7B, 8A (last year)
> 9A (a minute ago), 10B
> 11B (before), 12A (on our last school trip)
> 13A (had), 14B (Let's have)
> 15B, 16A (yesterday)
> 17A (last night), 18B

> **Activity Book Answers**
> **Language Diary**
> **2**
> Students' own answers
> **Exercise 1**
> 2 d   3 b   4 e   5 c   6 a
> **Exercise 2**
> 2 She hasn't been there before.
> 3 Have they lost him?
> 4 They haven't had lunch.
> 5 They have/'ve brought sandwiches.
> 6 They have/'ve enjoyed the morning.
> **Exercise 3**
> 3 did you get   4 got   5 Have you ever broken
> 6 have   7 did you break   8 broke
> 9 Has he ever been   10 hasn't   11 has/'s never left
> **Exercise 4**
> *Vicki:*
> 2 She saw elephants at the Bristol Zoo.
> 3 Yes, she has. It was for Art./It was the first prize in the Art competition.
> *You:* Students' own answers
> **Exercise 5**
> 2 went   3 left   4 have saved   5 hasn't been
> 6 haven't done

6 Crazy Reporters

Lesson objectives

Structures
Present Perfect: *just, already, yet*

Functions
Describing a race

Skills
Speaking: useful phrases

Key vocabulary
Racing: *champion, cheer, fall off, (starting/finishing) line, overtake, race, record, slow down, title, track, wave, wobble*

Background information
A *mollusc* is one of a class of animals with soft bodies and often hard shells, e.g. oysters, mussels, cuttlefish, snails and slugs.
Jake's new world record of being the slowest man on two wheels would be a suitable entry in the *Guinness Book of Records*, a collection of unusual records, e.g. the tallest person, the greatest number of people in a car, the oldest tortoise.

Before class
- Make a set of pictures from Resource 6 (page 126) for each pair or group.

Presentation
Exercise 1
- Find out how many of the class like cycling and if any of them have entered races. ('Did they enjoy racing?' 'Did they win?')
- Ask the class to look at the big picture of Jake and describe his appearance.
- Ask the class to look at the set of small pictures and see if they can guess what the story is about. Ss can then check their guesses as they listen and read.
- Play the recording twice for Ss to listen and read the text.
- Check Ss' general comprehension by asking: 'Why is Jake called "the Snail"?' 'Does he win the race?'

Comprehension
Exercise 2
- Ss work individually, referring back to the text and putting the pictures in the correct order.

Answers
2 c   3 e   4 a   5 b   6 d

Vocabulary
Exercise 3
- Ask Ss to repeat the words in the box after you to practise pronunciation.
- Ask one of the Ss to read out the example in sentence 1.
- Ss complete the exercise working individually.
- Check Ss' answers by asking individuals to read out the complete sentences.

Answers
2 track   3 line   4 record   5 title   6 champion

Language box   Present Perfect: *just, already, yet*
- Ask individual Ss to read out the sentences in the box illustrating positive, negative and questions. Draw Ss' attention to the position of *just, already* and *yet* in the sentences.
- Ask Ss to look back at the text in Exercise 1 and find and read out more sentences with *just, already* and *yet*.
- If any of the class ask about the use of *already* and *just* in questions, tell them that this is possible. Give them some examples, e.g.:
  Has the race just/already started?
  Has he just arrived?
  Has he already told her?

Practice
Exercise 4
- Ask one of the Ss to read out the example in sentence 1.
- Ss complete the exercise working individually.
- They can compare answers in pairs before checking answers as a class.

Answers
2 has already heard the story
3 hasn't finished yet
4 has just won the race
5 has already broken the record three times

- Depending on your class, you could point out that the auxiliary verb can also be contracted in 2, 4 and 5, especially in spoken English.

Extension
- Ask the class to look back at the pictures in Exercise 1. Ss work in pairs, choosing one of the pictures and writing a detailed description (five or six sentences) of what is happening in the picture. Go round and monitor the activity, helping with vocabulary where necessary and pointing out any errors to be corrected.
- The pairs can then form groups of four or six and read out their descriptions to each other.

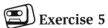 **Exercise 5**

- Give Ss time to read through the statements before you play the recording.
- Play the recording twice for Ss to listen and decide if the statements are true or false.
- Check Ss' answers by playing the recording again, pausing after each answer. Ask Ss to correct the false statements.

Tapescript

Harry: I went along to Kings Youth Club to find out about another kind of race, this time with real snails! Kathy, tell me about snail racing.

Kathy: Well, it's just a laugh really. I mean, it isn't very serious. I heard about snail racing on the radio, and I thought it sounded like fun.

Harry: Right, so there are six people here, and their snails are on the starting line. Umm, where do the snails come from?

Kathy: They're from our gardens. We'll put them back afterwards.

Harry: So what happens next?

Kathy: Well, we have a starting line here, and there's the finishing line, look. The track's two metres long.

Harry: Sorry. I didn't hear you. What did you say?

Kathy: The track – it's two metres long.

Harry: Oh, I see. And which snail will win in your opinion?

Kathy: Well, I haven't used my snail before, it's his first race, but he looks fast. I think he'll win.

Harry: Hmm. When will the race start?

Kathy: Oh! It's already started! It started half an hour ago!

Harry: Ah.

Answers
2 ✓ 3 ✗ 4 ✓ 5 ✗

Speaking skills: useful phrases

- Ask Ss to repeat the phrases in the box after you to practise stress and intonation patterns.
- Ask Ss if they can suggest any other expressions for these functions, e.g. *Pardon?* or *Sorry?* (with rising intonation) when you want someone to repeat something.

Extension

- Play the recording for Exercise 5 again and ask Ss to listen for one of the phrases in the box. (Sorry. I didn't hear you. What did you say?)

 Exercise 6

- Read out the instructions and point out that there may be more then one correct answer. Advise Ss to read through the dialogue before they start completing it.
- Ss can work in pairs, if you wish, reading out the dialogue and deciding what the missing phrases are.
- Play the recording for the class to hear the original dialogue and see if they have chosen the same phrases.

Answers
2 Could you say that again 3 What does … mean?
4 What do you 5 a minute 6 What did you

 Extension

- Play the recording again for the class to listen particularly to stress and intonation patterns.
- Ask pairs of Ss to practise reading the dialogue together. Go round and monitor.
- Then one or two pairs can read their dialogue for the class to hear.

Resource 6 (page 126)

Interaction: pair or group work (groups of three)
Exercise type: responding to picture clues
Aim: to practise the Present Perfect with *just* and *yet*
Language: She has just had a shower. She hasn't had breakfast yet.

- Before the activity make sure that Ss remember the past participle of the following verbs: *do, send, write, tidy up, have, wake up, find, fall off, win, read, meet, pass, drink.*
- Give a set of pictures from Resource 6 to each pair or group of Ss. Make sure that the cards are well shuffled and the pictures are face down. One S chooses a picture from the pile, shows it to the other S or the rest of the group and elicits a sentence: 'She has just had a shower', 'She hasn't had breakfast yet.' If it is group work, the S who answered first and correctly chooses another picture to elicit a sentence.

Extension

- You can use the same set of pictures to practise *yet* in questions and negatives. Copy the pictures, cross them out and produce a set that has some pictures crossed out and some not. Ss choose a picture and ask their partner: 'Has he won the race yet?'. The other S answers: 'Yes, he has.' (if the picture is without a cross) or 'No, he hasn't.' (if the picture is with a cross).

Activity Book Answers
Language Diary
2
Students' own answers
Exercise 1
2 a 3 f 4 e 5 c 6 b
Exercise 2
2 record 3 title 4 champion 5 line 6 track
Exercise 3
2 They haven't eaten their dinner yet.
3 Somebody has already eaten the sweets.
4 The train has just left the station.
5 Have you tidied your room yet?
Exercise 4
2 just 3 already 4 yet 5 just 6 yet
Exercise 5
2 have/'ve already heard
3 hasn't seen (them) yet
4 Have you read about Jake's race yet?
5 has/'s just finished
6 have/'ve already interviewed
Exercise 6
2 haven't 3 yet 4 ago 5 just 6 already

---

7 Friends' Club

Lesson objectives

Structure
Present Perfect: *for, since*

Functions
Describing people's talents and lives
Asking and answering questions about famous people

Key vocabulary
Adjectives describing people: *ambitious, bored, busy, friendly, gifted, unusual*

Background information
The National Association for Gifted Children (NAGC) is a UK organisation for promoting the needs of gifted children. The Youth Café, an online Cyber-Café, is the virtual branch of NAGC for young people aged eleven and over.

Before class
Make a copy of Resource 7 (page 127) for each pair of Ss.
Bring a picture of Britney Spears or one of her songs to the class (Exercise 7).

Exercise 1
- Play the recording twice for Ss to listen and read the text.
- Ask Ss to find another word in the text that means the same as *talented*. (gifted)

Presentation
Exercise 2
- Ask Ss to look at the title of the article and the pictures and guess what José is good at.
- Play the recording twice for Ss to listen and read the text. They can find out if their guess is correct.

Extension
- Ask Ss which academic subjects are mentioned in the text (Maths, Physics, Astronomy) and if they study these subjects at their own school.
- Elicit the names of other school subjects that the Ss study at their school.

Comprehension
Exercise 3
- Ask one of the Ss to read out the example item.
- Ss work individually, referring back to the text and completing the matching exercise.
- Check Ss' answers by asking individuals to read out the complete sentences.

> **Answers**
> 2 c   3 a   4 e   5 b   6 f

Vocabulary
Exercise 4
- Ask Ss to repeat the words in the box after you to practise pronunciation.
- Ask one of the Ss to read out the example in sentence 1.
- Ss complete the exercise working individually.
- Check Ss' answers by asking individuals to read out the whole sentences.

> **Answers**
> 2 unusual   3 bored   4 ambitious   5 friendly   6 busy

Language box   Present Perfect: *for, since*
- Ask individual Ss to read out the two sentences in the box and the time expressions with *for* and *since*.
- Write two sentences on the board to remind Ss that *for* is used for a period of time and *since* is used when we say the start of the period, e.g.:
  He has been at summer school for a month.
  He has been at summer school since last Monday.
  If necessary, draw time lines to illustrate the two sentences.

Extension
- Write on the board:
  I/We have lived/studied/known/been/had … for/since … .
- Ss work in pairs, making sentences about themselves, using the Present Perfect and *for* or *since*. If necessary, give the class one or two examples.
- Some of the pairs can then read out their sentences for the class to hear.

Practice
Exercise 5
- Ask one of the Ss to read out the first sentence of the text.
- Advise Ss to read through the text first, before doing the exercise.
- Ss can compare their answers in pairs before checking answers as a class.
- Check Ss' answers by asking individuals to read out the sentences.

> **Answers**
> 3 has not/hasn't seen   4 since   5 has/'s made
> 6 have not/haven't known   7 for   8 have/'ve been
> 9 since   10 has/'s been   11 for
> 12 have not/haven't had   13 for

Exercise 6
- Ask Ss to look at the title and the picture and to say what special talent the children in the picture have.

- Ask Ss what the two meanings of *stars* are in the titles 'Stars in His Eyes' (Exercise 2) and 'Young Stars' (Exercise 6).
- Ask Ss to read the text quickly and see if they can guess any of the missing words. They can check their guesses when they listen to the recording.
- Play the recording twice for Ss to listen and complete the text.
- Check Ss' answers by asking individuals to read out the sentences.

Tapescript

Ally: Maggie, tell me a bit about your job. You're a teacher, aren't you?

Maggie: Yes, that's right. I teach at the Russell Stage Academy in New York.

Ally: But you're not American, are you?

Maggie: No, I'm British, actually. But I visited a friend in New York about six years ago. I loved it, so I decided to come and live here. I've lived here for five years.

Ally: When did you start working at the Academy?

Maggie: I started at the beginning of the school year.

Ally: So, you've been a teacher there since September.

Maggie: That's right.

Ally: And what exactly do you teach?

Maggie: Well, it's called 'Performing Arts'. The kids have lessons in acting, dancing and singing. They are all very talented and ambitious.

Ally: So it's an easy job, I suppose?

Maggie: Well, no, it isn't. Gifted children get bored very quickly in class, so it's a real challenge. But I love my job, and I wouldn't change it for anything.

Ally: Are your students going to be stars?

Maggie: Yes, I think a lot of them will be famous one day. Would you like some autographs?

Ally: Good idea.

Answers
2 Britain   3 five
4 September/the beginning of the school year
5 acting   6 dancing   7 singing   8 easy

 Exercise 7

- If you've brought a picture of Britney Spears or a song, show/play this to Ss. Then read out the instructions to the class and ask two Ss to read out the example exchange. Elicit examples of more questions to ask the famous person, e.g. 'How long have you been married?'
- Ss work in pairs, preparing an interview with a famous talented person. Tell Ss they can invent some information if they wish. Go round and help Ss with vocabulary, if necessary.
- The pairs then take turns to perform their interviews for the class. If some of the pairs have chosen the same famous person, the class can see how different or similar the interviews are.

Exercise 8

- Read out the example sentences to the class. Explain that Ss can write about any of the people they heard about in Exercise 7. They need not

choose to write about the person in their own interview.
- Go round and monitor the activity, paying particular attention to correct use of verb forms.
- Ss then form groups of three or four and read each other's texts.

Resource 7 (page 127)

Interaction: pair work
Exercise type: completing a table
Aim: to practise the Present Perfect with *for* and *since*

- Give a copy of Resource 7 to each pair of Ss. Explain that 'Present' refers to this year. Ss should make the connection between the past and present and write sentences about Emma using the Present Perfect tense.
- As a follow-up, Ss should write similar sentences about themselves. They should write sentences in the Past Simple and the Present Simple first and then in the Present Perfect using *since* and *for*.

Answers (assuming that 'Present' means 2003)
1 She has lived in Cambridge since 1992/for eleven years.
2 She has played the violin since 1997/for six years.
3 She has studied at … school since 1998/for five years.
4 She hasn't watched TV for a month/since last month.
5 She has attended summer classes in dancing since 2001/for two years.
6 She has known Jo since 1998/for five years.
7 She has had a cat since 1999/for four years and a dog since 2000/for three years.

Activity Book Answers
Language Diary
2 Students' own answers
Exercise 1
2 g   3 a   4 f   5 i   6 e
Extra sentences: b, d, h
Exercise 2
for: a year, ten minutes, a month
since: yesterday, April, last winter, my birthday
Exercise 3
2 for   3 since   4 for   5 since   6 since
Exercise 4
4 has been   5 since   6 have you known
7 have/'ve been   8 for   9 have/'ve known   10 since
11 haven't seen   12 since   13 have/'ve been
14 haven't seen   15 for
Exercise 5
Students write their own numbers in the dotted spaces.
2 I started school … years ago.
3 I have/'ve been a pupil at this school for … .
4 I have/'ve studied English since … .
5 I have/'ve known my teacher for … .
6 I opened this book … ago.
Exercise 6
The numbers in the brackets are subject to change depending on the current date.
2 Stan has been interested in space for (eleven) years.
3 Stan went to the Space Academy (ten) years ago.
4 Stan has been an astronaut since 1998.
5 Stan has been an astronaut for (five) years.
6 Stan went into space for the first time (three) years ago.
Exercise 7
2 ambitious   3 scientist   4 student   5 friendly
6 beginning

8 Story Time

Lesson objectives

Structures
Past Simple, Past Continuous and Present Perfect

Functions
Describing events in the past
Describing people's feelings

Key vocabulary
Adjectives describing feelings: *curious, disappointed, embarrassed, exciting, familiar, jealous*
Filming: *ad, audition, camera, extra, film crew*

Before class
Make a set of cards from Resource 8 (page 128) for each pair or group.

Exercise 1
- Ss work in pairs, completing the text about 'Summer Meeting 1'. Tell them they can refer back to Unit 4 if they wish.
- Check Ss' answers by having individuals read out the sentences.

> **Answers**
> 2 Scott   3 Jilly   4 special   5 terrible

Extension
- Ask the class if they can remember what happened the next day. Ss pool their ideas and narrate the story. (See Unit 4, Exercises 5 and 6.)

Presentation
Exercise 2
- Ask Ss to talk about the picture and guess what is happening.
- Play the recording twice for Ss to listen and read the text.
- Ask the class what the TV crew are making. (a commercial/an ad/an advertisement)

Comprehension
Exercise 3
- Ss do the exercise working individually and referring back to the text if they wish.
- Check Ss' answers by asking individuals to read and answer the questions.

> **Suggested answers**
> 1 A film crew were making an ad.
> 2 She heard Scott and his friends.
> 3 No, she didn't.
> 4 She acted with Scott.
> 5 She felt happy.

Extension
- Ss work in pairs or groups of three. Tell the class to look back at the text in Exercise 2 and to think of more questions to ask about the story. Give them one or two examples, e.g.:
  'What time did Scott and his friends arrive at the beach?' (9 o'clock)
  Each group of Ss writes down two or three questions about the story.
- Go round and monitor the activity, offering ideas where appropriate.
- The groups take turns to ask the rest of the class one of their questions. If you wish, points can be given for a correct question form and a correct answer.

Vocabulary
Exercise 4
- Ask Ss to say the words in the box after you to practise pronunciation.
- Ask one of the Ss to read out the example sentences in question 1.
- Ss complete the exercise working individually.
- Check Ss' answers by asking individuals to read out the sentences.

> **Answers**
> 2 curious   3 familiar   4 embarrassed   5 disappointed
> 6 jealous

 Extension
- Ss work in groups of three or four, making sentences about themselves using some of the words in the box, e.g. talking about something that was exciting. Go round and monitor the activity, helping with vocabulary if necessary.

Language box Past Simple, Past Continuous and Present Perfect
- Read out the sentences in the box to the class.
- Ask Ss if they can explain when each verb form is used, e.g. The Past Simple describes a completed action in the past. If Ss have difficulty understanding when to use each verb form, a timeline may help them.
- Elicit more sentences using each verb form and appropriate time expressions from the class.

Practice

Exercise 5

- Advise Ss to read through the diary before completing it.
- Do the first sentence with the whole class. Ss then complete the exercise working individually.
- They can compare answers in pairs before checking answers as a class. Check Ss' answers by asking individuals to read out the sentences.

Answers	
2 have already made	8 liked
3 have not/haven't met	9 was
4 happened	10 have/'ve been
5 was walking	11 said
6 were playing	12 asked
7 spoke	13 has not/hasn't phoned

 Extension

- Ss work in pairs and write Harriet's diary for the day of the filming. Go round and monitor the activity, pointing out any errors to be corrected.
- Some of the Ss can then read out their diary entry for the rest of the class to hear.
- Ask the class what they think happens next to Harriet, Scott and Jilly.

 Exercise 6

- Read out the prompts to the class and ask two Ss to read out the example exchange. Elicit suggestions from the class for more prompts, e.g. *get lost, be embarrassed, go to sleep in a lesson, run away from home.*
- Ss work in groups of three or four, taking turns to ask and answer questions, using the prompts in the box and their own ideas. Go round and monitor the activity, paying particular attention to the use of correct verb forms.

Exercise 7

- Ask one of the Ss to read out the example. Elicit suggestions from the class for continuing the second sentence.
- Ss work individually, writing about one of the Ss in their group and the things they have or haven't done. Go round and monitor the activity.
- Some of the Ss can then read out their texts to the rest of the class.

Resource 8 (page 128)

Interaction: pair or group work
Exercise type: responding to word clues
Aim: to practise the Past Simple, the Past Continuous and the Present Perfect

- Give a set of cards with time expressions to each pair or group of three or four Ss. Make sure that the cards are well shuffled and that the words are face down. Ss choose a card from the pile and, depending on the time expression, form a sentence in either the Past Simple, the Past Continuous or the Present Perfect.

Activity Book Answers
Language Diary
2
Students' own answers
Exercise 1
2 familiar   3 embarrassed   4 curious   5 jealous
6 disappointed
Exercise 2
2 d   3 f   4 a   5 b   6 e
Exercise 3
2 has never lived   3 did she meet   4 met, have been
5 was watching, heard   6 didn't like   7 has met
8 hasn't met
Exercise 4
2 never   3 Did   4 didn't   5 was   6 since   7 yet
8 haven't
Exercise 5
2 acted   3 spoke   4 chose   5 were running   6 fell
7 haven't seen   8 has/have already given
Exercise 6
2 A   3 B   4 B   5 C   6 A

Revision 2

Language revised

Vocabulary

Adjectives describing people
Phrases with *get* and *have*
Sport

Pronunciation

Sentence stress
End rhymes

Grammar

Present Perfect and Past Simple
Present Perfect: *already*, *just*, *yet*
Present Perfect: *for*, *since*
Past Simple, Past Continuous, Present Perfect

Vocabulary

Exercise 1

- Read out the example item to the class.
- Ss complete the exercise working individually.
- Check Ss' answers by asking individuals to read out the sentences and the matched adjective.

> **Answers**
> 2 b   3 e   4 a   5 f   6 c

Exercise 2

- Ask one of the Ss to read out the example in sentence 1.
- Ss complete the exercise working individually.
- Check Ss' answers by asking individuals to read out the sentences.

> **Answers**
> 2 get   3 have   4 get   5 have   6 have

Exercise 3

- Read out the instructions to the class. Ask Ss what words match the arrows. (*across* and *down*)
- Ss can do the exercise working in pairs, if you wish.

> **Answers**
> champion   record   line   title   track

Pronunciation chant

 Exercise 4

- Ask Ss to look at the pictures. Use the pictures to present *Mount Everest* and *President*.

- Ask Ss to listen to the recording and focus on the stressed syllables. Ask Ss what word rhymes with *plane* (Spain) and what word rhymes with *fair* (everywhere).
- Play the recording again for Ss to listen and repeat the chant two or three times.

 Extension

- Divide Ss into teams of three or four.
- Give Ss a few minutes to practise the chant in their groups, before presenting it to the class to see which group is the best.

Grammar

Exercise 5

- Ask Ss to look at the first picture. Read out the example in sentence 1 and elicit the second sentence from the Ss.
- Ss complete the exercise working individually.
- They can compare answers in pairs before checking answers as a class.

> **Answers**
> 1 The others haven't finished yet.
> 2 He hasn't seen the film yet. She's already seen it.
> 3 He hasn't opened his present yet. She's just/already opened hers.

Exercise 6

- Ask one of the Ss to read out the example in sentence 1.
- Ss complete the exercise working individually.
- They can compare answers in pairs before checking answers as a class.

> **Answers**
> 2 for   3 for   4 since   5 since

Exercise 7

- Ask Ss to look at and describe the pictures.
- Advise Ss to read through each mini-dialogue before they start to complete it. Ss complete the exercise working individually.
- Check Ss' answers by asking pairs of Ss to read out each dialogue.

> **Answers**
> **Dialogue 1**
> 2 have   3 did you go   4 went   5 Did you see
> 6 did   7 didn't see
> **Dialogue 2**
> 1 Have you ever won   2 won   3 did you draw
> 4 drew   5 Did you get   6 did   7 got

Exercise 8

- Read out the instructions to the class and point out that Ss don't have to tell the truth.
- Ask two Ss to read out the example exchange and elicit suggestions from the class to complete the answer to the question.
- Elicit suggestions from the Ss for further questions, e.g.:
  'Have you ever been on television/flown in a helicopter?'
  What/Where/When/Who/How … ?
- Ss work in pairs, taking turns to ask and answer questions. Go round and monitor the activity, paying particular attention to the correct use of the Present Perfect and the Past Simple.
- Each pair performs one of their dialogues for the class to hear. The class then decides whether the speaker has told the truth.

Exercise 9

- Read out the instructions. Elicit from the class the Past Simple, the Past Continuous and the Present Perfect forms of the verbs *make* and *be*.
- Read out the first two sentences of the text to the class and elicit from the Ss the correct form of the verb *ring*.
- Ss complete the exercise working individually.
- Check Ss' answers by asking individuals to read out the sentences.

Answers	
2 rang	6 went
3 Have you been	7 saw
4 met	8 were swimming
5 were waiting	9 have/'ve never seen

 Fun Time

- Ask Ss to explain what *bluff* and *call my bluff* mean. Tell them they can look it up in their dictionaries.
- Read out the first stage in the box and the example sentence using the expression *three years ago*.
- Group Ss (A and B) in pairs. Group A writes sentences containing the expressions on Card A and Group B writes sentences containing the expressions on Card B. Go round and monitor the activity, pointing out any errors to be corrected.
- Read out Stage 2 in the box and ask two Ss to read out the example dialogue. Tell Ss to ask questions about each of their partner's sentences to try and find out if the sentence is true or not.
- Ss work in pairs, taking turns to read out each of their sentences and answer their partner's questions. Each S asks their partner questions about their sentences and guesses which of their partner's sentences is true.
- The class can then find out how many of them guessed their partner's true sentence.

 Check Yourself Units 5–8 – Activity Book page 20

 Check Units 5–8 – Teacher's Book page 112

Language Tests A/B Units 5–8 – Test Book pages 10–13

Lesson objectives

Skills

To express opinions about different types of fiction
To match vocabulary and visuals
To practise reading for specific information
To use visuals to predict events in a story
To practise listening for specific details in a story
To write the next part of a story
To make a board game

Key vocabulary

Jumanji: *board game, cup, dice, knife, lion, monkey, mosquito, plate, square, token*

Background information

Jumanji was written and illustrated by Chris Van Allsburg and published in 1981. It was made into a film starring Robin Williams in 1995.

Before class

- Ss will need large sheets of paper to make their board games, plus dice and tokens to play with (Project).

Exercise 1

- Ask Ss to look at the front cover of the book. Have any of them read this book or seen the film? What do they think the story is about?
- Ss read the text, working in pairs.
- Ask the class:
  'What is Jumanji?' (a dangerous game in a box)
  'Who plays it first?' (Alan and Sarah)
  'Who plays it years later?' (Peter and Judy)
- As a whole class, Ss discuss if they like adventure books and, if not, what sort of books they like to read.

Exercise 2

- Look at the example item with the class.
- Ss work in pairs, completing the matching exercise. Tell them not to use their dictionaries, but to start with the vocabulary they know and, by a process of elimination, guess the meaning of any words they are not sure of.
- After checking Ss' answers, ask them to make sentences using some of the words.

> **Answers**
> 2 c 3 i 4 a 5 f 6 h 7 d 8 g 9 j 10 b

Reading

Exercise 3

- Give Ss time to read through the questions.
- Play the recording once for Ss to listen and read the text.
- See if Ss can answer the questions after reading and listening to the text once. If necessary, play the recording again.
- Check Ss' answers by asking pairs of Ss to read out the questions and their answers.

> **Answers**
> 1 Peter and Judy
> 2 They heard a noise and followed it.
> 3 four
> 4 a glass eye
> 5 mosquitoes
> 6 They were as big as small birds.

Listening

Exercise 4

- Read out the instructions to the class.
- Ss work in pairs, looking at the picture and making a list of words they might hear.
- The pairs report back to the class and see how many words they have thought of. Check the spelling and pronunciation of words that may cause difficulty.

Exercise 5

- Ask one of the Ss to read out the example in sentence 1.
- Give Ss time to read through the remaining sentences before you play the recording.
- Play the recording twice for Ss to listen and complete the sentences.
- Check Ss' answers by asking individuals to read out the sentences.
- After checking Ss' answers, play the recording again for them to listen for extra information. As a whole class, Ss then pool what they can remember about the story.

> **Tapescript**
> New words came into the glass eye in the centre. *It has a long tail and lives in a tree. But is it dangerous? Wait and see!* Crashing noises came from below. Judy ran out of the room, and Peter took the dice and followed her. They ran downstairs to the kitchen. They could hear breaking plates and strange screams. Judy pushed open the kitchen door. Inside were twelve brown monkeys. Some threw plates and cups and food across the room. Others threw knives! Judy quickly closed the door.
> 'We must have another look at the game,' she said. When they were back in the room at the top of the house again, she said, 'Throw the dice and move. You threw two of the same number, so you can throw again.' The front door shut with a CRASH! and they

ran across to the window. Below, the monkeys ran out into the road.

'We must stop them!' said Peter.

'No, we must finish the game, then it will all go away,' said Judy. 'Quickly, throw the dice.' Peter threw a three and a five. His token moved across the board, and more words came into the glass eye: *This animal is very hungry. Be careful now! Don't make it angry!*

Answers
2 twelve 3 the room at the top of the house
4 the road 5 Peter 6 hungry

Speaking

Exercise 6

- If necessary, give Ss time to look back through the texts they have read so far in the lesson.
- Ask one of the Ss to read out the example sentence and elicit the following sentence from the class. Ask Ss what other sequencing linkers they know (e.g. *Next, After that, When, Suddenly, Later, Finally*) and write these on the board.
- Ss work in pairs, taking turns to tell the story so far. Go round and monitor the activity, making a note of any points to be revised with the whole class.
- As a whole class, Ss can tell the story, taking turns to add a sentence.

Writing

Exercise 7

- Read out the instructions and questions to the class.
- Ask one of the Ss to read out the example sentences. Elicit ideas from the class for continuing the story.
- Ss work individually, writing the next part of the story. Remind them that they have to write out only the next part of the story, they need not finish it. Tell them to write between six and ten sentences. Go round and monitor the activity, helping with vocabulary, if necessary, and pointing out any errors to be corrected.
- Ss form groups of three or four and read out their texts to the rest of the group.
- Some of the Ss can then read out their texts to the rest of the class.

Project

- Ask Ss to look at the board and suggest what sort of board games they could make. Elicit suggestions for useful language expressions in board games and write these on the board, e.g.:
  Move/Go (back).
  Have an extra turn.
  Lose a turn.
- Ss can work in pairs or groups of three, if you wish, using large sheets of paper to make their board and writing out instructions for it. Go round and monitor the activity, helping if necessary.
- Each group then tests their game by using dice and tokens to play their own game.
- Each group can then present their board game to the class. If time, the groups can play some of the other games.

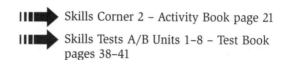

Skills Corner 2 – Activity Book page 21

Skills Tests A/B Units 1–8 – Test Book pages 38–41

Activity Book Answers for Skills Corner 2
Exercise 1
2 c 3 e 4 a 5 b
Exercise 2
Students' own answers
Possible answer:
The weather was very windy. We were running when suddenly the wind blew somebody's hat off their head. The hat flew in the air and landed on Alan's head. It covered his face and Alan fell down. The others in the race started to fall on top of him. Only Zoe was running. She overtook everybody and won. Everybody clapped and laughed. Zoe got a wonderful prize. It was very funny. I haven't laughed so much for ages.

---

9 The LONDONERS

Lesson objectives

Structures
will, *may/might*

Functions
Talking about school subjects and exams
Talking about certain and uncertain future plans

Skills
Writing: linking words

Key vocabulary
School and exams: *get a mark, go to/leave school, fail/pass/take an exam*

Background information

Between the ages of 11 and 16, pupils in Britain attend secondary school, sometimes called high school. Most secondary schools are comprehensives, which means that they teach pupils of all abilities. There are a few grammar schools, which select pupils who pass the 'eleven-plus' exam. State secondary schools have to follow the National Curriculum and assess pupils at the ages of 14 and 16. Core subjects such as English and Maths are compulsory subjects for GCSE but pupils may choose between non-core subjects, e.g. between Geography and History.

More recently, City Technology Colleges have been created, where the National Curriculum is followed but with more emphasis on Maths, Science and Technology. The number of specialist schools should reach 1,500 by 2005, and the ultimate aim is for all secondary schools to specialise.

Students take 'A level' (advanced level) exams when they are 18, usually as preparation for entering university.

Before class
- Make a copy of Resources 9A and 9B (page 129) for each pair of Ss.

Presentation

Exercise 1
- Ask the class what they know about the school system in Britain and encourage them to pool their ideas. Ss can then check if they are correct when they read and listen to the text.
- Play the recording twice for Ss to listen and read the text.
- Working in pairs, Ss list the differences and similarities between British schools and schools in their own country. The pairs then report back to the whole class and see if there is general agreement about the differences and similarities.

- Ask the class if there are any features that seem better or worse in the British system, compared with their own system.

Extension
- Build up on the board a similar text (using the Present Simple tense) about schools in the Ss' own country. Write the beginning of the text on the board:
  'In my country, children go to school from the age of ... to the age of ... .
  When children are ... , they leave their primary school and go to ... .'
- Elicit suggestions from the Ss for sentences to continue the text and encourage them to discuss the most logical sequence for the information.

Exercise 2
- Ask Ss to look at and talk about the picture, describing the people and discussing where they are and what they could be talking about.
- Play the recording twice for Ss to listen and read the text.
- Ask the class which subject each of the four Ss likes best. (Mark/Geography, Rob/Football, Vicki/Art, Kim/Acting)
- Point out to the class that, in Rob's first speech, he says, *I don't think I'll pass the exam* (not *I think I won't ...*).

Comprehension

Exercise 3
- Ask one of the Ss to read out the instruction and the example item. Ask the class to look back at the text in Exercise 2 and to find and read out the words that tell us that Mark is good at Geography. (I really like geography – it's my favourite subject. I'll definitely do Geography GCSE.)
- Ss complete the exercise working individually and referring back to the text in Exercise 2.
- Ss can compare their answers in pairs before checking answers as a class.
- When checking Ss' answers, ask them to read out the section in the text in Exercise 2 that supports their answer.

> **Answers**
> 2 no   3 maybe   4 yes   5 maybe   6 Ss' own answers

Vocabulary

Exercise 4
- Ask one of the Ss to read out the example in sentence 1.
- Advise Ss to read through the exercise quickly before they complete the sentences.
- Check Ss' answers by asking individuals to read out the complete sentences.

Answers
2 leave   3 go   4 get   5 pass   6 fail

Language box *will, may (not)/ might (not)*

- Read out the sentences in the box to the class. At this stage, Ss use *may* and *might* interchangeably to express uncertainty.
- Ask Ss to look back at the text in Exercise 2 and find and read out more sentences containing *will* (I'll definitely do Geography GCSE), *may* (I may not be a footballer) and *might* (You might not fail it).

 ## Extension

- Write on the board:
  'I'm sure I'll … .'
  'I won't … .'
  'I may/might … .'
  'I may not/might not … .'
- Ss work in groups of three or four, taking turns to make sentences about themselves using the prompts on the board. Go round and monitor the activity, paying particular attention to the correct form and use of these verbs.
- Each S then says one of their sentences for the class to hear.

Practice

Exercise 5

- Read out the instructions and example in sentence 1 to the class.
- Tell the class they can use *may* or *might* for the 'unsure' sentences.
- Check Ss' answers by asking individuals to read out the complete sentences.

Answers
2 Mark may/might get a good mark.
3 Rob may/might be a famous footballer one day.
4 Kim may/might not go to university.
5 Rob won't do Geography A level.
6 Vicki will be successful.

Writing Skills: linking words

- Read out the explanation and examples in the box.
- Tell the class that *but* is more informal and common in speech, whereas *although* and *however* are more formal and usually found in writing or formal speech.
- Draw Ss' attention to the positions in the sentences of *although* (at the beginning and in the middle) and *however* (at the end and at the beginning), and the punctuation (use of commas).

 ## Extension

- Ss work in pairs, writing four sentences, using *and*, *but*, *however* and *although*. Tell them that they can write about any topic and that they can choose the position of *however* and *although* in their sentences. Go round and monitor the activity.
- The pairs then form groups of four or six and read each other's sentences.

 ## Exercise 6

- Ask individual Ss to read out the notes about Rob and the example in sentence 1.
- Ss work in pairs and complete the text.

Answers
2 he hates Geography   3 watching football on TV
4 doesn't watch much TV   5 he doesn't like rap
6 he might be a footballer

 ## Extension

- Ss work in pairs, interviewing each other about sport, school, hobbies, music and the future.
- Each S writes three or four sentences about their partner using some of the linking words. Go round and monitor the activity.
- Each S then reads out one of their sentences for the class to hear.

Resource 9 (page 129)

Interaction: pair work
Exercise type: a questionnaire and a class survey
Aim: to practise *will*, *won't*, *may* and *might* for talking about certain and uncertain future plans

- Ss work in pairs. Give one S in a pair Questionnaire A and the other S Questionnaire B from Resource 9A. First, Ss complete the part about themselves by ticking the appropriate boxes in the table under 'I'. Next, they interview their partners and tick the appropriate boxes in the table under 'My partner'.
- When Ss are about to finish, give each pair Resource 9B. Using the results of their interviews, Ss now have to tick the actions that they both will/won't/may/might undertake in the future.
- Ss present the results in Resource 9B to the other groups and a class comparison can then be made.

Activity Book Answers
Language Diary
2
Students' own answers
Exercise 1
2 get   3 failed   4 passed   5 leave   6 go
Exercise 2
2 Rob might not pass the Geography exam.
3 Kim may become an actress one day.
4 Vicki will definitely be an artist.
5 I'm sure he won't have any problems.
Exercise 3
2 ✗   3 ?   4 ?   5 ✓   6 ?
Exercise 4
2 I might study Geography.
3 I may not be a teacher.
4 I might travel.
5 I will (definitely) get a job.
6 I may not live in London.
Exercise 5
2 She's good at English but she's bad at French.
3 You will/'ll definitely pass your exam.
4 It may not rain today.
5 Maybe we won't win.
6 He might phone tomorrow.

10 Crazy Reporters

Lesson objectives

Structures
First Conditional

Functions
Asking and answering questions
Saying what will happen under certain conditions
(*if* ...)

Key vocabulary
Quiz show: *final, the finals, get an answer right/wrong, get/lose a point, hear a sound, host a show, press the button, prize, team, time's up, your turn*

Background information
'The Gunge Show' is the name of the imaginary quiz show in this unit. *Gunge* is sticky, unpleasant, unidentifiable matter into which the losers will be dropped.

Before class
- Make a copy of Resource 10 (page 130) for each pair of Ss.
- You may wish to have some encyclopedias or general knowledge books available for Exercise 6 (part b) where Ss write their own quiz questions.

Presentation

Exercise 1
- Ask the class to look at the pictures and guess what happens in the story of the quiz show.
- Play the recording twice for Ss to listen and read the text and see if their guesses are correct.

Comprehension
Exercise 2
- Ss do the exercise working individually, referring back to the text in Exercise 1.
- When checking Ss' answers, ask them to correct the false statements.

> **Answers**
> 2 ✓ 3 ✓ 4 ✗ 5 ✓ 6 ✗

Extension
- Ask Ss if they watch TV quiz shows and, if so, what their favourite shows are and why.
- Find out if any of the Ss have ever been in a quiz show (not necessarily on TV). If so, encourage them to tell the class what happened and how they felt.

Language box First Conditional
- Ask Ss to repeat the sentences in the box after you.
- Draw Ss' attention to the different positions of the *if* clause in the sentences. Point out the use of the comma when the *if* clause comes first in the sentence.
- Ask Ss to reverse the other two sentences in the box. ('I'll press that button if you don't get the answer right.' 'If you get the next question right, what will happen?')

Extension
- Ask the class to look back at the text in Exercise 1. Choose six Ss to read aloud the parts of Harry, Claire, Jamie, Sarah, Adam and Cathy. The rest of the class listen and follow the text. Tell them to put their hands up when they hear a First Conditional sentence.

Practice
Exercise 3
- Ask one of the Ss to read out the example in sentence 1.
- Ss do the exercise working individually.
- They can compare answers in pairs before checking answers as a class. When checking Ss' answers, ask individual Ss to read out the complete sentences.

> **Answers**
> 2 is/won't know   3 gets/'ll win   4 Will he lose/gives
> 5 win/'ll have   6 will be/see

Be careful
- Ask one of the Ss to read out the two sentences. Draw Ss' attention to the difference in meaning between *if* and *when*.
- Give the class another example for Ss to explain the difference in meaning, e.g.:
  'I'll give you the money when I see you.'
  'I'll give you the money if I see you.'

Exercise 4
- Ask one of the Ss to read out the example in sentence 1.
- Ss complete the exercise working individually.
- Check Ss' answers by asking individuals to read out the sentences.

> **Answers**
> 2 when   3 If   4 when   5 If   6 if

Extension

- Write these prompts on the board:
  'My parents won't be pleased if … .'
  'My parents won't be pleased when … .'
  'Will the baby start crying when … .'
  'Will the baby start crying if … .'
- Ss work in pairs, completing the sentences. Go round and monitor the activity.
- The pairs then read out their sentences for the class to hear. Ss can find out how many different sentences they wrote.

Exercise 5

- Ask Ss to look at the picture and describe what they can see.
- Read the instructions to the class and check that Ss understand that they have to guess the answers.
- Ss work in pairs, reading the questions and guessing the answers.
- The pairs then discuss their suggested answers as a whole class and see how many different ideas they had.
- Play the recording twice for Ss to listen and check their answers.

> **Tapescript**
> Right. If you press the button, your light will go on. If you get the answer right, you'll get two points. But remember, if you give a wrong answer, you'll lose a point, and the other team will get one. If you get ten points, you'll get a prize. And if you get twenty points, you'll get two prizes, of course, and you'll go into the final!

Answers
1 You'll get two points.
2 You'll lose a point and the other team will get one.
3 You'll get a prize.
4 You'll get two prizes and you'll go into the final.

Exercise 6

(a)

- Ask one of the Ss to read out the six questions to think about when designing a class quiz.
- As a whole class, Ss discuss and agree on the answers to the questions. Write these 'rules' on the board for reference.

(b)

- Ask Ss to look back at the questions in the text in Exercise 1 and ask them similar questions, e.g.:
  'Name three countries/animals beginning with S.'
  (Spain, Sweden, Switzerland; snake, snail, squirrel)
  'Name the longest river in the world.' (Nile)
- Ss work in groups of three or four, writing four questions for the quiz. Tell them they must know the correct answers to their questions. If you have some encyclopedias or general knowledge books in the classroom, Ss can refer to these if they wish. Go round and monitor the activity, checking that questions are correctly formed.
- The groups write each of their four questions on four pieces of paper and put the papers in a bag.

(c)

- Choose the teams according to the answers the Ss agreed in part (a) of this exercise.
- Remind the class of the rules on the board that they agreed in part (a).
- Read out the questions from the bag in turn and keep the score for each team on the board. If possible, give the winning team some sweets or chocolate as their prize.

Resource 10 (page 130)

Interaction: pair work
Exercise type: dominoes
Aim: to practise the First Conditional

- Give one set of domino cards to each pair of Ss. Ss divide the cards between them so that each S in a pair has half of the cards.
- Student A puts a card down on the table and Student B tries to find a card to finish the sentence. If Student B doesn't have a card to finish the sentence, the turn passes back to Student A and the game continues.
- It is very important to monitor the activity closely to check if Ss' guesses are correct.
- The winner is the S who uses up all of their cards first.

Activity Book Answers
Language Diary
2
Students' own answers
Exercise 1
2 is asking a question   3 is answering a question
4 has got it wrong   5 has won a prize
6 is pressing a button
Exercise 2
2 baseball   3 capital   4 turn   5 carefully   6 round
Exercise 3
2 Will you watch the show if I am on it?
3 If she wins, she will/'ll get lots of prizes.
4 He will/'ll lose a point if he gets the answer wrong.
5 Will they fall in the gunge if they don't win?
6 If we fall in the gunge, our friends will laugh.
Exercise 4
2 when   3 if   4 if   5 If   6 when
Exercise 5
Students' own answers
Exercise 6
2 A   3 A   4 B   5 A   6 C

11 Friends' Club

Lesson objectives

Structures
Second Conditional

Functions
Talking about what kind of personality you have

Key vocabulary
Adjectives: *alone, brave, calm, cool, courageous, enormous, frightened, lonely, nervous, poisonous, quiet, shy, strange, terrified, unusual*

Before class
- Make a copy of Resource 11 (page 131) for each pair of Ss.
- You will need bilingual or monolingual dictionaries (Exercise 2).
- If you have any examples of quizzes from teenage or adult magazines in the Ss' first language, bring them to the lesson (Exercise 8 Extension).

 ## Exercise 1
- Play the recording once for Ss to listen and read the text. Check that Ss understand *brave* and *adventurous*.
- As a whole class, Ss discuss the two questions. Revise known vocabulary by asking Ss what kind of person each of them is. Ask Ss what sort of quizzes are in the magazines they read, and if they think quizzes can tell us the truth about ourselves.

Presentation
 ### Exercise 2
- Ask individual Ss to read out the five questions (e.g. 'What would you do if you heard a strange noise in the middle of the night?').
- Ss work in pairs, ticking the box/answer they want to choose. Tell them to look up any new words in their dictionaries. Go round and monitor the activity.

Exercise 3
- Each S adds up their score and reads the explanation for it.
- In pairs, Ss compare their scores and discuss how far they agree with the explanations.
- Ss then compare their scores as a whole class and see how many are in each group.

Vocabulary
Exercise 4
- Ask one of the Ss to read out the example matched words.

- Ss complete the exercise working individually.
- When checking Ss' answers, correct any pronunciation mistakes.

> **Answers**
> 2 e 3 f 4 b 5 d 6 a

Extension
- Elicit sentences from the class containing some of the adjectives in the exercise, e.g.:
  My sister is shy and doesn't like going to parties.
  I'm terrified of snakes.

Language box Second Conditional
- Read out the grammatical structure of the Second Conditional and show the class how this describes the first sentence:
  If + Past Simple, *would* + infinitive without *to*
  If I **saw** a ghost, I **wouldn't believe** my eyes.
- Ask individual Ss to read out the sentences in the box.
- Draw Ss' attention to the use of the comma when the sentence begins with the *if* clause. Ask Ss to reverse the order of the clauses in the other two sentences in the box.

Be careful
- Read out the two sentences to the class. Point out that *were* is used in formal spoken situations and nearly always in writing.
- Write these prompts on the board for Ss to make sentences:
  'I / on holiday now' / …
  (If I was/were on holiday now, I'd … .)
  'I / older' / …
  'I / a good (singer/footballer/artist) / …

Practice
 ### Exercise 5
- Ask one of the Ss to read out the example in sentence 1.
- Ss complete the exercise working in pairs. Tell them that *If I was* … or *If I were* … are both acceptable here because the exercise is describing what people say.
- Check Ss' answers by asking individuals to read out the complete sentences.

> **Answers**
> 2 would watch it
> 3 could speak French
> 4 was/were older
> 5 would ask for an autograph
> 6 would be lonely

Extension

- Write on the board:
  'I would be lonely/happy/sad/angry/surprised if ... .'
- Ask Ss to say sentences using the prompts and making their own endings.

Exercise 6

- Ask the class to look at the first email and ask who it is from and who it is to.
- Ask one of the Ss to read out the first sentence and the example answer. Then complete the first email with the whole class.
- Ss complete the exercise working individually.
- Ss can compare answers in pairs before checking answers as a class.

> **Answers**
> 2 would/'d run
> 3 was/were
> 4 would/'d catch
> 5 landed
> 6 wouldn't do
> 7 would/'d call

Extension

- After checking answers, ask Ss if they have any new ideas about what they would do in the situations in Exercise 2.
- Ask each S to tell the class their own suggestion for one of the situations.

Exercise 7

- Read out the instructions to the class.
- Ask two Ss to read out the example exchange and complete the second sentence. Elicit more suggestions from the class for what they would do if they were rich.
- Ss work in pairs, taking turns to ask and answer questions about what they would do in the four situations. Remind Ss that they can also use negative sentences, e.g. *If I were rich, I wouldn't worry about saving money/come to school every day.*
- Go round and monitor the activity, paying particular attention to correct form and use of the Second Conditional.
- Each pair then says one of their dialogues for the class to hear.

Exercise 8

- Read out the instructions and the example sentence to the class. Remind Ss to write about two of the questions in Exercise 7. Tell them to write three or four sentences for each of the two questions.
- Ss work individually. Go round and monitor the activity, helping with vocabulary if necessary and pointing out any errors to be corrected.
- Ss can then form groups of three or four and read each other's sentences.

Extension

- If you have brought to the lesson any quizzes from Ss' first language magazines, show these to the class and ask Ss what these quizzes are about.
- Ss work in pairs or groups of three, writing three questions for another quiz, using the structure *What would you do if ... ?* Remind Ss to write a score guide for their quiz. Ss may find it helpful to build up on the board an example item together, e.g.:
  'How honest are you?'
  '1 What would you do if you found a £20 note in the street?'
  a) 'I'd take it and keep it.'
  b) 'I'd take it to the police station.'
  c) 'I'd leave it in the street.'
- Go round and monitor the activity as Ss write their quizzes.
- The pairs and groups then exchange quizzes and do the quizzes for the other groups.

Resource 11 (page 131)

Interaction: pair work
Exercise type: completing a questionnaire
Aim: to practise the Second Conditional

- Ss work in pairs. Give one S in each pair Questionnaire A and the other S Questionnaire B. First, Ss complete the part about themselves (columns 'You' and 'Why?'). Then, they interview their partner and fill in the remaining two columns ('Your friend' and 'Why?').
- When Ss have completed the questionnaires, ask them to report back about their friend's choices.

> **Activity Book Answers**
> **Language Diary**
> **2**
> 1 would   2 saw   3 if
> **Exercise 1**
> 2 lonely   3 courageous   4 terrified   5 calm
> 6 enormous   7 shy
> **Exercise 2**
> 2 you didn't have any money
> 3 you saw an accident
> 4 you found some money
> 5 you didn't like the food at the party
> **Exercise 3**
> 2 I'd/wouldn't wash up. I wouldn't/'d run away.
> 3 I'd/wouldn't call for an ambulance. I wouldn't/'d panic.
> 4 I'd/wouldn't take it to a police station. I wouldn't/'d tell my parents.
> 5 I'd/wouldn't eat it. I wouldn't/'d leave it on the plate.
> **Exercise 4**
> 2 didn't have   3 had   4 would/'d go
> 5 wouldn't stay   6 would/'d get   7 did
> 8 Would you take   9 went   10 would
> **Exercise 5**
> 2 in   3 to   4 for   5 to   6 up

12 Story Time

Make a Wish 1

Lesson objectives

Structures
wish + Past Simple

Functions
Making wishes

Key vocabulary
Adjectives with opposite meanings:
careless – careful, interested – bored, messy – neat,
normal – weird, stupid – clever, unlucky – lucky

Background information
'Make a Wish' is a two-part story about a
schoolboy, Jimmy, who receives a message on his
mobile phone telling him he can make two wishes
and they will come true. In the first episode, Jimmy
wishes he didn't have any homework for the
weekend. To his surprise, he finds that all his
weekend homework has been completed for him.

Before class
- Make a copy of Resource 12 (page 132) for each
  group of four or five Ss. You will need a counter
  for each S and a dice for each group.

Exercise 1
- Ss work in pairs, looking at the picture and
  discussing the answers to the two questions.
- The pairs then exchange ideas about the answers
  to the two questions.
- Ask the class to describe what they can see in the
  bedroom, what the weather is like and what sport
  they think Jimmy likes.

Presentation
Exercise 2
- Play the recording twice for Ss to listen and read
  the text.
- Ask Ss what Jimmy's first wish was. (I wish I had
  something interesting to do.)
- Ask them what Jimmy had to do for his French,
  Geography and Science homework.

Extension
- Ask the class what homework they had last
  weekend. Which subjects? What tasks did they
  have to do in each subject? If necessary, revise the
  vocabulary of school subjects with the class.

Comprehension
Exercise 3
- Ask one of the Ss to read out the example in
  sentence 1.
- Ss complete the exercise working individually,
  referring back to the text if they wish.
- Check Ss' answers by asking individuals to read
  out the sentences.

> **Answers**
> 2 b   3 b   4 a   5 b   6 b

Vocabulary
Exercise 4
- Ask one of the Ss to read out the example in
  question 1.
- Ss complete the exercise working individually.
- They can compare answers in pairs before
  checking answers as a class. When checking Ss'
  answers, correct any pronunciation mistakes.

> **Answers**
> 2 bored   3 weird   4 lucky   5 neat   6 careful

Extension
- Ss work in pairs, choosing four words from the
  exercise and writing four sentences containing the
  words. Go round and monitor the activity,
  pointing out any errors that need correcting.
- Ss then form groups of four or six and read each
  other's sentences.
- Some of the Ss then read out one of their
  sentences for the class to hear.

Language box   *wish* + Past Simple
- Read out the sentences in the box to the class.
- Point out that we use the past after *wish* (*I wish I*
  had something to do) but that the meaning is
  present, not past.

Be careful
- Ask one of the Ss to read out the two sentences.
  Remind Ss of Unit 11, where they practised *If I*
  were/was alone, I'd panic (Second Conditional).

Practice
Exercise 5
- Ask one of the Ss to read out the example in
  sentence 1.
- Ss complete the exercise working individually.
- Check Ss' answers by asking individuals to read
  out the sentences.

> **Answers**
> 2 knew   3 weren't/wasn't   4 could   5 wasn't
> 6 was/were

Exercise 6

- Read out the instruction and check that Ss understand that they have to refer back to Exercise 5.
- Ask one of the Ss to read out the example in question 1.
- Ss complete the exercise working individually.
- They can compare answers in pairs before checking answers as a class.

Answers

2 no 3 yes 4 no 5 yes 6 no

Exercise 7

- Ss work individually, writing three wishes for themselves. Go round and monitor the activity, helping with vocabulary and pointing out any errors to be corrected.
- Ss form groups of three or four and read out their wishes to the rest of the group.
- Each S then reads out one of their wishes to the rest of the class.

Exercise 8

- Ask Ss how many of them send text messages. How many messages do they send a day? Who do they text most? (parents? friends?)
- Ask one of the Ss to read out the first question. Elicit the second question from the class.
- Ss work in pairs, writing out the rest of the text conversation.
- Check Ss' answers by asking individuals to read out the messages.

Answers

Are you OK? I want to see you.
Why?
I'll tell you when I see you. Maybe later today?
Sorry not today. Tomorrow?
Great! See you then!

Extension

- Ss work in pairs writing a question in the style of a text message. Go round and help, if necessary.
- The pairs form groups of four and exchange messages. Each pair writes a reply to the question. They then return the text message to the original pair who read the answer to their question.

Resource 12 (page 132)

Interaction: group work
Exercise type: board game
Aim: to practise *I wish* + Past Simple

- Put Ss into groups of four or five. Give each group a board.
- *Rules:* Ss should put their counters on the square which says 'START'. They take turns to throw the dice and move according to the number on the dice. If they land on a square with a verb, they have to make a correct sentence with that verb and *I wish*. If you wish, elicit a few examples from the class.
  Tell Ss that they can use *could* in many of their sentences, e.g.:
  I wish I could go to the party.
  If the sentence isn't correct or doesn't make sense, the player misses a turn.
  The winner is the player who reaches the 'FINISH' square first.

Activity Book Answers
Language Diary
2
2 didn't 3 could 4 Students' own answers
Exercise 1
2 c 3 f 4 d 5 a 6 e
Exercise 2
b 4 I wish I had lots of money.
c 3 I wish I could walk.
d 1 I wish he was asleep.
e 5 I wish I was him.
f 2 I wish I could go home.
Exercise 3
2 I wish I wasn't/weren't tired.
3 I wish my neighbours didn't have a horrible big dog.
4 I wish my friend could come out with me.
5 I wish I had my own bedroom.
6 I wish we weren't bored today.
7 I wish I could go to my friend's party.
Exercise 4
2 B 3 A 4 A 5 C 6 B

Revision 3

Language revised

Vocabulary
School
Adjectives

Pronunciation
Sentence stress in the Second Conditional

Grammar
will, won't, may, might
First Conditional
Second Conditional
wish

Vocabulary

Exercise 1
- Read out the first sentence of the text.
- Advise Ss to read through the text quickly before they start completing it. Ss do the exercise working individually.
- Check Ss' answers by asking individuals to read out the sentences.

> **Answers**
> 2 pass   3 get   4 fail   5 leave   6 go

Exercise 2
- Ss can do the exercise working in pairs, if you wish, putting the adjectives into positive and negative columns.
- After checking Ss' answers, ask them to make sentences using some of the adjectives, e.g. *It was very dark in the park and they were frightened.*

> **Answers**
> Positive adjectives: careful   cool   courageous lucky   neat
> Negative adjectives: careless   frightened   lonely messy   unlucky

Pronunciation chant

Exercise 3
- Ask Ss to look at the first two lines of the chant and identify the grammatical structure (Second Conditional).
- Play the recording for Ss to listen and read the text. Tell Ss to listen carefully to the stress and intonation patterns.
- Then play the recording for Ss to listen and repeat.
- Ask two or three pairs of Ss to read out the chant for the class to hear.

Grammar

Exercise 4
- Read out the instructions to the class. Remind Ss that *may* and *might* are used interchangeably. Point out that this exercise has two stages, first the pair work and then a writing activity.
- Give Ss time to read through the expressions in the table. Then ask two Ss to read out the example question and answer.
- Ask Ss to look at the second item (go to bed/no). Elicit the question and answer for this item from the class. (After school, will you go to bed? No, I won't.)
- Ss work in pairs, asking and answering the questions in the box and completing the table for their partner. Go round and monitor the activity, paying particular attention to the use of *will*, *won't* and *may/might*.
- Read out the example sentence about Adam and the sweet shop. Elicit the sentence for the second item. (Adam won't go to bed after school.)
- Ss then work individually, writing sentences about their partner. Go round and monitor the activity, pointing out any errors to be corrected.
- In pairs, Ss read their partner's sentences and see if they agree with them.

Exercise 5
- Ask Ss to look at the prompts for the first item and the picture. Read out the example to the class and elicit suggestions for completing the second sentence.
- Ss complete the exercise working individually. Remind Ss to put the comma in the correct place after the *if* clause.
- Check Ss' answers by asking individuals to read out the pairs of sentences.

> **Answers**
> 1 don't win, he'll be unhappy
> 2 If he passes, he'll have a party.
>   If he fails, he'll try again.
> 3 If he doesn't have the cake, he'll scream.
>   If he eats it all, he'll be ill.

Extension
- Ask Ss to reverse one sentence from each pair, reminding them to be careful with punctuation. (If they win, he'll sing. = He'll sing if they win.)

Exercise 6

- Ask Ss to look at prompts 1 and b while you read out the example sentence.
- Give Ss time to read through all the prompts and then do item 2 with the whole class.
- Ss complete the exercises working individually.
- They can compare answers in pairs before checking answers as a class.

Answers
2 c If I lived in England, I'd speak English all day.
3 a If I could sing, I'd be famous.
4 e If I could have a pet, I'd choose a dog.
5 f If I saw a ghost, I wouldn't be frightened.
6 d If I didn't have any homework, I'd be bored.

Exercise 7

- Ask Ss to look at the picture and tell you where the boy is and how he is feeling.
- Read out the first prompt and the example sentences. Remind Ss that both *I was* and *I were* are correct with *I wish*. Tell Ss there may be more than one correct answer. If necessary, elicit the second sentence as a further example.
- Ss work in pairs, writing sentences using *I wish … .*
- Check Ss' answers by asking pairs of Ss to read out the prompt and the second sentence with *I wish … .*

Suggested answers
2 I wish I liked swimming./I wish I didn't have to swim.
3 I wish I could dive.
4 I wish I wasn't/weren't hungry./I wish I had some chocolate.
5 I wish I had some money for food.
6 I wish we didn't come here every week.

Exercise 8

- Ask one of the Ss to read out the example in sentence 1. Tell Ss that the exercise uses both the First and the Second Conditionals.
- Ss complete the exercise working individually.
- Check Ss' answers by asking individuals to read out the sentences.

Answers
2 'd buy   3 would you do   4 plays   5 Will you help
6 had   7 saw   8 won't be   9 wouldn't walk
10 was/were

 Song Time

- Read out the text in Stage 1.
- In turn, each S tells the class their wish. Ss find out if any of them have the same wish.
- Ask Ss to look at Stage 2 in the box. Working in pairs, Ss see if they can complete the song with the expressions.
- Play the recording twice for Ss to check their answers.
- Play the recording again for Ss to say the song with the recording.

Answers
2 I had   3 some wings   4 who needs money
5 way up high

 Check Yourself Units 9–12 – Activity Book page 30

 Check Units 9–12 – Teacher's Book page 113

 Language Tests A/B Units 9–12 – Test Book pages 14–17

Culture Corner

England

Lesson objectives

To match visuals using general reading skills
To listen for specific information
To speak fluently about a favourite place
To write a postcard about a favourite place
To write and illustrate a legend from your own country

Key vocabulary

England: *countryside, cricket, punt, rose, symbol, thatched* (*roof*)

Background information

King Arthur is a fabled Celtic warrior of the sixth century. The myth of 'the sword in the stone' was that only one man would ever pull out the sword that was thrust into a huge stone. That man would then become the King of Britain. Arthur pulled out the sword and became king. The sword in the stone was not the only sword that featured in Arthur's life. According to the legend, Excalibur was the most powerful sword of all and Merlin the magician told Arthur where he could find it. It was held in a secret lake by 'the Lady of the Lake'.

Before class

- If you have any pictures or objects relating to the topics of this unit (e.g. Oxford, Cambridge, cricket, Hadrian's Wall), bring them to the lesson to show to the class at the appropriate time.

Reading

 ### Exercise 1

- Ask Ss to look at the map and say the names of the places after you.
- Give Ss time to look at the pictures and talk about them, using vocabulary they already know (e.g. they may know *roof* but not *thatched*). At this stage do not present new vocabulary but tell the class they should find the new words in the texts.
- Play the recording, pausing after each section for Ss to listen and read the text.
- Play the recording a second time for Ss to match the texts with the pictures.

Answers
1 e   2 c   3 b   4 a   5 d

- After checking Ss' answers, ask them to look at the pictures again and see if they now know the vocabulary they need to talk about them.
- As a whole class, Ss discuss which place they think is most interesting to visit – a university city like Oxford, a village in the south of England or Hadrian's Wall in the north.

Listening

 ### Exercise 2

- Ask Ss to look at the picture, not the questions, and guess what this place is and why it is interesting to visit.
- Play the recording once for Ss to listen for the name, location and other general information.
- Give Ss time to read through the questions, then play the recording again for Ss to answer the questions.

Tapescript
Cornwall is full of mystery and magic. There are lots of fascinating places. My favourite place in Cornwall is Tintagel. It's famous because legends say that King Arthur was born there, in the castle – the old castle walls are still there. There are lots of old stories about King Arthur, his beautiful wife Guinevere, Merlin the magician and the Knights of the Round Table. Some people say that their ghosts still walk around in the caves near the castle walls. The legends say that every year you can see the castle just like it was in Arthur's time. I'd love to see that!

Answers
1 in Cornwall
2 (legends say) King Arthur was born there
3 the old castle walls
4 in the caves near the castle walls
5 the castle just like it was in Arthur's time

- After checking Ss' answers, play the recording again and ask Ss to listen for any extra information.
- Ss then tell the class what else they can remember.

Speaking

 ### Exercise 3

- Read out the questions and the example sentences to the class.
- Give Ss time to think about their own answers to the questions.
- Ss then work in pairs, telling each other about their favourite place. Go round and monitor the activity, helping with vocabulary if necessary. Make a note of any general points to go over with the whole class before Ss move on to the next exercise.

Exercise 4

- Each S tells the class about their partner's favourite place. Ss can find out if any of them have chosen the same place.

Exercise 5

- Read out the instructions to the class.
- Ask Ss to look at the example postcard. Ask them if Jane Williams is writing the postcard and where she lives. Elicit suggestions from the class for continuing the first sentence. (Hi! I'm ...)
- Ss work individually, writing a postcard from their favourite place. Tell them to write five or six sentences. Go round and monitor the activity, pointing out any errors to be corrected.
- Ss then work in groups of three or four, reading each other's postcards.

Project

- See Background information for the story of 'The Sword in the Stone'. Tell the class the story and ask Ss to complete the text. (One day ...)
- Elicit the names of several legends about their own country from the Ss.
- Each S chooses a legend from their own country and writes and illustrates the story. Tell Ss to write a draft for you to check before they write the final version and illustrate it. Go round and monitor the activity, helping with vocabulary and pointing out any errors to be corrected.
- Ss can make a wall display of their illustrated stories.

Cartoon

- Ask one of the Ss to read the caption in the cartoon. Ask Ss what impression the cartoon gives of cricket (e.g. it isn't exciting; the spectators go to sleep, get cold and stay in one place for a long time).
- Ask Ss what they can remember about cricket from the text in Exercise 1 (without looking back at the text).
- Ask Ss what their favourite sports are and which sports are boring to watch. Encourage them to speak about this as a class.

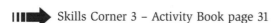 Skills Corner 3 – Activity Book page 31

Activity Book Answers for Skills Corner 3
Exercise 1
1 E   2 A   3 F   4 C, D
Exercise 2
Students' own answers

13 The LONDONERS

Presentation

Exercise 1

- Read out the first question to the class, and ask Ss if they can suggest how most people travel in London.
- Play the recording once for Ss to listen and read and see if their suggestions are correct. (by car, by bicycle, on foot, by boat, by bus, by underground/tube)
- Remind Ss that we say *on foot*.
- Read out the second question and elicit how Ss usually travel (to school? when they go on holiday?).
- Ask the class how people get around their country's capital or big cities.

Exercise 2

- Ask the class to look at the picture of the Londoners at London's Transport Museum and talk about what they can see in the picture.
- Ask the class to tell you about any projects they have done for their History lessons or any history trips they have been on.
- Play the recording twice for Ss to listen and read the text.

Comprehension

Exercise 3

- Ask one of the Ss to read the example answer and then ask the class to correct this false statement.
- Ss complete the exercise working individually.
- When checking Ss' answers, ask the class to correct the false statements.

Answers
2 ✓   3 ✓   4 ✗   5 ✓   6 ✗

Exercise 4

- Ask Ss to repeat the words in the box after you to practise pronunciation and word stress.
- Do the example in sentence 1 with the whole class.
- Ss complete the exercise working individually.
- Check Ss' answers by asking individuals to read out the sentences.

Answers
1 conductor   2 passengers   3 fare   4 underground
5 transport   6 escalators   7 tram

Language box   used to

- Read out the sentences in the box to the class. Draw Ss' attention to the structure of negative and question forms with *used to*.
- Ask Ss to look back at the text in Exercise 2 and find and read out more sentences containing *used to*.

Practice

Exercise 5

- Ask one of the Ss to read out the first sentence of the text. Elicit the correct form of *used to* in the next sentence.
- Ss work individually, completing the text.
- They can compare answers in pairs before listening to the recording.
- Play the recording twice for Ss to listen and check their answers.
- Ask individuals to read out the complete conversation so that you can check the answers and also Ss' pronunciation.

Answers
2 used to be   3 used to carry   4 didn't use to be
5 did they use to wash   6 used to have
7 didn't use to have   8 did they use to do
9 used to do   10 used to stand

Exercise 6

- Give Ss time to read through the questions before you play the recording.
- Play the beginning of the recording for Ss to hear the answer to the first question.
- Then play the recording twice for Ss to listen and answer the remaining questions. If necessary, pause the recording during the second playing for Ss to write down their answers.
- Check Ss' answers by asking pairs of Ss to read out the questions and answers.

Tapescript

Vicki: So what did you use to do in your spare time?

Ben: Well, we used to go to the Saturday morning pictures.

Vicki: What was that?

Ben: Oh, it was great. It was a special cinema show for children, every Saturday. They used to show two films.

Vicki: What about television when you were my age?

Ben: Well, only one family in our street had a TV, so all the children used to go and watch it at their house – but not very often. It was really exciting. It didn't use to be in colour, of course. It was all in black and white. And do you know, we didn't use to have CD players, we just had a radio.

Vicki: How did you use to get to school?

Ben: I used to go by bus most days. It was quite a long way. The journey used to take about half an hour.

Vicki: What kind of car did your dad use to have?

Ben: Well, it was an old one. It never used to start in the mornings, so when we went to school with him we were always late. I always used to miss the first lesson.

Vicki: Did you ever use to travel by plane?

Ben: Oh, no. I used to want to fly, but no, the fastest way I ever used to travel was by train. We used to go to the seaside by train every summer.

Vicki: What kind of food did you use to eat?

Ben: Ah, well, we didn't use to know about food from other countries, like pizza or Chinese food. I didn't use to like Chinese food but now I love it. And I think people used to cook more fresh food than we do now.

Vicki: Did you use to grow vegetables?

Ben: Yes, we did. My dad used to grow a lot of vegetables in the garden. Lovely fresh vegetables. No need for all these supermarkets.

Answers

2 no   3 by bus   4 the seaside   5 by train   6 yes
7 their garden

Extension

- Play the recording again and ask Ss to listen for any extra information about Ben's life, e.g. one family in Ben's street had a black-and-white TV; Ben's family had a radio, not a CD player.
- As a whole class, Ss pool their information to see how much they can remember from the recording.

Exercise 7

- Ask the class to look at the picture while one S reads out the example sentence.
- If you wish, elicit a second sentence from the class.
- Ss then work in pairs, finding the mistakes and telling their partner. Go round and monitor the activity, paying particular attention to correct negative forms.
- Check Ss' answers by asking individuals to say their sentences.

Answers

They didn't use to drive cars.
They didn't use to wear jeans and T-shirts.
They didn't use to drink cola.
They didn't use to eat burgers.
They didn't use to play computer games.
They didn't use to watch television.

Extension

- Ask Ss to write five or six sentences about their (great-) grandparents' lives or to imagine what their lives were like. Tell Ss they can write positive and/or negative sentences. Write some prompts on the board for Ss to use if they wish:
  'When my grandparents were my age, they used to/didn't use to … '
  go wear live play learn like drink eat
- Go round and monitor the activity, helping with vocabulary if necessary and pointing out any errors to be corrected.
- Ss can then form groups of three or four and read each other's sentences.

Resource 13 (pages 133–134)

Interaction: pair work
Exercise type: information gap
Aim: to practise *used to*
Language: What did she use to do when she was four? Did she use to walk in her sleep?

- The aim of the task is to find out about Tina's and Jim's habits in the past and present and to fill in the table in Resource 13B.
- Ss work in pairs. Give one S the card for Student A and the other S the card for Student B, which you can find in Resource 13A. The cards contain ten pieces of information about Tina's and Jim's lives in the past and present.
- Ss are to exchange the information they have on their cards and complete Resource 13B with the results they get, using *used to*.
- When Ss finish, ask each pair to present one fact from Tina's or Jim's life, e.g. 'Tina used to walk in her sleep, but she doesn't do it now.'

Activity Book Answers
Language Diary
2
positive: used   *negative:* didn't   *question:* Did, use
Exercise 1
Shape of a means of transport: tram, double-decker, fare, tube, underground
Shape of a man: conductor, driver, passenger
Exercise 2
2 didn't use to live   3 used to have   4 used to get up
5 used to sell   6 used to help
Exercise 3
2 Did you use to walk to school?
3 My mother used to work on a farm.
4 Where did they use to live?
5 He didn't use to like Maths.
6 My grandparents didn't use to have a car.
Exercise 4
2 did you use to play   3 used to go
4 didn't use to understand   5 used to read
6 Did you use to play
Exercise 5
2 Where did you use to live when you were two?
3 Who did you use to play with?
4 Did you use to go to school when you were five?
5 What time did you use to go to bed when you were five?
Students write their own answers to all the questions.
Exercise 6
2 to   3 ago   4 have   5 since   6 use

14 Crazy Reporters

Lesson objectives

Structures
must/have to, don't have to, mustn't

Functions
Explaining how to play a game or sport

Key vocabulary
Sports: *boots, court, goal, net, pitch, racket, team, trainers*

Before class
- Make a copy of Resource 14 (page 135) for each pair of Ss.

Presentation

Exercise 1
- Ask the class to look at and describe each picture. Revise or present the key vocabulary shown in the pictures. Remind Ss that the reporters only report crazy things and encourage them to suggest what is crazy in these pictures. Ss can see if their guesses are right when they listen to the recording.
- Play the recording twice for Ss to listen and read the text.

Comprehension
Exercise 2
- Ss work individually, referring back to the text to answer the questions and writing down their answers.
- Check Ss' answers by asking pairs of Ss to read out the questions and their answers.

> **Suggested answers**
> 1 They like different sports.
> 2 It's half tennis, half football.
> 3 on a football pitch
> 4 a tennis ball (usually)
> 5 a net, two goals, rackets

Extension
- Tell the class to listen carefully to pronunciation, stress and intonation patterns as you play the recording from Exercise 1 again.
- Then choose eight Ss to read the parts of Harry, Claire, Kelly and Jonathan in the two sections of the text. Correct any major pronunciation mistakes made by the Ss.
- When Ss have finished reading the text, ask the class more comprehension questions, e.g.:
  'Can you play tenball in the garden?' (yes)
  'Have Kelly and Jonathan got two goal posts?'
  (No. They use their jumpers.)

Vocabulary
Exercise 3
- Ask the class to look at the example item and then say the words after you to practise pronunciation.
- Ss do the matching exercise working individually.
- They can compare answers in pairs before checking answers as a class.

> **Answers**
> b 4   c 2   d 6   e 8   f 3   g 7   h 1

Extension
- Ss work in pairs, choosing three of the words and writing three sentences containing their words. Go round and monitor the activity, helping with vocabulary if necessary and pointing out any errors to be corrected.
- The pairs form groups of four or six and read each other's sentences.

Language box   *must/have to, don't have to, mustn't*
- Read out the sentences in the box to the class.
- Elicit from the Ss the difference in meaning between *don't have to* (it is not necessary) and *mustn't* (it is forbidden). The positive forms of *must* and *have to* are used interchangeably here. If Ss ask about the difference and you feel it is appropriate to explain this to your class, tell Ss that we use *must* when we give our personal feelings, e.g. *I must visit my aunt today* (I feel it is necessary), and we use *have to* for facts, not personal feelings, e.g. *They have to wear school uniform* (it's a school rule). Tell Ss that if they are not sure which to use, it is usually safer to use *have to*.
- Ask Ss to look back at the text in Exercise 1 and find and read out examples of sentences containing *must* or *have to* (positive, negative and question forms).

Practice
Exercise 4
- Ask one of the Ss to read out the example in sentence 1.
- Ss can do the exercise working in pairs, if you wish.
- Check Ss' answers by asking individuals to read out the sentences.

> **Answers**
> 2 have to   3 must   4 don't have to   5 have to
> 6 mustn't

Extension

- Ss work in pairs, writing three or four sentences (using *must/mustn't, have to/don't have to*) about another sport, e.g. basketball, hockey. Go round and monitor the activity, pointing out any errors that need correcting.
- The pairs can then read out some of their sentences for the class to hear.

Exercise 5

- Ask Ss to look at the picture and guess what happens in this crazy sport.
- Give Ss time to read through the phrases (a–e). Then ask one of the Ss to read out the first section of the text, including answer b.
- Advise Ss to read through the text quickly before they start completing the gaps. Ss do the exercise working individually.
- They can compare answers in pairs before checking answers as a class.
- Check Ss' answers by asking individuals to read out the text.

> **Answers**
> 2 a 3 c 4 e 5 d

 ## Exercise 6

- Ask individual Ss to read out the questions.
- One S then reads out the sentences about the swimming pool game. Ss complete the description of this game by answering the remaining questions:
  'What do you need?'
  'What are the rules?'
  'What is your crazy sport called?'
- Ss work in groups of four or five, writing about their own crazy sport and answering the questions about it. Tell Ss that they can draw diagrams to accompany their written text, if they wish. Go round and monitor the activity, helping with vocabulary where necessary and pointing out any errors to be corrected.
- Each group then presents their sport to the class, reading out the text and drawing diagrams on the board. After each presentation, the rest of the class can ask questions about the sport.
- At the end of the presentations, the class votes for the craziest sport.

Resource 14 (page 135)

Interaction: pair work
Exercise type: picture description
Aim: to practise *must, have to, mustn't*
Language: The elderly lady mustn't feed the ducks.

- Tell your Ss that they are in a very restrictive park where many things are forbidden and people have to behave in a particular way. They have to read all the signs and find all the people who don't obey the rules. Elicit an example using the target language, e.g.:
  'People have to keep to the paths.'
  'People mustn't walk on the grass.'
- Divide Ss into pairs.
- Tell your Ss that they have three minutes to look at the picture and spot all the people who are not following the signs. Tell the Ss to write down as many sentences describing the picture as they can remember. They should use *have to, must* or *mustn't*. If you want to turn this activity into a competition, set a time limit, e.g. two minutes. The pair who manage to write the most sentences are the winners. (It is not necessary to make Ss memorise the actions in the picture. You can simply make them write the sentences looking at it.)

> **Activity Book Answers**
> **Language Diary**
> **2**
> Students' own answers
> **Exercise 1**
> *across:* racket, goal, team, pitch
> *down:* tennis, trainers, court, net, football
> **Exercise 2**
> 2 You mustn't go swimming.
> 3 I mustn't forget.
> 4 We don't have to pay.
> 5 She doesn't have to take a coat.
> 6 You mustn't be late.
> **Exercise 3**
> 2 ✗ 3 ✓ 4 ✗ 5 ✓ 6 ✓
> **Exercise 4**
> 2 don't have to   3 don't have to   4 mustn't
> 5 mustn't 6 must
> **Exercise 5**
> 2 C   3 C   4 B   5 A   6 B

15 Friends' Club

Lesson objectives

Structures
make, let

Functions
Talking about sports and activities usually associated with boys or girls

Skills
Reading: guessing words from context

Key vocabulary
Films: *acting, award, critic, (big) hit, play a part, (film) star*
Other words: *keep in touch with, let it go to (his) head, recommend*

Background information
The film *Billy Elliot* starred Jamie Bell and Julie Walters. It was directed by Stephen Daldry and received Oscar nominations in 2000.

Before class
- Make a copy of Resource 15 (page 136) for each pair of Ss.
- A set of monolingual dictionaries (Reading Skills, Exercise 4)
- You could prepare a short video clip from 'Billy Elliot'.

Exercise 1
- Play the recording once for Ss to listen and read the text.
- Ask Ss if they think some activities are only for boys and others only for girls – encourage them to give contrary examples. Find out how many girls in the class play (or have played) football. Is there a women's football team in their country?

Presentation

Exercise 2
- Ask Ss to read the title of the article and look at the photograph. Ask Ss what they think the article is about.
- Play the recording twice for Ss to listen and read the text. Ss can see if they guessed the content of the article correctly. Tell Ss not to worry if they do not understand all the words. At this stage it is important to understand the main content of the article. Ss will practise guessing the meaning of unknown words later in this unit.
- If any of the Ss ask why the Present Simple form is used here, tell them that stories are usually told using this tense.

Extension
- Ask Ss if any of them have heard of or seen this film and, if so, ask them to tell the class about it. If not, encourage Ss to discuss films they have seen starring a child (or children).

Comprehension
Exercise 3
- Ask one of the Ss to read out the example in sentence 1.
- Ss complete the exercise, referring back to the text if necessary.

> **Answers**
> 2 Jamie   3 little   4 Some people   5 isn't   6 didn't stop

Reading Skills: guessing words from context
- Read out the sections in the box, one by one, using the example sentence to illustrate the strategies. Tell Ss that if a teacher is not available, they can check the meaning in a dictionary. If you and the Ss have monolingual dictionaries available, ask Ss to check the meaning of *give up* in their dictionaries.
- Give the class one or two more examples of sentences containing *give up* so Ss can see how the verb is used in other contexts, e.g.:
  'He gave up playing football because he hurt his back'.

Exercise 4
- Read the instructions to the class.
- Ask one S to read out the speech bubble.
- With the whole class, go through the steps in the Reading skills box, relating it to the process in the speech bubble.
- Ss work in pairs, completing the exercise and writing down the meanings of the numbered words or expressions. If Ss have dictionaries, ask them to check their guesses in them. Tell Ss that there is more than one possible synonym for each answer.

> **Suggested answers**
> 1 helped/supported
> 2 a great success
> 3 became rich
> 4 he didn't get big-headed/he didn't become arrogant
> 5 kept/remained in contact with
> 6 think it is good/think I'd like

Language box *make* and *let*
- Ask individual Ss to read out the sentences in the box. Point out that *make* and *let* have the structure:
  verb + object + infinitive (without *to*).
- Draw Ss' attention to the past forms of *let* and *make*.

Practice

Exercise 5

- Ask one of the Ss to read out the example in sentence 1.
- Ss complete the exercise working individually.
- They can compare answers in pairs before checking answers as a class.

Answers
2 made   3 let   4 let   5 makes, lets   6 made

 ### Exercise 6

- Read out the sentences to the class and ask Ss to predict if each statement is true or false, using the picture to help them.
- Play the recording once for Ss to do the exercise and check their predictions.
- Check Ss' answers by playing the recording again, pausing after each answer. Ask Ss to correct the false statements.

Tapescript

Alex: Emma, you're the film critic for your school magazine, aren't you?
Emma: Yes, I am.
Alex: Which film are you going to recommend today?
Emma: Well I really enjoyed *Bend it like Beckham*.
Alex: I've heard of that. It's a comedy, isn't it?
Emma: Yes, it is.
Alex: So, what's the story about?
Emma: Well, there's a girl called Jess, and she wants to play football. She's really good at it. She meets another girl footballer called Jules and joins the women's football club.
Alex: That's not very funny, is it?
Emma: Well, yes it is, because you see Jess's parents don't let her play football. So she has to play football in secret. Lots of funny things happen.
Alex: Does her friend Jules have the same problem?
Emma: Well, her parents let her play football, but her mother wants her to be a 'normal' girl … you know, she makes her wear pretty dresses although Jules hates them.
Alex: What happens in the end?
Emma: I'm not going to tell you. But it's a happy ending!
Alex: Good.

Answers
2 ✓   3 ✓   4 ✗   5 ✗   6 ✓

Extension

- Ask the class to listen to the recording again and try to find any extra information in the interview.
- Ss then report back to the class, either in small groups or as a whole, the extra information that they have remembered.

Exercise 7

- Ask one of the Ss to read out the example sentences and then elicit one more.
- Ss work in pairs, saying true sentences about themselves, using the ideas in the box. When the pairs have talked about all the ideas in the box,

tell them to think of some new ideas to use with *let* and *make*, e.g.:
'stay up late at the weekend'
'eat a lot of vegetables'
'paint my room black'.
Go round and monitor the activity, paying particular attention to the correct use of *make* and *let*.

- Each S then says one of their sentences for the class to hear.

Resource 15 (page 136)

Interaction: pair work
Exercise type: reacting to text clues
Aim: to practise *make* and *let*

- Tell your Ss that they are going to read about Mike and the people in his life. Write the following people on the board:
'grandmother' 'father' 'mother' 'teacher'
'older brother' 'sister' 'friend'
Tell Ss that their task is to guess who Mike has described in his little stories.
- Ask each pair of Ss to do it as quickly as possible. You can give a time limit of five minutes. Check answers with the whole class.

Extension

- Ask Ss to write similar descriptions of different people in their life. They can write them in pairs and present them to the rest of the class to guess or they can write them individually and ask their partner to guess.

Answers
1 his friend   2 his mother   3 his teacher
4 his older brother   5 his grandmother   6 his father
7 his sister

Activity Book Answers
Language Diary
2
Students' own answers
Exercise 1
across: 2 star   4 critic   6 award
down: 3 recommend   5 play
Exercise 2
2 My parents didn't let me go out last night.
3 Does your mother make you clean your room every week?
4 Does your English teacher make you work hard?
5 My friend let me borrow his bike yesterday.
6 My brother never lets me use his bike.
Exercise 3
2 d   3 b   4 f   5 e   6 c
Exercise 4
1 h   2 d, f   3 e, g   4 b, i   5 c, j
Exercise 5
2 dancing   3 famous   4 unusual   5 successful
6 funny

16 Story Time

Make a Wish 2

Lesson objectives

Structures
have to: past, present and future

Functions
Describing events in the past

Skills
Reading: skimming

Key vocabulary
School: *exam, sports day, swimming gala, uniform*
Other words and phrases: *go for a walk, have fun, hurry up, keep it secret, pick up, pull out, put on clothes, take your time*

Before class
- Make a copy of Resource 16 (page 137) for each pair of Ss.
- Work out how to group Ss in pairs for Exercises 5 and 6. Decide which Ss are to read Version 1 and which are to read Version 2 of Part 3 of the story.

Exercise 1
- Ss work in pairs, reading and completing the text.
- Check Ss' answers by asking individuals to read out the sentences.

> **Answers**
> 2 two   3 homework   4 one   5 careful

Extension
- Ask the class what else they can remember from Episode 1 of the story, e.g.:
  'What school subjects did Jimmy have for homework?'

Presentation

Exercise 2
- Ask Ss to look at and describe each picture.
- Play the recording twice for Ss to listen and read the text.

Comprehension
Exercise 3
- Ask one of the Ss to read out the example in sentence 1.
- Ss do the exercise working individually.
- They can compare answers in pairs before checking answers as a class. Tell Ss that there may be more than one possible answer for some of the items because the sentences can be corrected in different ways.

> **Answers**
> 2 ✓   3 ✗   4 ✓   5 ✗   6 ✓

Language box   have to
- Read out the sentences in the box to the class, pointing out that the third person singular in the present tense uses *has*.

Extension
- Ask Ss to make similar sentences about themselves or members of their family in the past, present and future. Write time prompts on the board and give some examples, e.g.:
  'Yesterday/Last week (I had to get up early/tidy my room).'
  'Today (our class has to do a French exam/I have to look after my sister).'
  'Tomorrow (my brother won't have to go to college/I'll have to apologise).'
- Give Ss time to write down three or four sentences. Go round and monitor the activity.
- Ss then take turns to read out some of their sentences to the class.

Be careful
- Ask Ss to study the expressions in the box. Draw their attention to the past and future forms of *must* (*had to* and *will have to*).

Extension
- Say some sentences containing *must* to the class and ask Ss to put the sentences in the past or future, e.g.:
  1 'Today I must clean the car.' (Yesterday …/ Tomorrow …)
  2 'Today we must start revising for the exams.' (Yesterday …/Tomorrow …)
  3 'Today I must visit my aunt in hospital.' (Yesterday …/Tomorrow …)

Practice
Exercise 4
- Ask one of the Ss to read out the prompts and example in sentence 1.
- Ss complete the exercise working individually.
- They can compare answers in pairs before checking answers as a class.
- Check Ss' answers by asking individuals to read out both the prompt sentence and their answer sentence.

> **Answers**
> 2 had to go to school
> 3 didn't have to run for the bus
> 4 won't have to do any work tomorrow
> 5 has to wear a tie every day
> 6 will have to work hard next week

Reading Skills: skimming

- Tell the class to look up the meaning of *skimming* in their dictionaries or encourage them to guess the meaning from example sentences such as:
  'He always skims quickly through the newspaper to find the main stories.'
  'The birds skimmed over the lake, hardly touching the water.'
- Read out the instructions in the box to the class.
- Ask Ss what reading material they usually skim through in their first language. For example, they might skim through a novel or magazine before deciding to buy it.
- Remind Ss of the strategies they practised in Unit 15 to guess the meaning of unknown words from the context.

 Exercise 5

- Read the instructions and the two questions out to the class. Group the Ss in pairs and say which is Student A and which is Student B. If you have an odd number of Ss in the class, make a group of three, with two (weaker) Ss reading the same text.
- Remind Ss to skim their texts to find the answers to the two questions. Give Ss one minute to read their texts.
- Ask the Ss who read Version 1 to answer the two questions and then ask the Ss who read Version 2 to answer the two questions.

 Exercise 6

- Give Ss time to read their texts again so that they can tell their partner more about their version.
- Ss work in pairs, taking turns to tell each other what happened in their version of the story. Go round and monitor the activity, helping where necessary.

 Extension

- In pairs, Ss read both versions of Part 3 of the story.
- Write these expressions from each text on the board:
  'Jimmy crossed his fingers' (Version 1)
  'Better luck next time' (Version 2)
  Ask the class to explain in English what people do or say in their own culture and language to bring 'good luck'.

 Exercise 7

- Ask one of the Ss to read out the example sentences.
- Ss work in groups of three or four, discussing which version they think is better, and giving their reasons.
- The groups then report back to the class and Ss see which is the more popular ending.

 Extension

- Elicit from the class some suggestions for alternative endings to the story.
- Ss then work in groups of three or four, discussing and writing their own endings to the story. Go round and monitor the activity, helping with vocabulary where necessary and pointing out any errors to be corrected.
- Each group then reads out its ending to the rest of the class.
- The class can then vote for the best ending.

Resource 16 (page 137)

Interaction: pair work
Exercise type: information gap
Aim: to practise *have to* – past, present and future
Language: What did she have to do on 21 December? She had to buy Christmas gifts./What does she have to do today? She has to prepare for the party./What will she have to do next year? She will have to study French.

- Divide your Ss into pairs and give each S a copy of Resource 16 (either the 'Student A' card or the 'Student B' card). Tell your Ss that they are going to look at Mary's 'things to do' notes. Some notes refer to the past, some to the present and some to the future. Ask Ss to imagine that today is 31 December. They have to ask questions and give answers about things that she had/has/will have to do, using an appropriate tense.
- For a follow-up, ask Ss to write about what they have to do over the next weekend, month or year. Then they should compare notes in pairs and tell the class what they are planning to do.

Activity Book Answers
Language Diary
2
past: didn't, Did, have
present: has, Does, have
future: will have, won't
Exercise 1
2 Go for a walk!   3 Keep it secret!   4 Hurry up!
5 Get up!   6 Put on your coat!
Exercise 2
2 had to   3 will/'ll have to   4 has to
5 won't/doesn't have to   6 had to   7 won't have to
8 didn't have to
Exercise 3
1 Yesterday Jimmy had to buy a new pencil case and (he had to) make sandwiches.
2 Now he has to write about his holidays and (he has to) draw a picture.
3 Tonight he will/'ll have to do homework and (he will/'ll have to) finish the picture.
Exercise 4
Students' own answers
Exercise 5
2 A   3 C   4 B   5 B   6 B

Revision 4

Language revised

Vocabulary
Sport
Transport

Pronunciation
Sentence stress in questions and answers with *have to* and *must*

Grammar
used to, didn't use to
must, mustn't, have to, don't have to
make and *let*
have to: past, present and future

Vocabulary

Exercise 1

- Ss work individually, labelling the picture.
- When checking Ss' answers, also check spelling.

> **Answers**
> 2 goal 3 net 4 court 5 racket 6 boots 7 football
> 8 trainers

Exercise 2

- Read out the first clue and answer.
- Elicit the second answer from the class.
- Ss complete the exercise working in pairs, if you wish.
- Check Ss' answers by asking individuals to complete the crossword on the board.

> **Answers**
> Keyword: transport
> 2 fare 3 escalators 4 underground 5 station
> 6 passengers 7 conductor 8 driver 9 tram

Pronunciation chant

Exercise 3

- Play the recording the first time for Ss to listen and read the chant.
- Then play the recording for Ss to listen and repeat.
- Ask four Ss to repeat the four sections of the chant as you play the recording again.

Grammar

Exercise 4

- Ask Ss to look at the two pictures and describe the girl/woman and what's happening in each picture.
- Read the instructions and the example sentence to the class.
- Ss work in pairs, completing the exercise and reading out the sentences to their partners.

> **Answers**
> 2 She used to have lots of pets.
> 3 She didn't use to have short hair.
> 4 She used to travel by bus.
> 5 She used to live with her parents.
> 6 She didn't use to have a mobile phone.

Exercise 5

- Read out the instructions to the class and ask one of the Ss to read out the example.
- Ss complete the exercise working individually.
- They can compare answers in pairs before checking answers as a class. (Answers may vary from school to school.)

Exercise 6

- Ask one of the Ss to read out the example in sentence 1.
- Ss complete the exercise working individually.
- Check Ss' answers by asking individuals to read out the sentences.

> **Answers**
> 2 have to 3 had to 4 Does he have to
> 5 didn't have to 6 won't have to

Exercise 7

- Ask Ss to look at the picture and say how the boy and the mother are feeling.
- Ask one of the Ss to read out the example sentence.
- Advise Ss to read through all the prompts before they start matching them.
- Ss do the exercise working in pairs.
- Check Ss' answers by asking individuals to read out the sentences.

> **Answers**
> 2 c He didn't like the food but his mother made him eat it.
> 3 d He wanted the last biscuit but his mother let his brother eat it.
> 4 f He wasn't tired but his mother made him go to bed.
> 5 a He was tired but his mother didn't let him stay in bed.
> 6 b He was doing his homework but his mother let his brother make a noise.

Exercise 8

- Ss work in pairs, Student A looking at the table on page 49 and Student B looking at the table on page 105. Read out the given questions to the class and elicit suggestions for more 'yes/no' questions, e.g.:
  'Do you play on a court?'
  'Is there a net?'
  'Is the ball big?'
- Ss work in pairs, asking questions to guess their partner's sport and answering their partner's questions.
- When the pairs have guessed the sports that are given in their tables, they can think of other sports and play the game again. Go round and monitor the activity, making a note of any points that need to be revised with the whole class.

 ## Song Time

- Ask Ss to repeat the words in the box after you, and point out that the words rhyme.
- Ss work in pairs, reading the song and completing it with some of the words.
- Check Ss' answers by asking individuals to read out the lines of the song.

Answers
2 you   3 true   4 you   5 through   6 you

- Ask Ss what *blue* in the second line means. (unhappy/sad)
- Ask Ss if they can guess which colours are used with jealousy (green) and anger (red). Is it the same in their first language?

Extension

- Give Ss more practice in identifying rhyming words by writing these groups of words on the board. Ask Ss which is the odd one out in each group because it doesn't rhyme with the others:

1 who   go   do
2 zoo   clue   now
3 show   flew   glue

Answers
1 go   2 now   3 show

 Check Yourself Units 13–16 – Activity Book page 40

 Check Units 13–16 – Teacher's Book page 114

 Language Tests A/B Units 13–16 – Test Book pages 18–21

Reading Corner

Lesson objectives

Skills

To practise reading for gist
To practise reading for specific information
To practise listening for specific information
To listen and match a story and a sequence of pictures
To write the end of a story

Key vocabulary

A Christmas Carol: chain, character, cry, ghost

Background information

Charles Dickens (1812–70) was a popular English novelist, many of whose novels have been made into films, e.g. *Oliver Twist* and *Great Expectations*. This extract replicates the Penguin Reader, but does not follow the original novel where all three ghosts appear during the same night.

Before class

• If you have any novels by Charles Dickens, bring them to the lesson for Ss to see (Exercise 1).

 Exercise 1

• Ask Ss to look at the pictures and guess what the story is about in pairs.
• Give Ss time to read the text silently to themselves then ask them:
  'What's the title of the story?'
  'Who wrote it?'
• If you have any novels by Charles Dickens, bring them to the lesson for Ss to look at.

Reading

 Exercise 2

• Give Ss time to read through the questions before you play the recording.
• Play the recording twice for Ss to listen, read the text and answer the questions.
• Check Ss' answers by asking pairs of Ss to read out the questions and answers.
• After checking Ss' answers, ask Ss to look back at the text and study the dialogue between Scrooge and the ghost.

Answers
1 yes   2 Jacob Marley   3 yes
4 He wanted to help Scrooge.
5 through the open window

Extension

• Ask pairs of Ss to read out the conversation between Scrooge and the ghost, omitting the narrative parts.

Listening

 Exercise 3

• Ask Ss to describe the pictures in pairs and guess what happens next in the story.
• Ss listen to the recording and match the picture and number.
• If necessary, play the recording again for Ss to check their answers.

Answers
a 3   b 1   c 2

Tapescript

Girl:	So what happened after the ghost of Jacob Marley disappeared?
Man:	Well, Scrooge went to bed and he went to sleep. After a few hours he woke up. He heard the clock. It was nearly one o'clock. He remembered the ghost's words, but he didn't really believe them. He heard the clock again. It was one o'clock. Nothing happened … and then, suddenly, there was a ghost in his bedroom!
Girl:	What was it like?
Man:	It had long white hair, like an old man. But it had a child's face.
Girl:	What happened next?
Man:	The ghost took Scrooge back in time. It showed Scrooge his past. Scrooge remembered his friends and he remembered his family. He wanted to have friends again, and he was very sad.
Girl:	Did more ghosts come, like Jacob Marley said?
Man:	Yes, two more. The second ghost was very fat and happy. It didn't take Scrooge back in time. It stayed in the present time. It showed Scrooge some poor people. They had no money, but they were enjoying Christmas. Scrooge wanted to help them, and he wanted to enjoy Christmas too.
Girl:	What about the third ghost? What happened next?
Man:	The third ghost came to Scrooge at twelve o'clock at night. It was tall and thin and it was wearing black clothes. Scrooge couldn't see its face. It didn't speak and it didn't move. It showed Scrooge the future. It was terrible.

Exercise 4

• Play the recording again (same Tapescript as for Exercise 3) and ask Ss to make notes for Questions 1, 2 and 3. If necessary, play the recording again.
• Get Ss to pool their answers in pairs or small groups, then choose groups to give their answers for the different questions.

Answers
1 his past (his friends and family)
2 the present time (some poor people)
3 the future (terrible)

Speaking

Exercise 5

- Ask Ss to look at the picture. Ask three Ss to read out the example conversation.
- Ss work in groups of three or four, discussing how the story ends and how they think Scrooge behaves and feels.
- The groups can then share their ideas with the whole class.

Writing

Exercise 6

- Read out the instructions to the class and elicit Ss' suggestions for completing the example sentence.
- Ss work individually, using their ideas from Exercise 5 to write the end of the story. Tell them to write one paragraph of six to ten sentences. Go round and monitor the activity, pointing out any mistakes to be corrected.
- Ss then work in pairs, reading each other's texts.
- Two or three Ss can read out their texts for the class to hear.

 Skills Corner 4 – Activity Book page 41

 Skills Tests A/B Units 9–16 – Test Book pages 42–45

Activity Book Answers for Skills Corner 4

Exercise 1

2 She usually played/used to play with her brother and sister.

3 They sometimes had their tea in a house under the table.

4 She used to like cheese most.

5 No, she didn't. (Her mother didn't let her watch a lot of TV.)

6 She didn't like *Teletubbies*.

Exercise 2

2 people from a house near your house   3 look for

4 not real   5 hated   6 loved

Exercise 3

Students' own answers

Lesson objectives

Structures

Passive Voice: Present Simple positive
made of

Functions

Asking and answering questions about the sequences of a process

Key vocabulary

Materials: *cotton, glass, metal, paper, plastic, plasticine, rubber, wood, wool*
Animation: *animator, cartoon film, dialogue, drawings, model, scene, script, storyboard, studio*

Background information

The first *Shrek* film, an American animated quasi-fairytale, was made in 2001.
The West End of London is the entertainment centre of London. The East End, where Cockneys originally come from, is the shipping and commercial centre.

Before class

- Make a copy of Resource 17 (page 138) for each pair of Ss.
- Bring some objects (e.g. a notebook, a wooden or plastic ruler, a coin, a leather or plastic bag or purse) to the lesson to demonstrate the use of *made of* (Be careful).
- Ask those Ss who like cartoon films to bring in a picture of their favourite cartoon character (Exercise 7 Extension).

Presentation

Exercise 1

- Read out the first question to the class.
- Play the recording once for Ss to listen and read and to find the answer to the question.
- Check further comprehension by asking:
  'Who is Patrick?'
  'What does he do?'
  'Where does he work?'
- As a whole class, Ss discuss the answer to the second question.

Extension

- Find out how many of the class like animated films. Ask Ss if they have seen the film *Shrek*. If so, what did they think of it?

Exercise 2

- Ask Ss to look at the picture and describe what is happening. Ask them what sort of person they think Patrick is.
- Play the recording twice for Ss to listen and read the text.
- Ask the class:
  'What exactly does Patrick do in the animation studio?' (He does the drawings.)
  'Are animations with models more difficult than those with drawings?' (No, not really.)
  'Why does Vicki say that "it's just like primary school"?' (Because children play with plasticine at primary school.)
- If you wish, present the expressions *2-D/two-dimensional* and *3-D/three-dimensional* to the class.

Comprehension

Exercise 3

- Ask one of the Ss to read out the example answer, which describes the first stage of making a cartoon.
- Ss complete the exercise working individually, and referring back to the text in Exercise 2.
- Ss can compare answers in pairs before checking answers as a class.

> **Answers**
> a 5   b 4   c 3   e 2

Language box   Passive Voice: Present Simple positive

- Ask individual Ss to read out the sentences in the box. Demonstrate on the board how the sentences match the grammatical form of the passive, e.g.:
  Subject +   to be +   Past Participle
  The script   is   written
- Ask Ss to look back at the text in Exercise 2 and to find and read out more examples of sentences containing the Present Simple passive.

Practice

Exercise 4

- Read out the pair of sentences in question 1 to the class. Point out that *somebody* is not needed in the passive sentence.
- Ss complete the exercise working individually.
- Check Ss' answers by asking individuals to read out the sentences.

> **Answers**
> 2 The pictures are chosen.
> 3 The pictures are put on the board.
> 4 The script and the pictures are matched.
> 5 The dialogue is recorded.
> 6 The animations are made.

Exercise 5

- Ask Ss to look at the pictures and pool what they know about Wallace (and Gromit).
- Ask one of the Ss to read out the first sentence. Elicit the second verb form from the class.
- Ss complete the text working individually.
- Play the recording twice for Ss to check their answers.

Answers
2 are changed   3 is taken   4 is put   5 is taken
6 are kept   7 are used

Extension

- Ss work in pairs, practising reading out the text to each other. Go round and monitor the activity.

Be careful

- Read out the example sentence to the class.
- If you have brought some objects to the class, hold them up one by one and ask the class: 'What's it/are they made of?' (It's/They're made of plastic/leather/paper/wood/metal, etc.)

Vocabulary

Exercise 6

- Ask the class to repeat the words after you to practise pronunciation.
- Ask one of the Ss to read out the example sentence.
- Ss complete the exercise working in pairs.
- They can compare answers in pairs before checking answers as a class.

Answers
2 It's made of rubber.   6 It's made of metal.
3 It's made of plastic.   7 It's made of cotton.
4 It's made of paper.   8 It's made of wool.
5 It's made of wood.   9 It's made of glass.

Exercise 7

- Ss work in pairs, looking at the pictures and discussing the answers to the questions. Go round and monitor the activity, helping where necessary.
- The pairs report back to the class.
- Ss find out how many of the class have seen the films and how many think one of these characters is their favourite.

Extension

- Ss work individually, writing five or six sentences about their favourite cartoon character. This can be one of the characters in Exercise 7 or another character. If Ss have brought in a picture of their favourite character, ask them to put the picture with their text. If any of the Ss do not like cartoon films, ask them to choose another character from a film. Go round and monitor the activity, helping with vocabulary where necessary and pointing out any errors to be corrected.
- Ss then form groups of three or four. In turn, Ss show their pictures to the rest of their group and read out their texts.

Resource 17 (page 138)

Interaction: pair work
Exercise type: general knowledge quiz
Aim: to practise the Passive Voice – Present Simple positive

- Give a copy of Resource 17 to each pair of Ss. They do the quiz together.
- Pairs swap their answers with another pair so they can mark each other's answers as you read out the correct answers.

Answers

1 b	6 a	11 b	16 a
2 b	7 a	12 c	17 b
3 a	8 a	13 b	18 a
4 c	9 b	14 c	19 a
5 c	10 c	15 a	20 b

Activity Book Answers
Language Diary
2
1 asked   2 is written   3 makes
Exercise 1
2 cotton   3 wood   4 glass   5 wool   6 metal
Extra words: plastic, plasticine, rubber
Exercise 2
2 is taken   3 is held   4 are chosen   5 are made
6 is made
Exercise 3
2 The parents are asked to help.
3 This room is cleaned every evening.
4 The streets are swept every day.
5 Rice is grown in China.
6 Oranges are grown in Florida.
Exercise 4
2 CDs are made of plastic.
3 Rice is grown under water.
4 Gold is found in the ground.
5 Football is played on a pitch.
6 Apples are sold at the greengrocer's.
Exercise 5
2 are performed   3 is shown   4 are driven
5 are often filmed   6 are always dressed
Exercise 6
2 are   3 them   4 is   5 is   6 haven't

18 Crazy Reporters

Before class
- Copy Resource 18A (page 139) and Resource 18B (page 140) for each pair or group.
- If any of the Ss have designed their own website, ask them to bring a printout of it to the lesson (Exercise 6 Extension).

Presentation
Exercise 1
- Ask the class to look at the pictures and describe what they can see. Use this as an opportunity to revise or present some of the key computer vocabulary, e.g. *computer screen, website, icon*.
- Play the recording twice for Ss to listen and read the text.
- Ask the class some general comprehension questions, e.g.:
  'What is the website called?' (Crazydaze)
  'What are two of the pages about?' (jokes, a competition)
  'What is the prize in the competition?' (a toy spider)

Comprehension
Exercise 2
- Ask two Ss to read out the pair of sentences in question 1.
- Ss complete the exercise working individually, and referring back to the text to check the facts.
- Check Ss' answers by asking individuals to read out each pair of incorrect and correct sentences.

Answers
2 Jesse replies to the emails.
3 Lots of people write the jokes.
4 Jesse's friends draw the cartoons.
5 Everybody in the class chooses the winner of the competition.

Vocabulary
Exercise 3
- Ask Ss to repeat the words in the box after you to practise pronunciation.
- Ss discuss if the words are similar in their first language and, if so, whether they are pronounced the same.
- Read out the beginning of the example sentence and elicit suitable sentence endings from the class.
- Ss can work in groups of three or four, discussing and writing down the definitions of the remaining words.
- The groups then read out their sentences to the class and the class chooses the best definition for each word.

Suggested answers
the Internet: a computer network made up of millions of linked computers
email: electronic mail; it is a way of sending and receiving messages from one computer to another
icon: a picture on the screen you can click on to make the computer do something
mouse: the equipment that you move by hand and use to operate items on the screen
website: the collection of pages belonging to one address

Exercise 4
- Ask one of the Ss to read out the example in sentence 1.
- Ss complete the exercise working individually.
- Check Ss' answers by asking individuals to read out the sentences.

Answers
2 Connect   3 Visit   4 Send   5 Print

Extension
- Ask Ss to choose three or four of the words from Exercises 3 and 4 and write sentences containing these words. Go round and monitor the activity.
- Ss form groups of three or four and read each other's sentences.

Language box Passive Voice: Present Simple negative and questions
- Read out the sentences in the box.
- Write on the board the positive, negative and question forms for one of the sentences so that Ss can study and compare the structure of each sentence, e.g.:
  'I am connected.'
  'I am not connected.'
  'Am I connected?'

Practice

Exercise 5

- Ask one of the Ss to read out the example in sentence 1.
- Ss complete the exercise working individually, writing negative sentences or questions.
- Ss can compare answers in pairs before checking answers as a class.
- Check Ss' answers by asking individuals to read out the sentences.

> **Answers**
> 2 are sent   3 isn't changed   4 Is it visited
> 5 is the winner chosen   6 are read by Jesse

Be careful

- Read out the two sentences to the class. Point out that we do not use *by somebody* or other non-specific words, e.g. *a person/people*. We only use *by* if we are giving more information, e.g. *by a lot of people*.
- If you wish, write some more examples on the board, e.g.:
  'Cars are made (by people) in Germany.'
  'The paintings are bought by very rich people.'
  'Shoes are made (by people) in Italy.'
  'Breakfast is served (by somebody) at seven o'clock.'
  'The meals are cooked by Italian chefs.'

Exercise 6

- Ask one of the Ss to read out the pair of sentences in question 1.
- Ss complete the exercise working individually.
- Check Ss' answers by asking individuals to read out the sentences.

> **Answers**
> 2 are written by the teachers
> 3 is always sent by Jesse
> 4 is won every week
> 5 is chosen by the class
> 6 is drawn every week

Extension

- If some of the Ss have brought printouts of their own web pages to the lesson, ask them to show the class their pages and talk about them. The rest of the class can ask questions about the web pages. If a lot of Ss have brought their web pages, do the activity in groups, rather than as a whole class.

 ### Exercise 7

- Read out the four sentences (a–d) as Ss look at the pictures.
- Ss work in pairs, completing the four speech bubbles with the four sentences.
- Play the recording once for Ss to check their answers.
- Then, in their pairs, Ss practise reading out the exchanges.

> **Answers**
> 1 c and a   2 b and d

Extension

- Elicit some examples from the class of two-line jokes in the Ss' first language.
- Choose one of these jokes and, as a whole class, Ss try to translate the joke into English and discuss how easy or difficult it is to translate jokes from one language into another.

Resource 18 (pages 139–140)

Interaction: pairs or groups of four
Exercise type: responding to text and picture clues
Aim: to practise the Passive Voice – positive and questions
Language: Who are eyes tested by? Eyes are tested by an optician.

- Divide Ss into pairs or groups of four.
- Tell the Ss that they are going to look at eight pictures of jobs very quickly and then answer questions about them. They know some jobs well from the other levels of *Friends*, but some will be new to them. Their task is to make a sentence describing what the person does in his/her job.
- Give Resource 18A to one S/pair and Resource 18B to the other(s). If you wish, elicit an example of a passive sentence.

> **Activity Book Answers**
> **Language Diary**
> **2**
> *negative:* not, are
> *questions:* Am, Is, Are
> **Exercise 1**
> 2 c   3 b   4 f   5 a   6 d
> **Exercise 2**
> 2 Is it designed by the teachers?
> 3 No, it's designed by the pupils.
> 4 Its pages are changed every week.
> 5 The articles are written by our class.
> 6 The pictures aren't drawn by the teacher.
> **Exercise 3**
> 2 isn't connected   3 is it fed   4 isn't fed   5 is fed
> 6 are they grown   7 aren't grown
> **Exercise 4**
> 2 Computers are used by millions of people.
> 3 Thousands of emails are sent every minute.
> 4 Stories are sent across the world.
> 5 The Internet is used by students and teachers.
> 6 New websites are designed every day.
> **Exercise 5**
> 2 All the children use the computers.
> 3 Is the website changed every week?
> 4 Is the grass cut every week?
> 5 The children don't do the housework.
> 6 The gardening is done by my mother.

19 Friends' Club

Lesson objectives

Structures

Passive Voice: Past Simple

Functions

Describing amazing places around the world

Skills

Listening for detail

Key vocabulary

Measurements: *age, height, length, size, weight, width*

Other words: *discover, discovery, invent, invention, material*

Before class

- Make a set of Resource 19 (page 141) for each pair.
- Large world map (Exercise 1).
- Ask Ss to bring a picture of an amazing place in their own country to the lesson (Exercise 8 Extension).

Exercise 1

- Play the recording twice for Ss to listen and read the text.
- Ask the class if they know anything about the Nasca lines in Peru or the clay army at Xian, or if they can guess what these things are. Ask them if they can guess what Hesham from Egypt will be talking about.
- Show the class a large wall map of the world and ask individual Ss to point to Peru, China, Xian, Egypt and Cairo.

Presentation

Exercise 2

- Ask the class to look at the pictures, describe what they can see and guess what the lines are.
- Before playing the recording, read out to the class the five questions in Exercise 3. Tell Ss to focus on the answers to these questions the first time they listen and read the text.
- Play the recording twice for Ss to listen and read the text.

Comprehension

Exercise 3

- Give Ss time to refer back to the text and write down their answers to the questions.
- Check Ss' answers by asking pairs of Ss to read out the questions and answers.

Answers

1 in Peru   2 1500–2500 years ago
3 birds, animals and insects   4 to please the sky gods
5 because they are so big

Extension

- Ask Ss to look back at the text in Exercise 2, and ask them further comprehension questions, e.g.:
'When were the drawings made?'
'What do BC and AD mean?'
'Why weren't the drawings found for thousands of years?'
'Who found the drawings in the 1920s?'
'What happened to the Nascans?'

Language box Passive Voice: Past Simple

- Read out the sentences in the box to the class and draw Ss' attention to the use of *was/were*.
- Ask Ss to look back at the text in Exercise 2 and to find and read out more examples of sentences containing the Past Simple Passive.

Practice

Exercise 4

- Ask one of the Ss to read out the first paragraph of the letter.
- Ss complete the exercise working individually.
- Check Ss' answers by asking individuals to read out the sentences in the letter.

Answers

2 were made   3 was buried
4 were not/weren't discovered   5 were found
6 were they made   7 Were they built

Vocabulary

Exercise 5

- Read out the example matching pair to the class.
- Ss complete the exercise working individually.

Answers

2 c   3 f   4 e   5 d   6 a

Listening Skills: listening for detail

- Read out the first step to the class and explain these are ways of preparing yourself for a listening exercise.
- Ask the class what questions and answers could go with other important words, e.g. *size*. (What size shoes does he take? Size 40.)
- Read out Steps 2 and 3 to the class. Ask Ss if this is what they usually do. Do they find it difficult not to write down things when they first listen?

Exercise 6

- Read out the example question and answer to the class and check that Ss understand what to do.
- Ss complete the exercise working in pairs.
- Check Ss' answers by asking pairs to read out the matching questions and answers.

Answers
weight 3 a   material 4 f   address 6 c
size 1 b   height 5 d

Exercise 7

- Give Ss time to read the notes, so that they know what information they need to find out.
- Play the recording twice for Ss to complete the notes.
- Check Ss' answers by playing the recording again, pausing after each answer.

Tapescript

Alex:	Tell me about the pyramids, Hesham. When were they built?
Hesham:	The first pyramids were built more than 4500 years ago. They're made of huge blocks of stone.
Alex:	How did they carry them?
Hesham:	They were carried by boats down the river Nile. However, nobody knows how the pyramids were actually built.
Alex:	How big are they?
Hesham:	They are not all the same size, but the biggest pyramids are about 100 metres high.
Alex:	Wow, that's huge! They were tombs for the kings, weren't they?
Hesham:	Yes, they were.

Answers
2 stone   3 boats   4 one hundred metres
5 tombs for the kings

Exercise 8

- Ss use their notes from Exercise 7 to write a paragraph about the pyramids. If necessary, play the recording again before Ss start writing.
- Go round and monitor the activity, helping where necessary and pointing out any errors to be corrected.
- Ss can then work in pairs reading and comparing their paragraphs.

Extension

- Tell Ss they are going to write about an amazing place in their own country. Write on the board some question prompts, e.g.: 'What is it?' 'Where is it?'   'How old is it?'   'How big is it?' 'Have you been there?'   'Why is it amazing?'
- If Ss have brought a picture of an amazing place, get them to ask and answer questions about it.
- Ss work in pairs or individually, writing a first draft about an amazing place in their own country.
- If Ss have brought a picture of the place to the lesson, they can attach the picture to the final version of their text.
- Ss can pass round the texts for everyone to read, or make a wall display of them.

Resource 19 (page 141)

Interaction: pair work
Exercise type: general knowledge domino
Aim: to practise the Passive Voice – Past Simple

- Give one set of domino cards to each pair and ask them to put down a card and try to find the other card to finish the sentence. They then try to find the new sentence/card and so on.
- The game continues until the Ss use up all the cards. If the domino cards are put down correctly, they form a closed square.
- Monitor the activity closely, and keep checking to see if Ss' guesses are right.
- If you want to make the activity more competitive, you can set a time limit and tell the Ss that the winner is a pair which finishes the activity first.

Answers
Jurassic Park was directed by Steven Spielberg.
The theory of evolution was developed by Darwin.
President J. F. Kennedy was shot in the sixties.
Hamlet was written by William Shakespeare.
The Theory of Relativity was discovered by Albert Einstein.
Radium was discovered by Marie Curie.
The opera *Don Giovanni* was composed by Wolfgang Amadeus Mozart.
The first jeans were made by Levi Strauss in 1873.
Television was invented in 1926.
Rock and roll music was created in the fifties.
The Statue of Liberty was given to the Americans by the French.
The first hamburgers were sold in 1895 in America.
Bikes were invented in France in 1865.
Books about Sherlock Holmes were written by Conan Doyle.
Shrek was created by DreamWorks.
Sandwiches were invented by Lord Sandwich.
Star Wars was directed by George Lucas.
Yellow Submarine was sung by the Beatles.
Harry Potter was written by J. K. Rowling.
The telephone was invented by Alexander G. Bell.

Activity Book Answers
Language Diary
2 1 was/wasn't   2 were/weren't   3 was/wasn't
Exercise 1
adjectives across: wide, high, big, old
nouns across: width, height, age
adjectives down: heavy   *nouns down:* weight, size
Exercise 2
2 width   3 age   4 height   5 weight   6 size
Exercise 3
2 We were amazed by the drawings.
3 When were the drawings made?
4 The first drawing was made thousands of years ago.
5 They weren't noticed for a long time.
6 Perhaps hot-air balloons were invented by the Nascans.
Exercise 4
2 were filled   3 were stolen   4 was found
5 was buried   6 were put
Exercise 5
2 a   3 d   4 e   5 b   6 c
Exercise 6
2 high   3 invent   4 long   5 width   6 sight

20 Story Time

The Story of Magnus 1

Lesson objectives

Structures
Gerunds and infinitives

Functions
Narrating a story
Expressing opinions

Key vocabulary
Dragon: *claws*, *face*, *flames*, *heat*
Sea: *horizon*, *nets*, *shore*, *voyage*

Background information
The term *Viking* refers to any of the Scandinavian sea-robbers who raided the coasts of Europe from the eighth to the tenth centuries. Sometimes the Viking raids reached south to the Mediterranean and east to the White Sea.

Before class
- Copy and cut up one set of Resource 20 (pages 142–143) for the class.

Exercise 1
- Ask Ss to look at the picture and, as a whole class, discuss the answers to the two questions. Ss can see if they guessed the content of the story correctly when they listen to the recording in the next exercise.
- Use the picture to present vocabulary such as *Viking*, *longboat*, *dragon*, *breathe fire*, *claw* and *flame*.

Presentation

Exercise 2
- Play the recording twice for Ss to listen and read the text.
- Ask the class to cover the text. Ask Ss what they can remember about Magnus and encourage them to pool their ideas.

Comprehension
Exercise 3
- Ask one of the Ss to read out the example in sentence 1.
- Ss complete the exercise working individually, and referring back to the text.
- Check Ss' answers by asking individuals to read out the sentences.

> **Answers**
> 2 a farmer   3 food   4 hungry   5 flames   6 claws

Vocabulary
Exercise 4
- Ask Ss to say the words in the box after you to practise pronunciation.
- In groups of three or four, get Ss to find the meaning of any difficult words, reminding them of Unit 15 – guessing words from context. Go round and monitor this activity.
- Ss can then do the exercise in pairs.

> **Answers**
> a shore   b flames, heat   c face, claws

Extension
- Ss work in pairs, choosing three words from the list and writing three sentences containing those words. Give the class one or two examples, e.g.:
  'My cat has got long claws.'
  'We could see the flames from the bonfire on the hill.'
- Go round and monitor the activity, helping and correcting where necessary.
- The pairs form groups of four or six and read out their sentences to the rest of their group.
- Each S then reads out one of their sentences for the class to hear.

Language box   gerunds and infinitives
- Ask individual Ss to read out the sentences in the box.
- Draw Ss' attention to verbs followed by the gerund and verbs followed by the infinitive. Suggest that Ss start making a list of the two groups of verbs in their notebooks. They can then add more verbs to this list in the future.

Extension
- Give the class the beginnings of some sentences for Ss to continue and finish with a verb in the correct form, e.g.:
  'My father hates … .'
  'When I was little, I wanted … .'
  'Our cat loves … .'
  'My brother has decided … .'
  'I've never enjoyed … .'

Be careful
- Read out the sentences in the box. Draw Ss' attention to the different structure with *would like* + infinitive.

Extension
- Ask Ss to work in pairs, discussing and writing two sentences beginning:
  1 'We like … .'
  2 'We'd like … .'
- The pairs then read out their sentences to the class.

Practice
Exercise 5

- Ask one of the Ss to read out the example in sentence 1.
- Ss complete the exercise working individually.
- Check Ss' answers by asking individuals to read out the sentences.

> **Answers**
> 2 living 3 to sail 4 to explore 5 telling 6 being
> 7 to leave 8 to become

Extension

- Read out to the class the last sentence of the text in Exercise 2 (Magnus was lifted into the sky.). Elicit suggestions from the Ss for the continuation of the story, e.g.:
  'Where did the dragon take Magnus?'
  'What did the sailors do?'
  'What did Magnus do?'
  'Did he escape from the dragon?' (If so, how?)
  Ss can see if their predictions are correct in Lesson 24.

 ## Exercise 6

- Ask one of the Ss to read out the example sentence.
- Give Ss time to read through the prompts and to think of how to complete the sentences.
- Ss work in pairs, telling each other their sentences. Go round and monitor the activity, paying particular attention to the correct use of gerunds and infinitives.
- Each S tells the class something about their partner, e.g. '(Tom) would like to live in America'.

Exercise 7

- Ss use the ideas from Exercise 6 to write a paragraph about their partner. Go round and monitor the activity, pointing out any errors to be corrected.
- Ss then work with their original partner, reading their partner's text about themselves and seeing if all the information is true.

Resource 20 (pages 142–143)

Interaction: pair and group work
Exercise type: completing personal cards and matching
Aim: to practise gerunds and infinitives

- Check that Ss understand what a dating agency is.
- Divide Ss into pairs. Give 'Women' personal cards to half the class and 'Men' personal cards to the other half so that each pair gets a full set of either the 'Women' cards or the 'Men' cards.
- In pairs, Ss look at the cards and fill in the missing information using their own ideas and imagination.
- Put the pairs together so that the cards are now mixed. The group discusses and decides who should be paired up with whom.
- The group reports to the rest of the class who they paired up with whom and why.

> **Activity Book Answers**
> **Language Diary**
> **2**
> 1 b 2 a
> **Exercise 1**
> 2 flames 3 claws 4 horizon 5 shore 6 face
> **Exercise 2**
> 2 working 3 to sail 4 to join 5 to tell 6 to leave
> **Exercise 3**
> 2 liked 3 planned 4 wanted 5 would like 6 enjoy
> **Exercise 4**
> Students' own answers
> **Exercise 5**
> 2 sailor 3 fishing 4 heat 5 happier 6 stolen

Revision 5

Language revised

Vocabulary

Materials
Computers
Sea and dragons
Measurements

Pronunciation

Sentence stress and emphatic stress
Vowel sounds

Grammar

Passive Voice: Present Simple and Past Simple
Gerunds and infinitives

Vocabulary

Exercise 1

- Read out the example in question 1 to the class.
- Ss work individually, sorting out the words and matching them to the objects.
- Ss can compare answers in pairs before checking answers as a class.

> **Answers**
> 2 glass – h   6 plastic – a
> 3 metal – d   7 wood – f
> 4 rubber – b   8 cotton – g
> 5 paper – c

Exercise 2

- Ask one of the Ss to read out the example.
- Ss complete the exercise working individually.
- After checking Ss' answers, ask them to work in pairs, writing three sentences using three of the words.
- The pairs can then read out their sentences for the class to hear.

> **Answers**
> 2 e   3 b   4 d   5 c   6 a

Exercise 3

- Read out the example to the class.
- Ss do the exercise working individually.
- Check Ss' answers by asking pairs of Ss to ask and answer:
  'What's (four down)?' 'It's (height. H E I G H T)'
- Go round and monitor this activity, paying particular attention to the pronunciation of consonant clusters.

> **Answers**
> *Down:* 4 height   5 age
> *Across:* 2 width   3 length   6 weight

Pronunciation chant

Exercise 4

- Ask Ss to look at the picture and guess what the child is talking about with her mother.
- Play the recording once for Ss to listen and pay attention to the stress and intonation patterns.
- Play the recording again for Ss to listen and repeat.
- Ask pairs of Ss to say the chant, trying to use the stress and intonation patterns they heard on the recording.

Grammar

Exercise 5

- Ask one of the Ss to read out the example sentence.
- Advise Ss to read through all the items before they start matching them.
- Ss complete the exercise working in pairs.

> **Answers**
> 2 a   3 f   4 b   5 d   6 e

Exercise 6

- Ask two Ss to read out the example sentences.
- Ss work in pairs, correcting the facts and writing sentences in the Past Simple Passive.
- Check Ss' answers by asking pairs of Ss to read out the two sentences for each item.

> **Answers**
> 2 No, it wasn't. It was written by J.K. Rowling.
> 3 No, it wasn't. It was invented by Alexander Graham Bell.
> 4 No, it wasn't. It was sung by Michael Jackson.
> 5 No, it wasn't. It was made by Walt Disney.
> 6 No, it wasn't. It was painted by Leonardo da Vinci.

Exercise 7

- Students work in pairs, with Student A looking at page 61 and Student B looking at page 105. Explain that each S has one complete text. They have to answer questions about this text. Each S also has one incomplete text. They have to ask questions about this text so that they can complete it. Tell Ss to use the Passive Voice in their questions and answers. Each S has an example question.
- Give Ss' time to read through both their texts and, if necessary, ask two stronger Ss to give an example to the class.
- Ss then take turns to ask and answer questions about the texts. Go round and monitor the activity, paying particular attention to the use of the Passive Voice.

- Check Ss' answers by asking individuals to read out the sentences in the texts.

Answers
Student A
2 Where were the main parts of the Eye built?
3 How were the parts carried to Britain?
4 Where were they put together?
5 When was it opened to the public?
Student B
2 Who was it opened by?
3 When was it closed?
4 Why was it closed?
5 When was it opened again?

 Exercise 8

- Give Ss time to read through the prompts and the example sentence.
- Before Ss work in pairs, check that they remember which verbs take the gerund and which take the infinitive by asking Ss to make one sentence for each verb. (*like, love, hate* and *enjoy* take the gerund and the remaining verbs take the infinitive)
- Ss work in pairs, making as many true or false sentences as they can with the prompts. Go round and monitor the activity, paying particular attention to the correct use of gerund and the infinitive.
- Each S then says one of their sentences for the class to hear.

 Song Time

- Read out the instructions for the first stage of the activity.
- Ss work individually, matching the rhyming words.
- Check Ss' answers by asking them to say the words in each group to check that they rhyme.

Answers
1 train   2 care/hair   3 me/tree

- Read out the first two lines of the song and ask Ss to repeat them after you.
- Ss complete the song with the rhyming words.
- Play the recording twice for Ss to check their answers.

Answers
3 me   4 air   5 hair   6 care   7 train   8 rain
9 again

- Read out the questions and the example sentences in Stage 2 of the activity.
- Elicit from the class two or three advantages and disadvantages of living in cities and in the country.
- Ss work in pairs, telling their partner what they like and don't like about where they live. Go round and monitor the activity, noting down any general problems to be revised or corrected with the whole class.

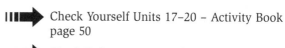 Check Yourself Units 17–20 – Activity Book page 50

 Check Units 17–20 – Teacher's Book page 115

Language Tests A/B Units 17–20 – Test Book pages 22–25

Ireland

Lesson objectives

To read and identify paragraph topics
To speculate about the content of a picture
To practise listening for specific information
To write a postcard
To ask 'yes/no' questions
To write about superstitions

Key vocabulary

Ireland: *emerald, fiddle, harp, leprechaun, shamrock*

Background information

St Patrick's Day is 17 March. He is the saint credited with bringing Christianity to Ireland and driving the snakes out of the country.
Great Britain includes England, Scotland and Wales, but not any part of Ireland. The UK (United Kingdom) includes Great Britain and Northern Ireland. The Republic of Ireland is also known as Eire.

Before class

- If you have any pictures/postcards or objects from Ireland bring them to the lesson to show the class.

Reading

Exercise 1

- Ask Ss to look at the map and repeat the names of the places after you.
- Ask Ss if they know anything about Ireland and, if so, ask them to tell the class.
- Play the recording twice, pausing after each section for Ss to read the texts and look at the pictures.

Exercise 2

- Look at the example matched items with the class.
- Ss work individually, reading the questions and matching them to the paragraphs.
- When checking Ss' answers, ask them if they have ever seen Irish dancing or heard a harp being played. Do they know any Irish surnames? (Murphy, O'Connor)

Answers
2 C 3 D 4 E 5 A 6 B

- After checking Ss' answers, ask the class if there is:
  – a national colour in their country. Do they think some colours are lucky and some are unlucky? Ss say what their favourite colour is.
  – a national flower or tree or plant in their country.
  – a traditional musical instrument.

Listening

Exercise 3

- Ask Ss to look at the picture.
- Ask one of the Ss to read out the example sentence. In pairs, Ss guess where the people are and what they are doing. At this stage, don't give the correct answers.

Exercise 4

- Give Ss time to read through the statements before you play the recording.
- Play the recording twice for Ss to listen and complete the exercise.
- When checking Ss' answers, ask them to correct the false statements.
- After checking Ss' answers, play the recording again for Ss to listen for extra information and more details about the story. Ss can then pool what they have remembered.

Tapescript
Irish people are good talkers – you know, we tell good stories – especially people who have kissed the Blarney Stone. They tell the best stories in the world. This is why it's visited – and kissed – by thousands of tourists every year. Well, people say the Blarney Stone is magic. You have to go to a village called Blarney. There's a castle there. The magic stone is part of the castle walls. There's a good story about the stone. An old woman fell into a river. She couldn't swim, but a king rescued her. The old woman gave the king the magic stone as a reward. Everybody who kisses the Blarney Stone becomes good at telling stories. The problem is, it's in a really difficult place, it isn't very easy to touch it!

Answers
2 ✓ 3 ✗ 4 ✓ 5 ✓ 6 ✗

Writing

Exercise 5

- Ask one of the Ss to read out the text on the postcard.
- Elicit suggestions from the class for the next sentence.
- Ask Ss how they can end the postcard. (Love, See you soon)
- Ss work individually, completing the postcard. Tell them to write four or five sentences. Go round and monitor the work, pointing out any mistakes to be corrected.
- Ss then work in pairs, reading each other's postcards.
- Ask one or two Ss to read out their postcards for the class to hear.

Exercise 6

- Read out the instructions to the class and the example questions and answers. Elicit two or three more 'yes/no' questions from the Ss.
- Ss work in groups of three or four, trying to guess their friends' places. If you wish, tell Ss they can ask a maximum of ten questions then, if they haven't guessed the place, their friend tells them where it is. Go round and monitor the activity, paying particular attention to question formation.

Project

- Read out the instructions to the class.
- Ask Ss to look at the pictures while one of them reads out the example text. Ask Ss if there are similar superstitions in their own country about small spiders and black cats. Elicit some examples of superstitions from the class and ask Ss if they believe in any of these superstitions.
- Ss may need time to find out about superstitions in the library or at home before they write about them.
- Check Ss' draft texts before they write the final version. Each S writes about two or three superstitions and illustrates them.
- Ss make a classroom display of their work.
- In turn, each S reads out their texts and shows their pictures to the class.

Cartoon

- Ask Ss to look at the cartoon. Ask them to explain why the children think these tourists have been to Blarney.

|||➡ Skills Corner 5 – Activity Book page 51

Activity Book Answers for Skills Corner 5
Exercise 1
2 f 3 e 4 d 5 b 6 a
Exercise 2
Students' own answers

---

21 The LONDONERS

Lesson objectives

Structures

so do I/neither do I

Functions

Asking for and giving information about an airport
Agreeing and disagreeing

Skills

Speaking: agreeing and disagreeing

Key vocabulary

Airport: *arrivals, check-in, departures, flight information, lost luggage, passport control*

Background information

Heathrow airport is accessible by tube. Stansted is in Essex and Gatwick is in Sussex. There is also a fourth London airport: Luton, in Hertfordshire.

Before class

• Copy and cut up Resource 21A (page 144) and Resource 21B (page 145) for each pair of Ss.

Presentation

Exercise 1

• Ask Ss to look at the picture and see if they can find the name of one of London's airports. (Heathrow) Ask them if they know anything about Heathrow airport or any of the other London airports and, if so, ask them to tell the class.
• Read out the first question (Are all three airports near central London?) to the class.
• Play the recording once for Ss to find the names of the airports and if they are near central London. (No)
• Ask Ss the second question (What is the main airport in your country?) and ask:
'Have you ever been there?'
'If so, were you a passenger, or were you meeting somebody?'

Exercise 2

• Ask the class to look at the picture again and see if they can translate the words on the signs into their first language. Ask Ss:
'Where does the Heathrow Express go?' (to London and Terminals 1, 2 and 3)
'What is the opposite of a short stay car park?' (a long stay car park)
• Play the recording twice for Ss to listen and read the text.
• If you wish, point out that the Present Participle of the verb *queue* can be spelt *queuing* or *queueing*.

Comprehension

Exercise 3

• Ask one of the Ss to read out the example and then ask the class to make the false statement true (e.g. Kim and Vicki are not passengers/Kim and Vicki are meeting Kim's cousin/Kim's cousin is a passenger, not Kim and Vicki).
• Ss complete the exercise working individually and referring back to the text in Exercise 2.
• When checking Ss' answers, ask them to make the false statements true.

> **Answers**
> 2 ✓ 3 ✗ 4 ✓ 5 ✓ 6 ✗

Extension

• Ask the class to look back at the text in Exercise 2. Play the recording again and ask Ss to listen carefully to the pronunciation, stress and intonation patterns.
• Ss then work in pairs, reading the dialogue aloud and taking turns to be Kim and Vicki. Go round and monitor the activity, correcting pronunciation, stress and intonation patterns where necessary.
• Some of the pairs then read out sections of the text for the rest of the class to hear.

Vocabulary

Exercise 4

• Ask Ss to say the words (a–f) after you to practise pronunciation.
• Ask one of the Ss to read out the example matched item.
• Ss complete the exercise working individually.
• They can compare answers in pairs before checking answers as a class. Check Ss' answers by asking pairs of Ss to read out the prompt (2–6) and the reply (a–f).

> **Answers**
> 2 a 3 e 4 d 5 c 6 f

Language box *so do I, neither do I*

• Ask pairs of Ss to read out each sentence and the response first to agree and then to disagree.
• Draw Ss' attention to the verbs in bold in the box and point out that the verb in the response is a repeat of the verb *to be* or the auxiliary verb:
'I'm (am) lost.' 'So am I./I'm (am) not.'
'I want to go to the shops.' 'So do I./I don't.'
• If any Ss ask about the use of *nor* (Nor do I), explain that *nor* can be used instead of *neither* but that *neither* is more commonly used in spoken, modern English.
• Ss may ask about the difference between the British pronunciation of *neither* /'naɪðə/ and the American pronunciation /'niːðər/.

Extension

- Say sentences for Ss to agree or disagree with, e.g.:
  'I want to be rich.'
  'I'm hungry.'
  'I've lived here for five years.'
  'I can't speak Russian.'
  'I'll visit America next year.'
  'I wouldn't like to come to school on Sundays.'
  'I've bought a new bike.'

Practice

Exercise 5

- Ask two Ss to read out the example exchange.
- Ss complete the exercise working in pairs. Tell them to agree with the statements and to take turns making statements and agreeing.
- Go round and monitor the activity, correcting where necessary.
- Some of the pairs then say their exchanges for the class to hear.

> **Answers**
> 2 So did I.   3 So am I.   4 Neither have I.
> 5 Neither would I.   6 So am I.   7 Neither can I.
> 8 Neither will I.

Exercise 6

- Ask two Ss to read out the example exchange.
- Complete the exercise as a whole class, with pairs of Ss saying each exchange.

> **Answers**
> 2 I wouldn't.   3 I haven't.   4 I do.   5 I did.
> 6 I'm not.   7 I can't.   8 I have.

Speaking Skills: agreeing and disagreeing

- Read out the sentences in the box to the class.
- Draw Ss' attention to sentences 2 and 5. Explain that it is polite to give a reason or add another sentence rather than just saying *So/Neither do I*. This is especially important when disagreeing with someone.

Extension

- Ask Ss to look back at Exercises 5 and 6. As a whole class, pairs of Ss say the exchanges, but this time also give a reason or an additional sentence, e.g.:
  'I like chocolate.'   'So do I. I buy some almost every day.'
  'I'd love a sandwich.'   'I wouldn't. I had a big breakfast so I'm not hungry.'

Exercise 7

- Read out the subjects to the class.
- Ask three Ss to read out the example sentences.
- Ss work in groups of three or four, choosing one of the topics and discussing it in their groups. Go round and monitor the activity, helping with vocabulary if necessary.
- Tell the groups to make a note of their ideas. Give the groups time to organise their ideas so that they can present them to the class.
- Each group presents their ideas to the class. The rest of the class listen and can ask questions at the end of each presentation, if they wish.
- The class can see which topic and which ideas were most popular.

Resource 21 (pages 144–145)

Interaction: pair work
Exercise type: game of 'snap'
Aim: to practise *so … I, neither … I* – present, past and future

- Give one set of 'snap' cards to each pair. One S in a pair gets Resource 21A with *so* and *neither* and the other gets Resource 21B with the sentences. Ask Ss to shuffle the cards well. Each S keeps their cards in a pile, face down.
- To start the game, the S who has the sentences puts the first card on the desk. The other S puts the *so/neither* response next to it. Ss mustn't look at their cards before they put them face up on the desk. They put them down very quickly so that both Ss can see the cards at the same time. If the two cards form a correct pair, Ss should shout 'SNAP'. The student who shouts first takes all the cards on the desk (i.e. the ones being put down by Ss) and the game continues. Warn Ss that it sometimes takes many turns to get the correct pair of sentences.
- The game continues until Ss have all the cards on their personal piles. The winner is the S who has the most cards.

> **Activity Book Answers**
> **Language Diary**
> **2**
> *I agree:* So will I. Neither have I.
> *I disagree:* I did.
> **Exercise 1**
> 2 Arrivals   3 Departures   4 Flight Information
> 5 Check-in   6 Passport Control
> **Exercise 2**
> 2 did I   3 have I   4 can I   5 would I   6 am I
> 7 will I
> **Exercise 3**
> 2 So am I./I'm not.   3 So did I./I didn't.
> 4 So would I./I wouldn't.   5 So do I./I don't.
> 6 Neither have I./I have.   7 Neither do I./I do.
> 8 Neither did I./I did.
> **Exercise 4**
> 2 C   3 A   4 B   5 C   6 A

22 Crazy Reporters

Lesson objectives

Structures

Verbs with two objects: *give, pass, sell, send, show lend* and *borrow*

Functions

Describing how something works
Asking someone a favour and agreeing or refusing it

Key vocabulary

Electrical appliances: *battery, button, dial, plug, switch, thermometer*

Before class

- Make a copy of the auction sheet from Resource 22 (page 146) for each S.
- Bring to the lesson four or five small appliances for Ss to describe how they are operated, e.g. a torch, a battery-operated children's toy, a mobile phone, a cassette recorder, an alarm clock, a small hairdryer (Exercise 4 Extension).

Exercise 1

- Ask three Ss to read out the texts about the three inventions.
- In pairs, Ss talk about the advantages and disadvantages of each invention and decide if they would buy any of them.
- Ask Ss if they know of any other crazy inventions and, if so, ask them to tell the class about them.

Presentation

Exercise 2

- Ask Ss to look at the pictures, describe the woman's appearance and guess what invention we can see in each picture.
- Play the recording once for Ss to listen and read the text.
- Then play the recording again, pausing after each section to check comprehension of vocabulary.
  (Section 1: *battery, press this switch, pass that watering can*)
  (Section 2: *plug, turn the dial, air conditioning, press this button, thermometer*)
  (Section 3: *springs, catalogue*)

Comprehension

Exercise 3

- Ask one of the Ss to read out the example matched items in question 1.
- Ss complete the exercise working individually.
- Check Ss' answers by asking individuals to read out the complete sentences.

Answers
2 e   3 b   4 f   5 d   6 a

Vocabulary

Exercise 4

- Ss work individually, matching the pictures and the words.
- They can compare answers in pairs before checking answers as a class.

Answers
2 b   3 e   4 c   5 a   6 d

Extension

- Show the class four or five small appliances that you have brought with you. Hold up one of the objects and elicit from the Ss some sentences to describe how it works, e.g.:
  'Put in the battery. Switch it on.'
- Put Ss in groups of four or five. Give each group one of the objects. The groups write some sentences to describe how the object works.
- In turn, each group shows the class their object and reads out their sentences.

Language box Verbs with two objects

- Ask the class to repeat the sentences in the box after you.
- Draw Ss' attention to the use of *to* when the pronoun or person comes in the second position, e.g.:
  'Show the shoes to us/your mother/John.'

Extension

- Write some prompts on the board and ask Ss to make two sentences for each set of prompts, e.g.:
  'Send an email to Susan.'
  'Send Susan an email.'

email	the teacher	your homework
pass	Philip	the dictionary
send	Susan	your ruler
lend	me	
give		

Practice

Exercise 5

- Ask one of the Ss to read out the example in sentence 1.
- Ss complete the exercise working in pairs, if you wish, or individually.
- Check Ss' answers by asking individuals to read out the sentences.

Answers
2 Claris gave them a demonstration.
3 Harry passed her the watering can.
4 Claris didn't give Harry the shoes.
5 Did she lend them to him?
6 She will send a catalogue to Claire.

Be careful

- Read out the sentences in the box and draw Ss' attention to the difference in meaning between *lend* (the person has got money) and *borrow* (the person hasn't got money and wants it).

 ## Exercise 6

- Ask the class to look at the pictures and guess what the speakers are saying in each situation. Ss can see if they guessed correctly when they listen to the recording.
- Play the recording for the first conversation and ask Ss why it matches picture d.
- Continue playing the recording for Ss to match the remaining conversations and pictures.
- Check Ss' answers by playing the recording again, pausing after each conversation.

Tapescript

1
Boy 1: Can you lend me some money, please?
Boy 2: Sorry, I can't. I haven't got any.
Boy 3: Of course. Here you are.
Boy 1: Oh, thanks a lot.

2
Girl 1: Can I borrow your ruler, please?
Girl 2: No, you can't. Sorry.
Girl 3: Here you are. You can borrow mine.
Girl 1: Oh, thanks!

3
Girl 1: Oh dear, I haven't got my mirror. Can you lend me yours?
Girl 2: Sorry, I need it.
Girl 3: Here, borrow mine.
Girl 1: Thank you.

4
Boy 1: Oh, no! My bike's broken. Can I borrow yours, please?
Boy 2: No, sorry, I want it.
Boy 3: Here, take mine.
Boy 1: Thanks.

Answers
a 2   b 4   c 3   d 1

 ## Exercise 7

- Play the recording from Exercise 6 again for Ss to listen carefully to each dialogue.
- Ask three Ss to read out the example dialogue. Draw Ss' attention to the use of polite expressions such as *please* and *sorry*.
- Ss work in pairs or groups of three, practising the dialogues for each picture and taking turns to be the borrower and the lender. Tell them not to worry if their dialogues are not exactly the same as the ones on the recording. Go round and monitor the activity, paying particular attention to the correct use of *lend* and *borrow* and the use of polite expressions.
- Some groups then say one of their dialogues for the class to hear.

 ## Extension

- As a final activity for this unit, ask Ss to work in groups of three or four, designing a crazy invention. Elicit some suggestions for crazy inventions from the Ss, e.g. an alarm clock that always tells the wrong time.

- In turn each group explains their invention to the rest of the class.
- The class then votes for the craziest invention.

Resource 22 (page 146)

Interaction: whole class
Exercise type: sentence auction
Aim: to practise all grammar and vocabulary up to Unit 22, including verbs with two objects
Language:
Teacher: *The starting price is £100.00.*
Do I hear £150.00?
Going, going, gone.
Sold to Pietro and Sandra for £200.00.
Ss: *We give £100.00 for this sentence.*

- Before the activity explain the concept of an auction.
- Give each S a copy of the auction sheet in Resource 22 (cover 'Teacher's sentences' when you photocopy the material). Tell your Ss they have a budget of £5000 and that they have to buy as many sentences as possible and spend as little money as possible. The minimum price for a sentence is £100. Some sentences are correct, some aren't. If Ss buy a sentence with a mistake, they lose that money.
- Read the first sentence from 'Teacher's sentences'. (Try to read all the sentences in a very convincing way, without giving away sentences with mistakes.) Ss discuss in pairs if they want to buy the sentence and they start bidding. They might want to put them down in the auction sheet. When the sentence is bought, confirm if it's correct or not and therefore if Ss lose or keep their money. Then move on to the next one. It may happen (and in fact should) that Ss won't like to buy some of the sentences. If this is the case, move on after giving them some time to think.
- The winner is the pair which bought the biggest number of correct sentences and spent the least money.

Extension

- You can use this activity type for practising any other grammar point or as an error correction exercise. You just have to invent your own sentences.

Answers
Sentences 4, 8, 9, 12 and 13 have mistakes.

Activity Book Answers
Language Diary
2
1 Harry/him, shoes   2 me, catalogue
Exercise 1
across: 4 dial   5 plug   6 thermometer
down: 2 battery   3 button
Exercise 2
2 Give him the shoes.   3 Pass her the watering can.
4 Sell them the invention.   5 Send her the catalogue.
6 Lend him the rain alarm.
Exercise 3
2 them   3 to them   4 it   5 him   6 to him
Exercise 4
2 Give Harry the shoes.   3 Send it to Claire.
4 Pass the watering can to her.
5 Sell them to the customers.   6 Lend it to her.
Exercise 5
2 are   3 them   4 them   5 was   6 it

Lesson objectives

Structures
Relative pronouns: *who, which, that*

Functions
Asking for and giving factual information

Key vocabulary
Olympic Games: *athlete, ceremony, champion, compete in, flame, found, hold (a competition), host country, introduce, light (a fire), marathon, vote*

Background information
The host countries for recent and forthcoming summer Olympic Games are: 2000 Sydney, Australia; 2004 Athens, Greece; and 2008 Beijing, China.

Before class
- Copy and cut up Resource 23 (page 147) for each group.
- If you are working with this unit at the time of the winter or summer Olympics, bring to class some newspaper cuttings (in the Ss' first language) about the games (Exercise 1 Extension).

Exercise 1
- Play the recording twice, if necessary, for Ss to listen and read the text. Check that Ss understand the meanings of *founded* and *Olympic flame*.
- Ask Ss to answer the first question. (every four years)
- Answers to questions 2 and 3 (the last and the next Olympic Games) will depend on when you are using this unit.
- Ask the class to look again at the text and questions and to find and read out examples of the passive voice, e.g.:
  'How often are the Olympic Games held?'
  'The modern games were founded.'

Extension
- Ask Ss what else they know about the Olympic Games, and encourage them to pool their knowledge.
- If you have brought some newspaper cuttings about the Games to the lesson, give one cutting to each group of three or four Ss. Each group reads their text and writes a summary of it in English.
- Each group in turn shows their text to the class and reads out their summary.

Presentation
Exercise 2
- Ask Ss to look at and identify the Olympic sport illustrated in each picture. (judo, football, ice-skating, weightlifting, downhill skiing and ice hockey)
- Ask Ss if they do any of these sports and, if so, ask them to tell the class about their experiences.
- Ss do the quiz working in pairs. Tell them to look up any new words (e.g. *marathon*) in their dictionaries.

Exercise 3
- Ss check their answers to the quiz by listening to the recording.
- Find out if any of the Ss got all the answers right and which questions Ss found most difficult.

Answers
1 a   2 b   3 c   4 c   5 a   6 b

Language box   Relative pronouns: *who, which, that*
- Read out the sentences in the box to the class. Point out that only *that* can refer to people, animals and things.

Practice
Exercise 4
- Read out the instructions to the class and remind Ss not to use *that* in this exercise.
- Ask one of the Ss to read out the first sentence to the class.
- Advise Ss to read through the whole text quickly before they start completing the gaps. Ss do the exercise working individually.
- They can compare answers in pairs before checking answers as a class.
- Check Ss' answers by asking individuals to read out the sentences.

Answers
2 who   3 which   4 which   5 who   6 which

Extension
- Ask the class to suggest other sports or activities in which people have to train hard, e.g. musicians, dancers, footballers, wrestlers, marathon runners, tennis players or racing drivers.
- Ss work in pairs, writing three or four sentences for one of these people. If you wish, give them an example for a ballet dancer called Maria, e.g.:
  'Maria is a (ballet dancer) who was born in New York.'
  'Every day she (practises in a studio) which (is near her home).'

'She has a marvellous (teacher) who was a famous dancer in Russia.'

'She has a special diet which (is mainly vegetables, fruit and fish).'

- Ss work in pairs, writing their sentences. Go round and monitor the activity, helping with vocabulary, if necessary, and pointing out any errors to be corrected.
- Ss then form groups of four or six and read each other's sentences.

 Exercise 5

- Give Ss time to read through the text before doing the exercise.
- Ss work individually or in pairs completing the text with the phrases a–e.
- Play the recording for Ss to listen and check their answers.

Answers
2 d   3 a   4 c   5 e

 Extension

- Play the recording again and ask Ss to listen carefully to the pronunciation, stress and intonation patterns.
- Ss work in pairs, reading aloud the dialogue and taking turns to be Ally and Nikos.

 Exercise 6

- Ask one of the Ss to read out the example sentence about Christopher Columbus.
- Ss work in pairs, matching the items and then writing sentences using *who* or *which*. It's possible that the Ss will write sentences using *that*, but they should not be encouraged to do so.
- Check Ss' answers by asking individuals to read out the sentences.

Answers
2 e Hogwarts was the school which/that Harry Potter went to.
3 b Walt Disney was the man who/that invented Mickey Mouse.
4 f The *Titanic* was the ship which/that sank.
5 a George Lucas was the man who/that made *Star Wars*.
6 d Hobbits were the characters which/that appeared in *The Lord of the Rings*.

 Extension

- Write these prompts on the board and ask Ss to work in pairs completing the sentences using *who* or *which*:

  'A marathon runner is a person … .'
  'Athens is the city … .'
  'Mark Spitz is the swimmer … .'
  'Dragons are animals … .'
  'Claris is an inventor … .'
  'The rain alarm is an invention … .'
  'Heathrow is the airport … .'
- Go round and monitor the activity, pointing out any errors that need correcting.
- Ss then form groups of four or six and read out their sentences to the rest of their group.

Resource 23 (page 147)

Interaction: group work
Exercise type: guessing card game
Aim: to practise relative clauses with *who*, *which* and *that*. (Note: *that* can be used with each card, so you may wish to focus on *who* or *which*.)
Language: It is a very big country which is in Asia., It is a person who works on a ship.

- Put Ss into groups of three or four.
- Give a set of picture cards to each group. The cards should be well shuffled and should be put face down.
- The first S picks up a card. He/She must define the object or a person using a sentence containing *who*, *which* or *that*. The S who guesses what object or what person is in the picture gets the card. The next S in the group then picks up a card and defines an object or a person. The winner is the S who collects the most cards.

Activity Book Answers
Language Diary
2
1 c   2 b   3 a
1 who   2 which
Exercise 1
2 founded   3 held   4 lights/lit   5 introduced
6 voted
Exercise 2
2 who   3 which   4 which   5 who   6 who
Exercise 3
2 c   3 b   4 a   5 f   6 d
Exercise 4
2 b At the Olympic Games there are athletes who come from all over the world.
3 d The winners receive medals which are made of gold.
4 a Skiing and ice hockey are examples of sports which are played in the Winter Olympics.
5 e Carl Lewis and Mark Spitz are famous sportsmen who have won many Olympic medals.
Exercise 5
2 in   3 which/that   4 who/that   5 was
6 which/that

24 Story Time

The Story of Magnus 2

Lesson objectives

Structures
Subject and object questions

Functions
Asking for and giving factual information

Key vocabulary
Word formation: adjectives and nouns

Before class

- Make a copy of Resources 24A and B (pages 148–149) for each pair of Ss.

Exercise 1

- Ss work in pairs, completing the text. Tell them not to look back at Unit 20 but to try to complete the text from memory.
- Check Ss' answers by asking individuals to read out the sentences.

> **Answers**
> 2 fields   3 sail   4 boat   5 dragon

Extension

- Ask Ss what else they can remember about the first episode of the story, e.g.:
  'What was the dragon like?'
  'Why was life difficult in the village?'

Presentation

Exercise 2

- Ask Ss to look at the picture and predict what happens in the story. Ss can check their predictions as they listen to the recording.
- Play the recording twice for Ss to listen and read the text.
- Ask two general comprehension questions:
  'Why was the dragon roaring?'
  'Did Magnus open its claws?'

Comprehension

Exercise 3

- Read out the example in question 1 to the class.
- Ss complete the exercise working individually. Tell them to refer back to the text, if they wish.
- They can compare answers in pairs before checking answers as a class. If Ss disagree about any of the answers, ask them to look back at the text and read out the section that supports their answer.

> **Answers**
> 2 a   3 c   4 a   5 b

Vocabulary

Exercise 4

- Look at the example in question 1 with the class and ask Ss to find and read out the sentence in paragraph 1 containing the noun *horror*.
- Ss complete the exercise working individually.
- When checking Ss' answers, ask Ss to read out the pairs of adjectives and nouns. Correct pronunciation and word stress where necessary, e.g. cou*ra*geous, **cou**rage.

> **Answers**
> 2 amazement   3 terror   4 pain   5 anger   6 safety
> 7 courage   8 pride

Extension

- Ss work in pairs, choosing four or five of the nouns and adjectives in the exercise and writing sentences containing their chosen words.
- The pairs form groups of four or six and read out their sentences to the rest of their group.
- Each S then chooses one of their sentences to read out to the class.

Language box   Subject and Object questions

- Read out the questions in the box to the class and point out the position of the subject and object in each type of question.
- Ask Ss to find these four questions in paragraphs 1 and 4 of the text in Exercise 2. Read out each question again and ask Ss to answer it, e.g.:
  'What hurt the dragon?' (the sunlight)
  'Who saw it?' (the fishermen and Magnus)
  'What did you do?' (I used my knife)
  'Who did it take?' (Magnus)

Practice

Exercise 5

- Ask one of the Ss to read out the example pair of sentences in question 1.
- If you wish, do the second item with the whole class before Ss complete the exercise working individually.
- Check Ss' answers by asking individuals to read out the question and answer it, e.g.:
  'Who watched the dragon?' (the sailors)

> **Answers**
> 2 Who did the dragon attack?
> 3 What did Magnus remember?
> 4 What did the knife reflect?
> 5 What hurt the dragon's eyes?
> 6 Who hurt the dragon?
> 7 Who rescued Magnus from the sea?
> 8 What did the dragon hit?

 Exercise 6

- Ask Ss to look at the picture and predict what will happen at the end of the story, either in pairs or as a whole class.
- Give Ss time to read through the questions.
- Play the recording twice for Ss to listen and answer the questions.
- Check Ss' answers by playing the recording again, pausing after each answer.

Tapescript
'How Magnus sent the dragons away'
Magnus went away with the Viking sailors. He spent ten years with them and in that time he visited many lands and saw many things. But Magnus never forgot about his village. He often thought about the people there and the dragons too. One day, he called his friends and spoke to them. 'I have decided to return to my land,' he told them. 'I want to send the dragons away, and I have a plan. Who will come with me?' The Viking sailors loved Magnus. They never forgot his fight with the dragon. Soon Magnus had a hundred men to help him. He explained his plan and they started to prepare for the voyage. Soon they were ready. After many days and nights Magnus finally saw land. He was shouting to his men, when suddenly he heard a roar. He looked up and there was a huge dragon. The men were ready. Magnus shouted 'Now!' and they threw something up into the sky. It was a dragon, made of wood and paper. Its paper wings were gold and silver. The real dragon turned its head to look at this strange thing, and again the men threw something into the air. It was a huge fishing net. The net flew up and over the dragon's head, and the dragon fell into the sea. The water closed over its head. The dragon was dead. Then the sky went black. Hundreds of frightened dragons were flying away. While Magnus watched, they disappeared over the horizon. The sun shone again and the people cheered. And that's how Magnus sent the dragons away.

Answers
2 a hundred   3 a dragon
4 a dragon made of wood and paper, the real dragon turned its head to look
5 a huge fishing net, it went over the dragon's head, it fell into the sea
6 The dragons flew away.

 Extension

- Play the recording again and ask Ss to listen carefully for any more facts in the story.
- In groups of three, Ss retell the story.
- The group that remembers the most can then tell the class and, if you wish, you can encourage other Ss to join in and help with the narrating.

Exercise 7

- Ask one of the Ss to read out the example sentence. Elicit suggestions from the class for the next sentence.
- Ss write the story working individually. Go round and monitor the activity, pointing out any errors to be corrected.
- Ss can then work in pairs, reading each other's story and seeing how similar or different their stories are.

 Extension

- Ask the class what fables or legends there are in their own culture about dragons or other creatures.
- Ss work in groups. Each group chooses a fable or legend they all know and writes out the story.
- Each group in turn reads out its story to the class.

Resource 24 (pages 148–149)

Interaction: pair work
Exercise type: information gap
Aim: to practise object and subject questions

- Each S in a pair gets a copy of either Resource 24A or Resource 24B (one completed and one gapped text). Ss ask each other questions to complete the information missing in their texts. They should use either subject or object questions depending on the information they need to extract in order to complete the texts.
- Give Ss time to read through both their texts and, if necessary, ask two stronger Ss to give an example to the class.
- Ss then take turns to ask and answer questions about the texts. Go round and monitor the activity, paying particular attention to the use of object and subject questions.

Activity Book Answers
Language Diary
2
2 saw it   3 did you do   4 did it take
Exercise 1
2 pain   3 courage   4 Safety   5 anger   6 terror
7 amazement   8 pride
Exercise 2
2 Sigurd (killed the dragon).
3 (The birds were watching) Sigurd.
4 (Sigurd understood) the language of birds.
5 Regin (was planning to take all the gold).
6 (Sigurd took) the gold.
Exercise 3
2 Who hid in the hole?   3 Who fell asleep?
4 What did Sigurd fight?   5 What did Sigurd touch?
6 What was magic?
Exercise 4
2 horrible   3 painful   4 angry   5 terror   6 proud
7 safety   8 amazed

Revision 6

Language revised

Vocabulary
Airport
Electrical appliances
Word formation: adjectives and nouns

Pronunciation
Sentence stress

Grammar
So do I, Neither do I
Relative pronouns: *who* and *which*
Subject and Object questions
Verbs with two objects

Vocabulary

Exercise 1
- Ask Ss to look at the signs. Point out that the 'dropped' letters are in pairs and will fit in the two-letter spaces in the words.
- Ask Ss to look at the example item and complete it.
- Ss complete the exercise working individually.
- When checking Ss' answers, ask them to spell the words.

Answers
1 NF AT   2 AS RT OL   3 LO GA   4 HE   5 RI   6 TU

Exercise 2
- Ask the class to look at the example picture and word and to identify the other illustrations.
- Ss work in pairs, if you wish, finding the words in the square. Tell them the words are spelt across and down in the square.

Answers
battery   plug   dial   thermometer   button

Exercise 3
- Read out the example in sentence 1 to the class.
- Ss complete the exercise working individually.
- When checking Ss' answers, ask them to spell the adjectives.

Answers
2 courageous   3 painful   4 proud   5 terrified
6 angry

Pronunciation chant

Exercise 4
- The rhyme about the Prince of Wales refers to Edward, the eldest son of George V. In the 1920s, he was the leader of the 'Bright Young Things'. He enjoyed travelling, dancing and socialising and was at the forefront of fashion. He became king in 1936 and abdicated the same year.
- Play the recording once for Ss to listen and read the text.
- Play the recording two or three times for Ss to listen and repeat.

Grammar

Exercise 5
- Ask three Ss to read out the example exchange.
- Tell Ss to practise agreeing and disagreeing with each statement.
- Ss work in groups, taking turns to make statements and agree and disagree. Go round and monitor the activity.
- Check Ss' answers by asking pairs to say their exchanges for the class to hear.

Answers
2 Neither have I./I have.   6 Neither can I./I can.
3 So am I./I'm not.   7 So will I./I won't.
4 So have I./I haven't.   8 So would I./I wouldn't.
5 Neither do I./I do.

Exercise 6
- Read out the instructions and the example sentence to the class.
- Check that Ss understand that they have to match three parts of a sentence (1, F and b for the example item).
- Do the second item with the whole class.
- Ss work in pairs, completing the exercise. Check Ss' answers by asking individuals to read out the sentences.

Answers
2 C d Tenball is the game which was invented by twins.
3 G c Billy Elliot is/was the boy who liked ballet.
4 D e The Nasca lines are the drawings which were made thousands of years ago.
5 B g The Vikings were the people who built longboats.
6 A a Claris is/was the woman who invented the techno jacket.
7 E f Athens is the city which held the first modern Olympic Games.

Exercise 7

- Ask Ss to look at the picture and describe the place and the people. Ask Ss to guess what is happening in the picture.
- Ask individual Ss to read out the text. Ask the class if any of them have got to the counter in a shop and then found they didn't have enough money to pay. What did they do?
- Ask two Ss to read out the example question and answer. Point out that the questions are answered by the words in bold in the answers.
- Ss complete the exercise working individually.
- They can compare answers in pairs before checking answers as a class. Check Ss' answers by asking pairs to read out the questions and answers.

Answers
2 went with him   3 did he want   4 did he see
5 paid for the game   6 is he/Ted going to give Mr Franks

Exercise 8

- Ask one of the Ss to read out the example in question 1.
- Ss complete the exercise working individually.
- Check Ss' answers by asking individuals to read out the sentences.

Answers
2 She showed it to the teacher.
3 Pass the water to George.
4 Could you lend me £5?
5 I've sent a letter to John.
6 She gave me some advice.

 Song Time

- Read out the instructions to the class and ask individual Ss to read out the words in the box.
- Ss work in pairs, telling each other what makes them happy. Tell Ss they can use their own ideas as well as the words in the box.
- Each S tells the class two things that make them happy.
- Ask Ss to read through the text in Stage 2 and see if they can guess any of the missing phrases.
- Play the recording twice for Ss to listen and complete the text.

Answers
2 makes me happy   3 makes me want to dance

 Check Yourself Units 21–24 – Activity Book page 60

 Check Units 21–24 – Teacher's Book page 116

 Language Tests A/B Units 21–24 – Test Book pages 26–29

Lesson objectives

Skills

To practise reading for gist
To practise reading for specific information
To practise listening in order to sequence sentences
To speculate about what is going to happen next in a story
To discuss and plan a story
To write a story
To play *The Borrowers* game

Key vocabulary

The Borrowers: borrow, fridge, human beings, lend, mouse, spider, web

Background information

The Borrowers by Mary Norton appeared in 1952 and several sequels followed. It was made into a film in 1997. Mary Norton died in 1992.

Before class

- Groups of Ss will need dice and tokens for the board game in Fun Time.

Exercise 1

- Ss work in pairs, describing what they can see in the picture.
- Ss then read the text and answer the question. (The story is about little people who borrow things from human beings.)
- Check that Ss remember the difference between *borrow* and *lend* (from Unit 22) and elicit examples, such as:
  'Can I borrow a pencil, please?'
  'X has lent me a pencil.'
- Ask Ss to discuss (in their first language, if necessary) what the difference is between *borrowing* and *stealing*.
- Ask Ss to speculate about Mr Potter's reasons for wanting to destroy their house.

Reading

Exercise 2

- Play the recording twice for Ss to listen and read the text.
- Ask Ss:
  'What did Pete see inside the cupboard?' (a small light)
  'How did Pete catch Arrietty?' (He put a glass over her.)
  'Does Arrietty know that Pete must move to another house?' (yes)

Exercise 3

- Ss work in pairs, writing the names in the text in Exercise 2 in the two lists.

> **Answers**
> 1 Pete, Joe
> 2 Arrietty, Homily, Peagreen, Pod

Listening

Exercise 4

- Give Ss time to look at the picture and describe what is happening.
- Ss read the sentences (a–f). Tell them to guess the correct order of the sentences. They can check their guesses when they listen to the recording.
- Play the recording twice for Ss to listen and sequence the sentences.

> **Tapescript**
> Arrietty started to climb up the refrigerator in the Lenders' kitchen. It was very big. 'Where are you going?' Peagreen asked. 'We must stay here. Dad'll kill you.'
> 'I'm going to find some ice cream,' Arrietty said. 'You open the refrigerator door.' She climbed inside the refrigerator. She walked over to the ice cream, put her hand into it and put some into her mouth.
> 'Come on, Arrietty,' Peagreen said – but suddenly he fell and the refrigerator door closed! 'Dad!' he cried. 'Help!'
> 'Where's Arrietty?' Pod asked.
> Peagreen looked at the refrigerator. 'In there.'

> **Answers**
> a 4   b 3   c 6   e 2   f 5

Speaking

Exercise 5

- Elicit from the whole class some suggestions for what Arrietty does next.
- Ss work in pairs, discussing and deciding on their own ending for the story. Go round and monitor the activity, helping with vocabulary, if necessary.
- The pairs then tell the class their story. Ss can see how many different stories they thought of.

Exercise 6

- Read out the instructions and the given titles of the stories. Tell Ss they can use their own title, if they wish.
- Ss work in groups of three or four, discussing and deciding their story. Go round and monitor the activity, helping with vocabulary, if necessary.

Writing

Exercise 7

- Read out the example text to the class. Point out that the title is underlined at the top of the page and the important words in the title begin with a capital letter. Refer Ss back to the titles in Exercise 6 to illustrate the use of capital letters.
- Ss can work individually or in their groups, writing out their story from Exercise 6. Some Ss may like to illustrate their story, making a picture as in Exercise 4.
- Go round and monitor the activity, pointing out any errors to be corrected.
- Ss can then make a display of their stories or pass them round the class for the rest of the class to read.

Extension

- The groups could record their stories on cassette and then listen to all the stories as a whole class.
- To extend this further, each group could also write three or four comprehension questions about their story to ask the other groups.

 ## Fun Time

- Ss play the game in groups of three or four. Each group needs a dice and tokens.
- Ss take turns to throw the dice and move their tokens. When a S lands on a square, they have to make up a story about *The Borrowers* using the picture in their square. Go round and monitor the activity, making a note of points to go over with the whole class afterwards.

 Skills Corner 6 – Activity Book page 61

 Skills Tests A/B Units 17–24 – Test Book pages 46–49

Activity Book Answers for Skills Corner 6
Exercise 1
2 F   3 E   4 D   5 A   6 C
Exercise 2
2 ✗   3 ✗   4 ✓   5 ✓
Exercise 3
Students' own answers
Possible answer:
Mandy and Rosie were ready for the big race. They stood behind the starting line together with hundreds of runners. They had to wait ten minutes before they could cross the line but they were happy. The crowd were great and everybody cheered. The marathon began and the runners started running.

Suddenly Mandy stopped. She hurt her foot. She wanted to give up but Rosie decided to help her.

They decided to go to the bus stop and catch a bus. The bus took them to the finishing line. They got off and waited for the winners. When they appeared at the finishing line, Mandy and Rosie clapped.

Lesson objectives

Structures
must, can't (deduction)

Functions
Making deductions

Key vocabulary
End of school term: *award* (*prize*), *break up,*
celebrity, come top, guest speaker, make a speech
Adjectives: *cold, happy, hungry, late, strong, tired*

Background information
Schools in Scotland break up for the summer earlier
than schools in England and Wales, and the school
year in Scotland starts in August.
At present, British schools have a three-term year
with short half-term breaks within each term. In the
future, there are plans to have a six-term year, so
terms and holidays are more frequent and shorter.

Before class
- Make a copy of Resource 25 (page 150) for each
  pair of Ss.

Presentation

Exercise 1
- Read out the first question to the class and see if
  Ss can guess the answer.
- Play the recording once for Ss to see if their
  guesses are correct.
- Ask the class the second question:
  'When does your school year finish?'
- Ask Ss when they have school holidays, if they
  have speech days, if pupils are awarded prizes
  and if celebrities visit their school.

Exercise 2
- Ask Ss to look at the picture, describe what they
  can see and guess what is going to happen. Ss can
  check their guesses when they listen to the
  recording.
- Play the recording twice for Ss to listen and read
  the text.
- Ask Ss to find these words and phrases in the text
  and say what they mean: *embarrassing, stuck in*
  traffic, come top, guest speaker, scary.

Comprehension
Exercise 3
- Read out the example item to the class and ask Ss
  to find and read out the section in the text that
  gives this information.
- Ss complete the exercise working individually,
  referring back to the text in Exercise 2, if
  necessary.
- When checking Ss' answers, ask them to correct
  the false statements.

> **Answers**
> 2 ✓ 3 ✗ 4 ✓ 5 ✓ 6 ✗

Language box *must, can't* (deduction)
- Ask two Ss to read out the example sentences.
- Ask the class to find these two sentences in the
  text in Exercise 2 and explain why the speakers
  have made these deductions, i.e. they are certain
  that their deduction is correct.
- Ask Ss to look back at the text in Exercise 2 and
  find and read out more sentences with *must* or
  can't (deduction) in them.

Practice
Exercise 4
- Ask one of the Ss to read out the example
  sentences in question 1.
- Do the second item with the whole class, if you
  wish.
- Ss complete the exercise working individually.
- Ss can compare their answers in pairs before
  checking answers as a class. Check Ss' answers by
  asking individuals to read out the pairs of
  sentences.

> **Answers**
> 2 can't   3 must   4 must   5 can't
> 6 must   7 can't   8 can't

Exercise 5
- Read out the example in question 1 to the class.
- Ss complete the exercise working individually.
- Check Ss' answers by asking individuals to read
  out the pairs of sentences.

> **Answers**
> 2 She must be tired.   5 She can't be cold.
> 3 He must be late.   6 He must be hungry.
> 4 He/They can't be happy.

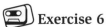 **Exercise 6**

- Give Ss time to read through the notes before you play the recording.
- Play the recording twice for Ss to listen and complete the notes.
- Ask individual Ss to read out their notes and see if the rest of the class agree.
- Then play the recording again, if necessary, for Ss to confirm their answers.

Tapescript

Kim: Hey, Vicki! I know who our guest speaker is. I've just found out a few things about her.

Vicki: Oh, really! Who is she then? She must be somebody famous if she's the guest speaker.

Kim: Yes, she is. Her name is Wanda Black and she used to be a pupil at the school.

Vicki: Oh, I see. When was that?

Kim: Um, fifteen years ago.

Vicki: So she must be – let's see – fifty years old.

Kim: Oh, come on Vicki. She can't be fifty. She must be about thirty. Fifteen years is not so long ago.

Vicki: You're right. What else did you find out?

Kim: She used to be in the drama club. She liked acting and she was in all the school plays. And she was good at music. One year she won the music prize.

Vicki: So what does she do now? Is she a musician?

Kim: No, she's a reporter. She writes for a Canadian newspaper.

Vicki: Canadian? How come?

Kim: Oh, Mrs Black doesn't live in England any more. She went to live in Canada five years ago. This year she decided to come back to England for a holiday and to visit some friends.

Vicki: I wonder if the school will ever invite us to be guest speakers some day?

Kim: Well, maybe – if we're famous.

Answers
2 thirty   3 acting   4 music   5 reporter   6 Canada

Be careful

- Read out the sentences in the box and point out the link between *woman* and *one*.
- Write these sentences on the board and ask Ss what *one(s)* refers to in each sentence:
  1 'A woman bought the trousers.'   'Which *one*?'
  'The tall woman.' (*one* refers to the woman)
  2 'A woman bought the trousers.'   'Which *ones*?'
  'The black ones.' (*ones* refers to the trousers)

Exercise 7

- Ask two Ss to read out the example dialogue.
- Ss work in pairs, reading out the remaining dialogues and deciding what *one* means in each dialogue.
- Check Ss' answers by asking some of the pairs to read out the dialogues and say what *one* means in the dialogue.

Answers
2 boy   3 book

Exercise 8

- Read out the instructions to the class and remind Ss that they must ask 'yes/no' questions.
- Ask two Ss to read out the example questions and answers. Elicit more examples of 'yes/no' questions from the class, e.g.:
  'Does she live in … ?'
  'Is she sitting next to … ?'
  'Does she like … ?'
  'Is she good at … ?'
- Ss work in pairs, taking turns to think of a classmate and ask and answer questions. Go round and monitor the activity, checking that Ss are asking only 'yes/no' questions.

Resource 25 (page 150)

Interaction: pair work
Exercise type: responding to picture clues
Aim: to practise *must* and *can't* (deduction)
Language: Nancy must be John's wife. Jo can't be Nancy's daughter.

- Give a cut-up copy of Resource 25 to each pair of Ss.
- Ss speculate and decide on the age, profession and family relationship of the people in the pictures. It is purely speculation and guessing, there are no right or wrong answers.
- As a follow-up, ask pairs to present their decisions.

Activity Book Answers
Language Diary
2
must, can't
Exercise 1
2 break up   3 celebrity   4 speech   5 prize   6 top
Exercise 2
2 They can't be on holiday.   3 He can't like them.
4 He must be hungry.   5 It must be a mistake.
6 She can't come from England.
Exercise 3
2 must   3 can't   4 must   5 must   6 can't   7 must
Exercise 4
Possible answers:
2 No, they can't be cold because they're wearing light clothes.
3 Yes, she must go skating a lot because she is very good at skating.
4 Yes, he must like her because he's smiling.
5 No, he can't be good at skating because he's wobbling a lot.
Exercise 5
2 You must know the answer.
3 It can't be true.
4 They must have a lot of money.
5 He can't understand.
6 It must be him.

26 Crazy Reporters

Before class

- Copy Resource 26 (page 151) – one weekend plan for each group and one role card for each S.
- You will also need large sheets of paper for each group to draw their house design (Exercise 8).

Presentation

Exercise 1

- Ask Ss to look at the two pictures and describe what they can see. Ask them what they think is 'crazy' about the young man. Ss can check their ideas when they listen to the recording.
- Play the recording twice for Ss to listen and read the text.

Comprehension

Exercise 2

- Ask one of the Ss to read out the example question and answer in sentence 1.
- Ss complete the exercise working individually, referring back to the text in Exercise 1 if necessary.
- When checking Ss' answers, ask them to read out the sections of the text that support the answer.

Answers
2 a   3 c   4 a   5 a

Vocabulary

Exercise 3

- Ask Ss to look back at the text in Exercise 1 and find and read out sentences containing *see*, *look at* and *watch*. Ask Ss what the difference in meaning is between the expressions as used in these sentences, i.e.: *look at* is normally used with objects (*look at trees/a view*); *watch* is normally used with an action or event (*watch TV*); and *see* means to be able to use your eyes (*see for miles*).
- Ask one of the Ss to read out the example in sentence 1.
- Ss complete the exercise working individually.
- They can compare answers in pairs before checking answers as a class.

Answers
2 watch   3 see   4 Look at   5 watch   6 see

Language box *I prefer, I'd (= I would) rather*

- Read out the sentences in the box to the class. Draw Ss' attention to the difference in structure:
  prefer (noun) *to* (noun)
  prefer verb + *ing* (noun) *to* verb + *ing* (noun)
  would rather (infinitive) *than* (infinitive)
- If any of the Ss ask about other structures, explain that we can use *prefer* + verb, e.g. *I prefer to travel by train than by car.*

Be careful

- Ask one of the Ss to read out the sentence in the box.
- Ask Ss to make these sentences negative:
  'I'd rather look at TV.' (I'd rather not look at TV.)
  'I'd rather live in a tree.' (I'd rather not live in a tree.)
- If Ss ask about the negative with *prefer*, give them some examples, e.g.:
  'I prefer not to drink coffee at night.'
  'I prefer not to live in a city.'

Practice

Exercise 4

- Ask one of the Ss to read out the example in sentence 1.
- Advise Ss to read through the text quickly before they start completing it. Ss work in pairs, completing the text.
- Check Ss' answers by asking individuals to read out the sentences.

Answers
2 would   3 than   4 prefer   5 rather   6 not

Extension

- Write these prompts on the board:
  food   drink   sport   music   colour   travel   animals   holidays
- Give the class some examples of sentences about these topics, e.g.:
  'I'd rather not eat any sweets.' (food)
  'I prefer jazz to pop songs.' (music)
  'I'd rather have a cat than a dog.' (animals)
- Ss work in pairs writing five or six sentences, using the topics on the board. Go round and monitor the activity, helping with vocabulary where necessary and pointing out any errors to be corrected.
- The pairs then form groups of four or six and read out their sentences to the rest of their group.

Exercise 5

- Ask one of the Ss to read out the example sentence.
- Ask Ss to look at the pictures and identify each prompt, e.g.:
  (3) listen to music on my CD player/watch TV
  (5) have a shower/have a bath
  Elicit another example sentence, if necessary.
- Ss work in pairs, telling their partner which they prefer for each picture. Go round and monitor the activity, correcting where necessary.

Exercise 6

- Read out the example sentence to the class.
- Ss work individually, writing about their partner's preferences. Go round and monitor the activity, pointing out any errors to be corrected.
- When Ss have finished their writing, they can show their text to their partner, who reads it and sees if they agree with it.

 ## Exercise 7

- Give Ss time to look at the pictures and read the statements before you play the recording.
- Play the recording twice for Ss to listen and complete the exercise.
- Check Ss' answers by playing the recording again, pausing after each answer. Ask Ss to correct the false statements.

Tapescript

Harry: Hey, look at this crazy house. It's called the Flying Saucer House. Isn't it great?

Claire: Do you think so? I think it's horrible! It looks stupid. Does it actually fly?

Harry: No, of course not. It can't move. But it's great. I'd love to live somewhere like that.

Claire: I wouldn't. It must be very uncomfortable. I like unusual houses, but I'd rather live here.

Harry: What, on the water?

Claire: Yes. The people who live here can go wherever they like because their house floats.

Harry: I'd rather stay in one place, thank you very much. And the Flying Saucer House is in a beautiful place.

Claire: But it's so small! I'd rather live in a big house. This Floating House has got three bedrooms and a bathroom as well as a separate kitchen. And they can build more rooms if they want to.

Harry: I prefer the simple life. The Flying Saucer House hasn't got a kitchen at all, so they don't have to keep it clean! That's brilliant!

Claire: Where do they cook?

Harry: Outside.

Claire: Ugh, I hate camping! I prefer cooking and eating inside to sitting outside on the ground.

Answers
2 ✗ 3 ✗ 4 ✓ 5 ✓

Extension

- Play the recording again and ask Ss to listen carefully for more information.
- Ss pool their ideas and see how much of the text they have understood and remembered.
- Ask Ss which of these houses they would rather live in.

 ## Exercise 8

- Ask Ss if they know of any unusual houses. Have they read about them or seen them on TV?
- Ask one of the Ss to read out the example sentences. Elicit ideas from the class of other features of an underground house.
- Ss work in groups of three or four, discussing and designing their own crazy house. Tell each group to draw a plan of their house so that they can show it to the rest of the class. Go round and monitor the activity, helping with vocabulary where necessary.
- In turn, each group presents their house design to the rest of the class. The rest of the class can ask questions after each presentation.
- After all the presentations, the class can vote for the craziest house.

Resource 26 (page 151)

Interaction: groups of three or four
Exercise type: matching and roleplay
Aim: to practise *I prefer* and *I'd rather*
Language: Why don't we go to the cinema on Saturday evening? I'd rather watch television.

- Divide Ss into groups of three or four. Tell Ss that they have to make plans for a nice summer weekend. They have to decide on the six things they want to do together.
- Give out their role cards (A, B, C or D) and a copy of a diary and allow time for Ss to read and understand them.
- Ss discuss their preferences. They make suggestions and state preferences until they finally come to an agreement and fill in the weekend plan.
- As a follow-up, groups present their decisions to the class.

Answers
The six things that all four Ss want to do are: cycling, going to the cinema, going to the disco, going for a picnic, sleeping late and reading in bed, and playing tennis. How these activities are scheduled depends on a particular group.

Activity Book Answers
Language Diary
2 Students' own answers
Exercise 1
2 see 3 watch 4 Look at 5 look at 6 watch
Exercise 2
2 prefer 3 to 4 'd rather 5 playing, swimming
6 than
Exercise 3
Possible answers:
2 cakes to vegetables/salad; eating cakes to eating vegetables/salad 3 cook than wash up 4 playing tennis to shopping/doing the shopping 5 eat fruit than paint fruit 6 watching TV to cooking
Exercise 4
Students' own answers
Possible answers:
3 I prefer cats to dogs.
4 I'd rather eat pizza than pasta.
5 I prefer sleeping to working.
6 I'd rather drink cola than orange juice.
7 I prefer chocolate to ice cream.
8 I'd rather watch *The Simpsons* than *Friends*.
Exercise 5
2 than 3 not 4 to 5 prefers 6 rather

Lesson objectives

Structures

should, shouldn't
if I were you (advice)

Functions

Asking for and giving advice

Skills

Dictionary: finding the meaning of idioms and expressions

Key vocabulary

Adjectives: *common, fair, noisy, patient, selfish, tricky, upset*
Expressions: *change one's mind, get in the way, get on one's nerves, get on with someone, give someone a hand, have a chat*

Before class

- Copy and cut up Resource 27 (page 152) for each group.
- Bring to class (or ask Ss to bring) some teenage magazines with problem pages in them. If this is not practical, write down problems yourself on slips of paper (Exercise 7 Extension).
- You will also need monolingual dictionaries (Dictionary Skills).

 Exercise 1

- Play the recording once for Ss to listen and read the text.
- Read out the two questions to the class. As a whole class, Ss discuss the answers to the questions.
- Ask Ss which magazines they read and if they have problem pages. If so, ask Ss what kinds of problems are most common.

Presentation

 Exercise 2

- Play the recording twice for Ss to listen and read the texts.
- Ask Ss to cover the texts and, as a whole class, to say what the problem is in the three letters (1–3). Ss pool their ideas and see how much they can remember about the problems.

Comprehension

Exercise 3

- Ss work individually, reading the problems and replies again and matching them.
- Ss can compare answers in pairs before checking answers as a class.

Answers
1 b 2 c 3 a

Extension

- Ask the class if they agree with the advice given in the replies to the three problems.
- Ss work in groups of three or four, reading the three problems again and discussing alternative replies.
- The groups report back to the class and discuss their alternative advice.

Vocabulary

Exercise 4

- Ask the class to repeat the words after you to practise pronunciation.
- Ask one of the Ss to read out the example in question 1.
- Ss complete the exercise working individually.
- Check Ss' answers by asking individuals to read out the complete sentences.

Answers
2 upset 3 noisy 4 patient 5 tricky 6 common
7 selfish

Language box *should, shouldn't, if I were you* (advice)

- Ask individual Ss to read out the sentences in the box.
- Draw Ss' attention to the use of *wouldn't* with *If I were you, I …* to advise against an action.
- Draw Ss' attention to the use of a comma after *If I were you, I'd … .*
- Ask Ss to look back at the texts in Exercise 2 and find and read out more sentences containing *should, shouldn't* and *if I were you.*

Practice

Exercise 5

- Ask two Ss to read out the pair of sentences in question 1.
- Ss complete the exercise working individually.
- Check Ss' answers by asking pairs of Ss to read out the two sentences in each item.

Answers
2 You should get an alarm clock.
3 You should have some water.
4 You shouldn't go to bed late.
5 You should join a club.
6 You shouldn't watch horror films.

Exercise 6

- Ask two Ss to read out the pair of sentences in question 1.
- Ss can complete the exercises working individually or in pairs, if you wish.
- Check Ss' answers by asking pairs of Ss to read out the two sentences in each item.

<table>
<tr><td>

Answers
2 If I were you, I'd get a fish.
3 If I were you, I'd record it.
4 If I were you, I wouldn't go to school.
5 If I were you, I'd have a sandwich.
6 If I were you, I wouldn't eat it.

</td></tr>
</table>

Exercise 7

- Give Ss time to read the letter. Elicit suggestions for advice from the whole class.
- Ss work individually, writing their advice. Go round and monitor the activity, helping with vocabulary if necessary and pointing out any errors to be corrected.
- Ss then form pairs or groups of three and read out their advice to each other.

Extension

- If you and the Ss have brought to class some teenage magazines with problem pages, give each pair or group of three Ss one of the problem pages.
- Tell Ss to choose one or two of the problems in their magazine and summarise the problem in English, and then the advice given by the magazine.
- Go round and monitor the activity, helping with vocabulary where necessary and pointing out any errors to be corrected.
- The groups read out their summaries of the problems and advice to the class. The class discuss if the advice given is the best advice for each problem or they can write three or four sentences giving their own advice.
- *Option:* If you haven't got access to suitable teenage magazines, write 'problems' on pieces of paper. Give each pair or group of Ss some of these problems to work with.

Dictionary Skills: finding the meaning of idioms and expressions

- Read out the text to the class.
- Tell Ss that sometimes the expression might not be listed under each important word, e.g. in some dictionaries, *change your mind* might be listed under *mind* but not *change*.
- Write some expressions and idioms on the board, e.g.:
  'to break a promise'   'to be over the moon'
  'to make up your mind'   'to fit like a glove'
- Ss work in pairs, looking up the expressions in their dictionaries and then writing sentences containing the expressions. Go round and monitor the activity, helping where necessary.
- As a whole class, Ss discuss the meanings of the expressions. Then Ss read out their sentences for the class to hear.

 Exercise 8

- Read out the instructions and example item to the class. Tell Ss to use their strategies for guessing the meaning of new words from the context and then check their ideas in a dictionary.
- Ss complete the exercise working in pairs.
- They can compare answers in pairs before checking answers as a class.

<table>
<tr><td>

Suggested answers
2 annoy me   3 are a nuisance   4 help someone
5 opinion

</td></tr>
</table>

Exercise 9

- Ask one of the Ss to read out the example sentence.
- Ss work in pairs, discussing and writing sentences using the five expressions from Exercise 8. Go round and monitor the activity, helping Ss to use the expressions appropriately.
- Ss then read out their sentences to the rest of the class.

Resource 27 (page 152)

Interaction: groups of three or four
Exercise type: responding to text clues
Aim: to practise *should, shouldn't, if I were you* (advice for problems with learning English)
Language: If I were you, I would use polite expressions like …/You should listen to the tapes at home.

- Tell your Ss that this activity is their chance to be teachers and to help Ss with their problems in learning English. Most of the problems described in Resource 27 correspond with Skills boxes in the *Students' Book*. If Ss have problems with giving advice, they should refer to these boxes.
- Put Ss in groups and give each group a set of problem cards, which they place face down in a pile in front of them.
- Ss turn over the cards in turn. They read the card and explain their problem to the group, and then the other Ss have to give them advice.
- The S with the problem decides which of their classmates has given the best advice and gives them the problem card. The S who collects the largest number of problem cards is the winner.

Activity Book Answers
Language Diary
2
2 should   3 were   4 would
Exercise 1
2 patient   3 upset   4 tricky   5 fair   6 noisy
Exercise 2
2 e   3 d   4 a   5 f   6 c
Exercise 3
2 You shouldn't watch TV all day.
3 You should wash your hands.
4 If I were you, I wouldn't eat that./I wouldn't eat that if I were you.
5 You shouldn't buy this shirt.
Exercise 4
2 You shouldn't eat fast food. If I were you, I'd do more exercise.
3 You should say you're sorry. If I were you, I'd buy her a new one.
4 You shouldn't give up. If I were you, I'd ask the teacher for help.
5 You shouldn't go to bed late. If I were you, I'd relax in the evenings.
Exercise 5
2 c   3 a   4 b
Exercise 6
2 You should use a dictionary.
3 You shouldn't go.
4 If I were you, I wouldn't worry.
5 You shouldn't do that.
6 If I were you, I would/'d hurry.

28 Story Time

The Streetboys 1

Lesson objectives

Structures
allow, to be allowed to

Functions
Asking for and giving or refusing permission

Key vocabulary
Music: *agent, band, gig, guitar, instrument, keyboard, music shop, recording contract, youth club*

Before class
- Make a copy of Resource 28 (page 153) for each S.
- You will also need paper for Ss to write down their ideas for the story (Exercise 8).

Exercise 1
- Ask Ss to look at the picture. Find out how many Ss play the keyboard, the guitar or other musical instruments. See how many other instruments the class can brainstorm in a minute. Do any of them belong to a band? If so, encourage them to tell the class about it.
- Read out the instructions and four questions to the class.
- Ss work in pairs, discussing the answers to the questions.
- Ss exchange ideas as a whole class.

Presentation

Exercise 2
- Play the recording for Ss to listen and read the text.
- Then ask Ss to read through the questions in Exercise 3 so they know what information they need as you play the recording a second time for them to listen and read the text.

Comprehension
Exercise 3
- Ss write down the answers to the questions, referring back to the text if necessary.
- Check Ss' answers by asking pairs of Ss to read out the questions and answers.

Answers	
1 a music shop	4 Andy and Steve
2 in Ricky's (father's) garage	5 the Haven Club
3 Ricky	6 the keyboard

Extension
- Play the recording for Exercise 2 again and tell Ss to listen carefully to the pronunciation, stress and intonation patterns.
- Ss work in groups of four, reading out the text and taking turns to be the narrator, Lisa, Lisa's father (Mr Long) and Ricky. Go round and monitor the activity, correcting pronunciation, intonation and stress if necessary.

Language box *allow, to be allowed to*
- Remind Ss of the difference between the active and passive voice by asking them to make these sentences passive:
  1 'Ricky plays the keyboard.' (The keyboard is played by Ricky.)
  2 'Andy and Steve sing the songs.' (The songs are sung by Andy and Steve.)
- Read out the sentences in the box to the class and draw Ss' attention to the position of *to* in the active and passive sentences.
- Ask Ss to make the two sentences negative. (*does not allow them to … ./They are not allowed to … .*)
- Ask Ss to look back at the text in Exercise 2 and find and read out three sentences with forms of *allow* in them.

Practice
Exercise 4
- Ask one of the Ss to read out the pair of sentences in question 1.
- Ss complete the exercise working individually.
- Check Ss' answers by asking individuals to read out the pair of sentences in each item.

Answers
2 allowed to practise on the keyboard
3 him to practise at home
4 allowed to practise in his/Mr Long's shop
5 allow customers to touch the instruments

Exercise 5
- Ask one of the Ss to read out the sentence for the first picture. Tell Ss to begin each answer with *You're not allowed to … .*
- Ss work in pairs, discussing the pictures and writing the sentences.
- Check Ss' answers by asking individuals to read out the sentences.

Answers
2 You're not allowed to eat.
3 You're not allowed to take photographs.
4 You're not allowed to use a mobile phone.
5 You're not allowed to dive.
6 You're not allowed to cycle/ride a bicycle.

Extension

- Ask Ss to look at the six pictures again and, working in pairs, discuss where they might see these signs. For example, Picture 1 might be in a library or a recording studio.
- The pairs then exchange ideas as a whole class.

Be careful

- Read out the two sentences to the class. Point out that *to* is used with *allow* but not with *let*.
- Ask Ss to make the sentences negative (*does not allow them to …/does not let them …*) and interrogative (*Does he allow them to …/Does he let them …*).
- Tell Ss that *allow* is more formal than *let*, e.g. written warning signs use *allow* ('Dogs are not allowed in the playground/Cycling is not allowed').
- Ss may like to look back at Unit 15, where they practised using *let* and *make*.

Exercise 6

- Read out the first two lines of the text to the class.
- Advise Ss to read through the text quickly before they start completing it.
- Ss do the exercise working individually.
- They can compare answers in pairs before checking answers as a class.
- Check Ss' answers by asking individuals to read out the sentences.

Answers
2 to   3 let   4 not   5 let   6 to

Exercise 7

- Give Ss time to read through the list of activities (1–8).
- Ask two Ss to read out the example sentences.
- Tell Ss to talk to their partners about 'when I was eight', using *allow* and *let*. If you wish, elicit an example exchange from some stronger Ss. Go round and monitor the activity, paying particular attention to the correct use and form of *allow* and *let*.
- Each S then says one of their sentences for the class to hear.

Exercise 8

- Ask Ss to look back at the picture and text for Exercise 2.
- Elicit some ideas from the class for what might happen next in the story.
- Ss then work in pairs, discussing possible ways for the story to continue. Tell the pairs to write down their ideas on pieces of paper. Go round and monitor the activity, helping with vocabulary if necessary.
- The pairs exchange their ideas as a whole class and see how many different ideas they have had.
- Collect the pieces of paper and save them to use as an introduction to Unit 32.

Resource 28 (page 153)

Interaction: pair work
Exercise type: completing a questionnaire
Aim: to practise *let, make, to be allowed to*

- Give each S a copy of the questionnaire in Resource 28.
- Ss are to complete the questionnaire for themselves first. They give themselves points depending on the answer, either ten points or no points. When they have completed the table for themselves, they interview two Ss in the class.
- When Ss have completed the questionnaires they compare their answers and decide whose parents are the least and most strict. The least strict parents will get about 100 points.

Activity Book Answers
Language Diary
2
Students' own answers
Exercise 1
2 b   3 e   4 a   5 f   6 c
Exercise 2
2 Do your parents let you go out in the evenings?
3 I'm not allowed to go out on Sunday nights.
4 Are pupils at your school allowed to wear jeans?
(at your school *can also come at the end*)
5 Our teacher doesn't let us eat in class.
Exercise 3
2 You're allowed to play football.
3 You're allowed to eat in the park.
4 You're not allowed to feed the ducks.
5 You're not allowed to pick the flowers.
6 You're allowed to skateboard.
Exercise 4
2 Were they allowed to use the garage after that?
3 Did Mr Long allow Lisa to invite them to his shop?
4 Did Mr Long let Ricky borrow his keyboard?
5 Was Lisa allowed to go to the Haven Club?
6 Did her dad let her go alone?
Exercise 5
b 6   c 3   d 4   e 5   f 2
Exercise 6
2 We aren't allowed to wear jeans.
3 Do your parents allow you to have parties?
4 The dog isn't allowed to sleep on the bed.
5 Does your teacher let you talk in class?
6 We weren't allowed to play in the street.

Revision 7

Language revised

Vocabulary
Adjectives
look at, see, watch

Pronunciation
Sentence stress and intonation

Grammar
must, *can't* (deduction)
I prefer, I'd rather
should, shouldn't, if I were you (advice)
allow, to be allowed to

Vocabulary

Exercise 1
- Read out the example matched items to the class.
- Advise Ss to read through all the definitions before they start matching the items.
- Ss complete the exercise working individually.
- After checking Ss' answers, ask them to make sentences containing some of the words.

Answers
2 d   3 a   4 f   5 g   6 e   7 c

Exercise 2
- Before doing the exercise, write the three verbs on the board (*look at, see, watch*) and elicit from the Ss the differences in meaning (see Unit 26).
- Read out the example in sentence 1 to the class.
- Ss complete the exercise working individually.
- They can compare answers in pairs before checking answers as a class.

Answers
2 see   3 look at   4 watch   5 see   6 look at

Pronunciation chant

 Exercise 3
- Ask Ss to look at the picture and say what the child is going to do.
- Play the recording for Ss to listen and read the text. Tell them to listen carefully to stress and intonation patterns.
- Play the recording again for Ss to listen and repeat.
- Ss work in pairs, practising saying the chant to each other. Go round and monitor the activity.

Grammar

 Exercise 4
- Give Ss time to study the picture.
- Remind them of the use of *must* and *can't* for deduction.
- Read out the example sentence.
- Ss work in pairs, writing sentences for the prompts.
- Check Ss' answers by asking individual Ss to read out the sentences. If Ss disagree about any of the answers, ask them what gives the answer in the picture.

Answers
2 She can't like cats.
3 She must like music.
4 She can't be English.
5 She can't be keen on tennis.
6 She must take a lot of photographs.
7 She can't wear dresses every day.
8 She must read a lot.
9 She must play the guitar.
10 She must drink a lot of cola.

 Exercise 5
- Read out the example prompts and sentence to the class.
- Do the second item with the whole class.
- Ss complete the exercise working in pairs, writing and saying the sentences to each other. Tell them that they prefer the first prompt in each item.
- After checking Ss' answers, tell Ss to work in pairs again and this time say true statements about their own preferences, e.g.:
'I'd rather travel by ship/train than by plane.'

Answers
2 I prefer bananas to apples.
3 I'd rather play tennis than swim.
4 I prefer music to reading.
5 I'd rather cycle than walk.
6 I prefer pizzas to burgers.

Answers
Students' own answers

Exercise 6
- Ask Ss to look at the example matched items. Read out the example sentence.
- Remind Ss of the structures *should, shouldn't* and *if I were you*.
- Ss work individually, matching the pictures and prompts and writing sentences giving advice.

Answers
Picture 2: f If I were you, I wouldn't eat all of them.
Picture 3: a You should hurry up.
Picture 4: b You shouldn't do that.
Picture 5: d If I were you, I'd go to bed.
Picture 6: e If I were you, I wouldn't buy that.

Exercise 7

- Read out the prompts in the box. Ask one of the Ss to read out the example sentence.
- Do the second item (*jump in*) with the whole class.
- Ss then complete the exercise, working in pairs.

Answers
2 You're allowed to jump in.
3 You're not allowed to eat.
4 You're allowed to play ball.
5 You're not allowed to push.
6 You're not allowed to run.
7 You're not allowed to wear shoes.

Song Time

- Ask the class to repeat the three expressions after you.
- Ss work in pairs, completing the song. Tell them to think about the sounds at the end of sentences.
- Play the recording twice for Ss to check their answers.

Answers
1 the way I feel   2 Everything's new
3 I want to stay here

- Ask Ss to look at Stage 2 of 'Song Time'. Read out the instructions to the class.
- Ask one of the Ss to read out the example sentences. Elicit more sentences from the class to continue this dream of being a world famous pop star:
  'What about the house(s)? Food? Clothes? Friends? Travel?'
- Give Ss time to think about their best dream. Tell them that they can invent a dream, if they wish.
- Ss work in pairs telling their partner about their dream. Go round and monitor the activity, noting down any general points to revise with the whole class.

 Check Yourself Units 25–28 – Activity Book page 70

 Check Units 25–28 – Teacher's Book page 117

 Language Tests A/B Units 25–28 – Test Book pages 30–33

Wales

Lesson objectives

To practise reading for factual information
To match specific nouns with general nouns
To practise reading for specific information
To say why you've made a certain choice
To complete an email
To practise listening to a description and identifying the object
To describe an object in detail

Key vocabulary

Wales: *castle, daffodil, dragon, harp, leek, rugby*

Background information

St David's Day is 1 March. St David was one of the saints who spread Christianity in the sixth century and also founded a monastery in west Wales. The most famous festival is the Eisteddfod, a festival of oratory, poetry, singing and harp-playing. Snowdon (1086 metres high) is the highest mountain in England and Wales.

Before class

- If you have any pictures/postcards or objects from Wales, bring them to the lesson to show the class.
- Ss need coloured pencils/crayons for Exercise 8.

 Exercise 1

- Ask Ss to look at the picture and see if they can pronounce the words.
- Play the recording twice for Ss to listen.
- Ss can then say the Welsh word for 'Wales'.

Reading

 Exercise 2

- Ask Ss to look at the map and say the names of the places after you.
- Ask Ss if they know anything about Wales and, if so, to tell the class.
- Play the recording twice, pausing after each section for Ss to read the text and look at the pictures.
- Ask Ss:
  'What symbols of Wales are mentioned in the text?' (red dragon, leek, daffodil, harp)
  'What languages can you see on road signs in Wales?' (Welsh and English)
  'What do tourists like?' (beaches, mountains and castles)

Exercise 3

- Look at the example matched item with the class.
- Ss complete the exercise, referring back to the text in Exercise 2 if necessary.

Answers
2 a   3 e   4 b   5 d

Exercise 4

- Read out the questions (1–6) to the class.
- Ss work individually, reading the texts and answering the questions. Tell Ss not to worry about understanding every word in the texts but just to focus on answering the questions.
- Check Ss' answers by asking pairs of Ss to read out the questions and answers.

Answers
2 c St David's (Oceanarium and Marine Life Centre)
3 b Cardiff
4 c St David's (Cathedral)
5 a Snowdonia National Park
6 b Cardiff (Techniquest)

- After checking Ss' answers, ask individual Ss to read out the sentences in the texts. Correct pronunciation and check comprehension of the texts. Point out the use of the imperative (*Travel to …* , *Don't miss …*) in tourist texts like these.

Speaking

 Exercise 5

- Ss work in pairs, discussing which place they would choose to visit, using *prefer* or *would rather*. If necessary, remind Ss of this structure from Unit 26.
- Each pair then tells the class the place they prefer and gives two reasons for choosing it.

Writing

Exercise 6

- Read out the instructions to the class and then read out the text, pausing where there are spaces in the text.
- Ss work individually, completing the text. Go round and monitor the activity.
- Ss then work in groups of three or four, reading each other's emails.
- Two or three Ss read out their emails for the class to hear.

Listening

Exercise 7

- Give Ss time to study the flags and find the differences before you play the recording. If you wish, pre-teach or remind Ss of these prepositional phrases:
  'on the right/left'
  'at the top/bottom'
- Play the recording twice for Ss to listen and identify the Welsh flag.

Tapescript

The Welsh flag has a big red dragon on it. The dragon is looking left. That's important. Its tail is on the right and its face is on the left. Behind the dragon there are two colours, white and green. The white is at the top and the green is at the bottom.

Answer
3

Speaking

Exercise 8

- Draw an oblong flag shape on the board and use it to revise further vocabulary for positions:
  'on the left/right side'
  'in the middle'
  'in the top/bottom right-hand/left-hand corner'
  'above, below, opposite, between'
- Read out the instructions and the example sentence to the class.
- Give each S time to draw and colour their own flag.
- Ss then work in pairs, taking turns to describe their flag to their partner and to draw their partner's flag. Go round and monitor the activity, making a note of any general points to revise later with the whole class. The pairs can then compare their drawings and see how similar they are.

Extension

- Ss write a short description of their partner's flag. The descriptions can then be swapped, so Ss can check if they are accurate.
- Encourage Ss to think about what their flag could represent, e.g., a sports' club, a friends' club or a new country. Get Ss to exchange their ideas in groups of four or six.
- Groups choose their favourite flag and tell the class what it represents. The class can vote for the best idea, and the winning flag and other flags can be displayed.

Cartoon

- Ask Ss to look at the cartoon. Ss work in pairs discussing why the cartoon is amusing.
- Each pair of Ss presents their reason to the class.

 Skills Corner 7 – Activity Book page 71

Activity Book Answers for Skills Corner 7
Exercise 1
1 It's not fair!   2 I can't decide …
Exercise 2
a Steve   b Daisy
Exercise 3
Students' own answers

The LONDONERS

Lesson objectives

Structures

Adjectives: comparative, superlative
both, *the same as*, *different from*, *as … as*, *less than*

Functions

Describing places and speculating about their history

Key vocabulary

-ing, *-ed* adjectives

Background information

Stonehenge is situated on Salisbury Plain in Wiltshire where other historic sites are also found, e.g. the West Kennet Long Barrow (a burial mound), Silbury Hill (the largest artificial mound in Europe) and Avebury. While Stonehenge may have been dedicated to the worship of the sun and moon (the 'temple' is aligned with the summer solstice), Avebury seems to have been dedicated to the more human themes of birth, life and death.
The Seven Wonders of the Ancient World are the Pyramids of Egypt, the Hanging Gardens of Babylon, The Tomb of Mausolus at Halicarnassus, The Temple of Diana at Ephesus, the Statue of Jupiter (Zeus) at Olympia, the Colossus of Rhodes and the Pharos at Alexandria.

Before class

- Copy and cut up a set of Resource 29 (page 154) for each group.
- Bring to the lesson (or ask Ss to bring) some pictures of historic places in their own country or another country. Tell Ss that the most important thing is that they know something about the place and can talk about it (Exercise 7 Extension).

Presentation

Exercise 1

- Ask Ss to look at the picture and say if they recognise this place. Have any of them heard of Stonehenge? If so, ask them what they know about it.
- Play the recording twice for Ss to listen and read the text.
- Read out the first question and ask Ss the answer. (more than four thousand years old)
- In pairs or groups of three, Ss discuss the answer to the second question and then exchange views as a whole class.

Extension

- Ask Ss if they know any of the Seven Wonders of the Ancient World and, if so, ask them to tell the class about them.
- Ss may like to discuss what they would choose as the Seven Wonders of the Modern World.

Exercise 2

- Play the recording twice for Ss to listen and read the text.
- Ask the class if they think Vicki and Rob are enjoying their visit to Stonehenge. Ask Ss to find and read out parts of the text that tell us that they are enjoying themselves.

Comprehension

Exercise 3

- Ask one of the Ss to read out the example statement. Ask the class to correct this statement.
- Ss complete the exercise working individually and referring back to the text if necessary.
- When checking Ss' answers, ask them to correct the false statements.

> **Answers**
> 2 ✓ 3 ✗ 4 ✓ 5 ✗ 6 ✓

Be careful

- Read out the two sentences to the class.
- Write another pair of sentences on the board for Ss to complete, e.g.:
  'Jane thinks this is an … film.' (interesting)
  'Jane is … in films.' (interested)

Vocabulary

Exercise 4

- Ask one of the Ss to read out the example in sentence 1.
- Ss complete the exercise working individually.
- They can compare answers in pairs before checking answers as a class.
- Check Ss' answers by asking individuals to read out the sentences.

> **Answers**
> 2 interested   3 exciting   4 amazing   5 bored   6 tired

Extension

- Working in pairs, Ss choose four words from the exercise and write their own sentences containing these words. Go round and monitor the activity, checking that Ss are using the words appropriately.
- The pairs then form groups of four or six and read each other's sentences.

Language box comparative and superlative adjectives

- Read out the short, long and irregular adjective forms to the class.
- Ask individual Ss to say the three forms for other adjectives, e.g. *young, cheap, interesting, successful, bad.*
- Ask individual Ss to read out the six comparative sentences. Draw Ss' attention to the structure of each sentence.
- If appropriate, remind Ss of the use of the superlative with the Present Perfect and *ever/never*, e.g.:
  'She's the most intelligent girl I've ever met.'
  'I've never met such an intelligent girl.'
  'It's the best holiday we've ever had.'
  'We've never had such a good holiday.'

Practice

Exercise 5

- Ask one of the Ss to read out the first sentence of the text.
- Advise Ss to read through the text quickly before they start completing it. Ss do the exercise working individually.
- Check Ss' answers by asking individuals to read out the sentences.

> **Answers**
> 2 from   3 than   4 both   5 as   6 The

Exercise 6

- Read out the pair of sentences in question 1 to the class.
- Ss complete the exercise working individually.
- They can compare answers in pairs before checking answers as a class.
- Check Ss' answers by asking individuals to read out the pair of sentences in each item.

> **Answers**
> 2 different from   3 less interesting than   4 as big as
> 5 places are   6 the same age

Exercise 7

- Ask Ss to look at and talk about the picture:
  'What can they see?'
  'What's happening?'
- Ask one of the Ss to read out the example sentence. Remind Ss of polite ways of agreeing and disagreeing from Unit 21.
- Elicit suggestions from the class to explain why Stonehenge was built.
- Ss then work in pairs, discussing different explanations and trying to come to an agreement.
- The pairs can then report back to the class and see if there is any general agreement.

Extension

- If you and/or the Ss have brought pictures of historic places in the Ss' own country or another country, use these for Ss to work with in pairs or groups of three. Check that each group of Ss has a picture of a place they know about.

- If necessary, Ss can research their place in the library or at home.
- Each group writes five or six sentences about their place. Go round and help with vocabulary, if necessary, and point out any errors to be corrected.
- The groups then display their texts and pictures for the rest of the class to read.

Resource 29 (page 154)

Interaction: groups of three
Exercise type: roleplay
Aim: to practise adjectives (comparative, superlative) plus expressions like *both, the same as, different from*

- Review the vocabulary from the lesson (*amazing, ancient,* etc.) and the comparison expressions (*both, the same as,* etc.) and tell Ss that they have to use them in this activity.
- Put Ss in groups of three. If the class doesn't divide by three, one group can consist of two Ss. Give each S in the group one of the castle descriptions.
- Tell Ss that they are kings/queens and each of them has a fantastic castle. They have to discuss whose castle is bigger, more expensive, more beautiful, etc., using the comparatives, superlatives or other expressions. They also have to find similarities between the castles. They should not show their cards to other Ss. Ask Ss to put a lot of acting into the discussion. They have to try to be as convincing as possible when boasting about their castles.
- As a follow-up, Ss roleplay their discussion in front of the class.

> **Activity Book Answers**
> **Language Diary**
> **2**
> old – older – the oldest
> heavy – heavier – the heaviest
> big – bigger – the biggest
> mysterious – more mysterious – the most mysterious
> good – better – the best
> 1 as   2 same   3 as, as   4 from   5 are   6 than
> **Exercise 1**
> 2 amazing   3 tired   4 interesting   5 bored
> 6 amazed
> **Exercise 2**
> 2 ✓   3 ✗   4 ✗   5 ✓   6 ✗   7 ✓
> **Exercise 3**
> 2 Chinese/English is more difficult than English/Chinese.
> 3 Your cat is less friendly than mine.
> 4 Lions aren't as big as elephants.
> 5 Big Ben is one of the most famous buildings in Britain.
> 6 Bicycles are less expensive than cars.
> **Exercise 4**
> 2 Robin   3 No   4 Anna   5 Anna   6 No
> **Exercise 5**
> 2 Kenny is weaker than Fred.
> 3 Grace is as old as Sam.
> 4 Tom isn't as strong as Danny.
> 5 My dog is more intelligent than yours/your dog.
> 6 This picture is different from that one.

30 Crazy Reporters

Lesson objectives

Structures

Verbs of sense (*feel*, *look*, *smell*, *sound*, *taste*) + adjective

Functions

Talking about senses

Skills

Dictionary: words with several meanings

Key vocabulary

Adjectives with opposite meanings, e.g. *fizzy/still*, *well/ill*

Before class

- Make a copy of Resources 30A (page 155) and 30B (page 156) for each S.
- You will also need monolingual dictionaries (Exercise 8 Extension).

Presentation

Exercise 1

- Ask Ss to look at the three pictures and describe what they can see in each picture. Encourage them to guess what this 'crazy' story is about.
- Play the recording twice for Ss to listen and read the text.
- Ask Ss to cover the texts and pool what they can remember about Mike Robertson.

Comprehension

Exercise 2

- Ask one of the Ss to read out the first sentence in the text.
- Ss complete the text working individually, referring back to the text in Exercise 1 if necessary.
- Check Ss' answers by asking individuals to read out the sentences.

> **Answers**
> 2 carrot   3 chocolate   4 carrot   5 chocolate

Vocabulary

Exercise 3

- Get Ss to repeat the words after you to practise pronunciation.
- Ask one of the Ss to read out the example sentence.
- Ss do the matching exercise working in pairs.
- Check Ss' answers by asking individuals to make sentences like the example. (The opposite of X is Y.)

> **Answers**
> delicious/disgusting   fizzy/still   hard/soft   ill/well
> ordinary/odd   right/wrong   rough/smooth

Language box   *feel, look, smell, sound, taste* + adjective
feel, look, smell, sound, taste + *like* + noun

- Read out the sentences in the box to the class and point out the different structures used with verbs of sense.
- Ask Ss to look back at the text in Exercise 1 and find and read out sentences containing verbs of sense.

Practice

Exercise 4

- Ask one of the Ss to read out the example in sentence 1.
- Ss complete the exercise working individually before checking answers as a class.
- Check Ss' answers by asking individuals to read out the sentences.

> **Answers**
> 2 sounds   3 smells   4 looks   5 feels   6 taste

Exercise 5

- Give Ss time to read through the list of food before playing the recording.
- Play the recording twice for Ss to listen and complete the exercise.
- Check Ss' answers by playing the recording again, pausing after each answer.

> **Tapescript**
> **Harry:** Do we like food because it looks nice, or because it tastes nice? We decided to find out. Listen to what happened.
> **Mike:** Right, Harry. Would you like to test this ice cream?
> **Harry:** Yes, please. It looks delicious. Yuk! It tastes disgusting.
> **Claire:** What does it taste like, Harry?
> **Harry:** It tastes like … onions. Yuk! Right. It's Claire's turn, now, Mike.
> **Mike:** OK, Claire. Look at this bread.
> **Claire:** Oh yuk! It looks horrible. It's bright blue!
> **Mike:** Please taste it now.
> **Harry:** Ha, ha.
> **Claire:** Oh, just a little bit, then. Oh! It tastes just like ordinary bread. It's fine.
> **Harry:** Huh!
> **Mike:** Now, both of you, please put on these blindfolds. What does this smell like?
> **Harry:** Mmm, it smells lovely. It smells like pizza.
> **Claire:** Yes, it tastes like pizza too. It is pizza.
> **Mike:** Now look.
> **Harry:** Oh! It's cabbage. You tricked us.
> **Harry:** Well, we learnt something from that. Don't always believe your eyes …
> **Claire:** … or your mouth!

> **Answers**
> onions ✗   bread ✓   pizza ✗   cabbage ✓

Exercise 6

- Give Ss time to read through the sentences and guess the missing words before you play the recording again.
- Play the recording twice for Ss to complete the exercise.
- Check Ss' answers by asking individuals to read out the sentences.

Answers
2 onions 3 bread 4 pizza

Extension

- Ss work in pairs, designing some delicious or disgusting crazy food. Tell them to think about what it looks like, tastes like, smells like and feels like.
- In turn, the pairs tell the class about their crazy food.

Exercise 7

- Ask a pair of Ss to read out the first joke and another pair to read out the second. Pay particular attention to sentence stress and intonation.
- Ask Ss if they know of any similar jokes using the structures: sense + adjective, or sense + *like* + noun. If so, let them tell the class. If not, you could go on to Resource 30.

Dictionary Skills: words with several meanings

- If possible, choose one or two words from the Ss' first language which have several meanings. Ask the class to tell you the different meanings of these words.
- Read out the text in the box about *watch* to the class.

Extension

- Write on the board more examples of words which can be nouns or verbs, e.g.:
  'a telephone, to telephone'
  'a walk, to walk'
  'a play, to play'
- Ss work in pairs, writing six sentences using these words. Go round and monitor the activity.
- The pairs form groups of four or six and read out each other's sentences.

Exercise 8

- Ss can work in pairs, if you wish, finding the words in Exercise 1 and ticking the correct meaning.
- After checking Ss' answers, ask the class to make sentences containing these words with their other meanings, e.g. 'Three is an odd number'.

Answers
The first meaning is the 'correct' one for all four words.

Extension

- Ask Ss to look at the text in Exercise 1 and find the adjectives *still*, *soft* and *rough*.

- Ss use their monolingual dictionaries to look up these words and choose the correct meaning for the texts in Exercise 1.
- Ask the class what the other meaning(s) are. Elicit sentences from the class for some of these meanings.

Resource 30 (pages 155–156)

Interaction: pair work
Exercise type: information gap
Aim: to practise sense + adjective/sense + *like* + noun
Language: Number 1. It tastes fizzy and cold.
Vocabulary: fizzy/still, smooth/soft, lovely/beautiful, delicious/disgusting, heavy, sweet, expensive, loud/noisy, difficult

- Elicit some of the adjectives with opposite meanings from Unit 30, i.e. *fizzy/still, delicious/ disgusting*, etc.
- Ss should sit in pairs facing each other across the table with a book or folder between them so that neither can see what the other is doing.
- Give the picture cards (Resource 30A) and the frames (Resource 30B) to each S in the pair. Ask Student A to arrange any of his/her sixteen pictures in any order on the frame.
- The object of the game is for Student B to arrange the pictures in the same order. To do this, Student A must describe each picture in turn to Student B in terms of how the objects in the pictures taste, smell, look, sound and feel. Student B may ask questions. When Student B finishes arranging the pictures, Ss compare their frames.
- Ss should now reverse roles. Student B arranges pictures on his/her frame and describes them to Student A.

Activity Book Answers
Language Diary
2
Students' own answers
Exercise 1
2 a 3 e 4 b 5 c 6 h 7 d 8 g
Exercise 2
2 hard 3 well 4 right 5 well 6 odd 7 hard
8 right
Exercise 3
The verbs can be followed by any adjective that matches the picture.
Possible answers:
2 It smells (beautiful).
3 It tastes (disgusting).
4 She feels (cold).
5 It sounds (horrible).
6 She looks (great).
Exercise 4
2 It tastes like paper.
3 It sounds great.
4 They feel uncomfortable.
5 The kitchen smells like the baker's.
6 She looks like a model.
Exercise 5
Students' own answers (*make sure that students use either adjectives or 'like' and a noun after the verbs*)
Exercise 6
2 look like 3 sound 4 taste 5 smells 6 feel

Lesson objectives

Structures
Comparison of adverbs

Functions
Discussing people's strengths and weaknesses

Key vocabulary
Verb and noun collocations: *do business, go into business, have a go at something, make a decision, set up a company, take a chance*

Background information
Secondary school students who are studying Economics and Business Studies often carry out a project in which they plan and set up a small company and so gain experience in management and finance.

Before class
- Copy and cut up Resource 31 (page 157).

Exercise 1
- Play the recording once for Ss to listen and read the text.
- Ask Ss the names of the twins and how they do business.
- Read out the question to the class. Ask Ss if they can guess what kind of company it is from the picture. Ss can check their guesses when they listen to the recording.

Extension
- Read out the first question of the text. ('What are you going to do when you leave school?') Ask the class what form the answer can take, e.g.:
  'I don't know what I'm going to do/be.'
  'I (think) I'm going to … .'
- Ask each S to tell the class what they are going to do when they leave school.

Presentation

Exercise 2
- Play the recording twice for Ss to listen and read the text.
- Ask Ss what the company's problem is. (The company is growing more quickly than planned.)

Comprehension
Exercise 3
- Ask one of the Ss to read out the example in sentence 1.
- Ss complete the exercise working individually.

- Check Ss' answers by asking individuals to read out the sentences.

Answers
2 clothes 3 fashion 4 often 5 staff 6 write

Extension
- Play the recording for Exercise 2 again and ask Ss to listen carefully to the pronunciation, stress and intonation patterns.
- Ss work in pairs, reading out the dialogue in Exercise 2 and taking turns to be Alex and Sheila. Go round and monitor the activity, correcting pronunciation, stress and intonation where necessary.

Vocabulary
Exercise 4
- Ask one of the Ss to read out the first sentence of the text.
- Advise Ss to read through the text quickly before starting to complete it.
- Ss do the exercise working individually. Tell them to look back at the expressions in the dialogue in Exercise 2, if they wish.
- They can compare answers in pairs before checking answers as a class.

Answers
2 go 3 have 4 set 5 do 6 take

Language box Adverbs
- Ask individual Ss to read out the adjective, adverb and comparative adverb forms of the words in the box.
- Write on the board:
  1 'Ted's a brilliant designer.'
  'He designs brilliantly. He designs more brilliantly than Sheila.'
  2 'I come on an early train.'
  'My train arrives early. My train arrives earlier than his.'
  3 'She's a hard worker.'
  'She works hard. She works harder than her brother.'
- Ss work in pairs or groups of three, making similar sets of three sentences, using the words in the box. Go round and monitor the activity, paying particular attention to the correct use of adjectives and adverbs.

Practice
Exercise 5
- Read out the example in sentence 1 to the class, pointing out how the adjective *good* changes to the adverb *well* in the sentence.
- Ss complete the exercise working individually.

- Check Ss' answers by asking individuals to read out the sentences.

Answers
2 carefully 3 fast 4 better 5 earlier 6 harder

- Draw Ss attention to *started work earlier* in question 5 and ask Ss to find the similar phrase in Exercise 2. (We went into business earlier than most people.)

Exercise 6

- Ask two Ss to read out the example items. Draw Ss attention to how this exchange is recorded in the questionnaire.
- Ss work in pairs, taking turns to ask and answer questions and complete their questionnaire. Go round and monitor this activity.
- In groups of four or six, Ss tell their group about the comparisons they have found.

Exercise 7

- Ask one of the Ss to read out the example sentence. Elicit two or three sentences from Ss about themselves and their partners.
- Ss work individually, writing a paragraph comparing themselves and their partners. Go round and monitor the activity, pointing out any errors to be corrected.
- Ss then form pairs again, read their partner's paragraph and see if they agree with the content.

Resource 31 (page 157)

Interaction: whole class (fifteen Ss)
Exercise type: information gap
Aim: to practise adverbs
Language: Are you talking on your mobile happily?
- This activity may be done with the whole class if there are up to fifteen Ss. If the class is bigger, divide it into two and give as many cards as necessary to each group. Make sure that you use the cards in the order in which they are printed, e.g. if you have ten Ss in the group, use the first ten cards and amend the last one by deleting the line 'The person behind you … .' and substituting 'You are the last person in the queue.'
- Tell Ss that they are waiting in a bus queue.
- The aim of the activity is to reconstruct the queue as it was. To do this Ss have to find the person who is in front and behind them in the queue. They have to move around the class and either 'act' their own activity or ask each other questions about their activity. If you have two groups of Ss doing the activity at the same time, make sure that they don't mix as it may cause a lot of confusion.
- If you have two groups, you can make the activity more competitive by telling Ss that they have to do it very quickly and the winner is the group who manages to arrange itself in a queue first.
- When Ss have finished, check if they are standing in the correct order by asking some of them what they are doing.

Answers
1 Person 1 is talking on his/her mobile happily.
2 Person 2 is studying hard.
3 Person 3 is looking at his/her watch nervously.
4 Person 4 is playing the guitar nicely.
5 Person 5 is sad and is waiting quietly.
6 Person 6 is drinking cola very quickly.
7 Person 7 is playing tennis well.
8 Person 8 is playing tennis badly.
9 Person 9 is eating a hamburger carefully.
10 Person 10 is reading a book very slowly.
11 Person 11 is dancing brilliantly.
12 Person 12 is eating an ice cream very fast.
13 Person 13 is singing a song loudly.
14 Person 14 is singing a song awfully.
15 Person 15 is looking at everybody angrily.

Activity Book Answers
Language Diary
2
quick – quickly – more quickly
brilliant – brilliantly – more brilliantly
careful – carefully – more carefully
bad – badly – worse
good – well – better
early – early – earlier
late – late – later
fast – fast – faster
Exercise 1
2 Please hurry up and decide.
3 Let's try this puzzle!
4 My uncle wants to start his own company.
5 I'd like to go into business.
6 We'll have to do something dangerous.
Exercise 2
2 earlier 3 better 4 more slowly 5 harder
6 more loudly
Exercise 3
2 noisy 3 well 4 worse 5 hard 6 carefully
Exercise 4
2 brilliant 3 good 4 quickly 5 successful 6 well
7 carefully
Exercise 5
2 Kate runs more slowly than Paul.
3 Both Jack and Helen sing badly.
4 You know Maths better than me/I do.
5 I don't work as carefully as you.
6 You arrived later than me/I did.

32 Story Time 📖
The Streetboys 2

Lesson objectives

Structures

too + adjective/adverb + infinitive
not + adjective/adverb + *enough* + infinitive

Functions

Telling a story

Skills

Writing: story

Key vocabulary

Words and expressions: *backstage, go on tour, interviewer, limousine, manager*

Before class

- Copy and cut Resources 32A (page 158) and 32B (page 159).
- Bring to the lesson the Ss' pieces of paper you collected at the end of Lesson 28, Exercise 8 (Exercise 2).

Exercise 1

- Read out the first sentence of the text to the class.
- Ss work in pairs, completing the text. Tell Ss not to look back at Unit 28, but to see how much they can remember.
- Check Ss' answers by asking individuals to read out the sentences.

> **Answers**
> 2 music   3 keyboard   4 gig

Presentation

Exercise 2

- Give back to the Ss their papers from Unit 28 with their ideas for the ending of the story.
- Ss tell the class how they thought the story would continue. They can see how many different ideas they had. Ss can find out if any of their ideas are correct as they listen to the recording.
- Ask Ss to look at the picture and say what is happening.
- Play the recording twice for Ss to listen and read the text.
- Ask Ss if their own ideas for the ending of the story were correct. Ask them if they think the ending here is better than their own ideas.

Comprehension

Exercise 3

- Ss do the exercise working individually and referring back to the text in Exercise 2.
- Ss can compare answers in pairs before checking answers as a class.
- Check Ss' answers by asking pairs of Ss to read out the questions and answers.

> **Suggested answers**
> 1 She saw *The Streetboys* on TV.
> 2 at the Haven Club
> 3 go on tour
> 4 They were too expensive.
> 5 *The Streetboys'* manager
> 6 Ruth
> 7 by limousine
> 8 Lisa

Language box

too + adjective/adverb + infinitive
not + adjective/adverb + *enough* + infinitive

- Read out the sentences in the box to the class and point out the two sentence structures with *too* and *not … enough*.
- Draw Ss' attention to the meaning of these two sentences:
  'It was raining too hard to go out.' (= It was raining so they couldn't go out.) and
  'The tickets will be too expensive to buy.' (= The tickets will be expensive so we can't buy them.)

Extension

- Ask Ss to complete the two sentences using *early* and *late* for this situation: the film started at 7.00 p.m. and Carol arrived at 7.15 p.m.:
  1 'Carol didn't arrive … to see the beginning of the film.'
  2 'Carol arrived … to see the beginning of the film.'

Practice

Exercise 4

- Read out the sentences in question 1 to the class.
- Ss complete the exercise working individually.
- They can compare answers in pairs before checking answers as a class. Check Ss' answers by asking individuals to read out the sentences.

> **Answers**
> 2 too expensive to buy
> 3 good enough to be a hit
> 4 hard enough to play well
> 5 too excited to sleep
> 6 too badly to be a pop star

Writing Skills: story

- Ask Ss what sort of stories they like to read (in English or in their first language), e.g. adventure, travel, historical, romantic or detective. Ask Ss what makes a good story for them, e.g. fast action, interesting characters, good plot.
- Read out the advice in the Writing Skills box.

Exercise 5

- Give Ss time to read the first part of the story again (Unit 28).
- Ask Ss to look at the first picture as one of them reads out the text under the picture. Refer Ss back to the advice in Writing Skills:
  'Set the scene and describe the characters.'
  Elicit one or two sentences from the class to begin the story, e.g.:
  'Lisa Long and *The Streetboys* (Ricky, Dave, Frankie, Andy and Steve) went to the same youth club. Lisa's father allowed the boys to practise in his music shop.'
- Ask Ss to work in pairs, making notes and writing down useful vocabulary for pictures 2 and 3. Go round and monitor the activity, helping with vocabulary, if necessary.
- Ss work individually, writing the paragraphs for the last two pictures. Go round and monitor the activity, pointing out any errors to be corrected.
- Ss then form pairs or groups of three and read each other's stories.
- Some of the Ss can read out one of their paragraphs for the class to hear.

Exercise 6

- Read out the example sentences to the class and elicit suggestions for completing the second sentence.
- Give Ss time to plan and think about how they are going to tell the story from Lisa's point of view.
- Ss work in pairs or groups of three, taking turns to tell the story. Go round and monitor the activity. Make a note of any general points to mention to the class afterwards, but do not interrupt Ss' fluency.

Extension

- Give Ss more practice in narrating stories by asking them to work in pairs or groups of three and tell the story from the point of view of Ricky, one of the agents or Mr Long.

Resource 32 (pages 158–159)

Interaction: whole class
Exercise type: matching
Aim: to practise *too* + adjective/adverb, *not* + adjective/adverb + *enough*

- Divide the class into estate agents and house buyers, with a maximum of eight estate agents. The other Ss should work in pairs. In this way up to twenty-four Ss will be taking part in the activity at the same time. Give the pictures of houses (Resource 32B) to the estate agents. Each of them should get a minimum of at least one picture; if the group is small, up to three pictures. Avoid giving descriptions of similar houses to the same agent. The house buyers receive the description of the house they want to buy.
- House buyers go to an estate agent. You could arrange the classroom so that the estate agents are seated by their tables and the buyers rotate and visit them. The agents have to do everything they can to sell their house(s). The buyers should only buy the house that fulfils all the requirements described in their card. They shouldn't show their card to the estate agents. If you wish, elicit an example of the target structure (*It's too expensive for us.*, etc.).
- If the first estate agent does not have the house the buyers need, the buyers have to go to another one.
- The activity goes on until all buyers have bought the houses they want.

Activity Book Answers
Language Diary
2
1 too, No   2 enough, No
Exercise 1
2 backstage   3 manager   4 tour   5 interviewer
Exercise 2
2 f   3 b   4 a   5 d   6 e
Exercise 3
2a They arrived too late to get tickets.
2b They didn't arrive early enough to get tickets.
3a Lisa plays too badly to join a band.
3b Lisa doesn't play well enough to join a band.
4a They talk/are talking too fast for him to understand.
4b They don't talk/aren't talking slowly enough for him to understand.
5a Mr Long is too old to be a pop star.
5b Mr Long isn't young enough to be a pop star.
6a They are/'re too excited to sleep.
6b They aren't tired enough to sleep.
Exercise 4
2 We arrived too late to see the band.
3 She didn't work hard enough to pass the exam.
4 I didn't run fast enough to win.
5 They are too young to see that film.
Exercise 5
2 A   3 A   4 C   5 B   6 C

Revision 8

Vocabulary

Exercise 1

- Read out the example clue and answer to the class.
- Ss complete the crossword working in pairs, if you wish.
- Check Ss' answers by asking pairs of Ss to ask and answer:
  'What's (six across)?' 'It's serious (S E R I O U S).'

> **Answers**
> Down: 2 disgusting   5 ordinary   8 smooth
> Across: 3 ill   4 wrong   6 serious   7 delicious
> 9 fizzy

Exercise 2

- Ask one of the Ss to read out the example in sentence 1.
- Ss complete the exercise working individually.
- Check Ss' answers by asking individuals to read out the sentences.

> **Answers**
> 2 ed   3 ed   4 ing   5 ed   6 ed, ing   7 ing

Exercise 3

- Read out the matched pair to the class.
- Ss complete the exercise working individually.
- After checking Ss' answers, ask them to make sentences containing the expressions 1–4.

> **Answers**
> 2 a   3 d   4 c

Pronunciation chant

Exercise 4

- Play the recording once for Ss to listen and read the text.
- Play it again for Ss to listen and repeat.
- Ss practise saying the chant and saying the role of each of the two boys. Go round and monitor the activity.

Grammar

Exercise 5

- Give Ss time to read through the words in both boxes.
- Ask two Ss to read out the example sentences.
- Elicit one or two more sentences from the class, using the words in the boxes.
- Ss work in pairs, making as many sentences as they can about the two men. Go round and monitor the activity, paying particular attention to comparative structures.
- Check Ss' answers by asking each pair in turn to read out one of their sentences.

> **Suggested answers**
> Both men are fat.
> Frankie is shorter than/isn't as tall as Joe.
> Frankie's clothes are smarter than Joe's (clothes).
> Joe sings more loudly than/doesn't sing as quietly as Frankie.
> Joe sings better than Frankie./Frankie doesn't sing as well as Joe./Joe doesn't sing as badly as Frankie.
> Joe's songs are different from Frankie's (songs).

Exercise 6

- Ask one of the Ss to read out the example in sentence 1. Draw Ss' attention to the adverb (*badly*) and the verb of sense + adjective (*sounded awful*) in this sentence.
- Advise Ss to read through all the words in the box before they start completing the sentences.
- Ss complete the exercise working individually.
- Check Ss' answers by asking individuals to read out the sentences.

> **Answers**
> 2 early   3 delicious   4 faster   5 later   6 pretty
> 7 horrible   8 carefully

Exercise 7

- Ask Ss to look at the first picture and text. Read out the example answer to the class. Ask Ss if they can make a sentence with *enough* and *thin* for this picture. (*She's not thin enough to get through the door.*)
- Ss complete the exercise working in pairs, if you wish. Tell them they may be able to make two sentences (using *too* and *enough*) for some of the pictures.

> **Answers**
> 2 It's/That film is too frightening to watch.
> 3 He isn't running fast enough to catch the bus./He's too slow to catch the bus./He's running too slowly to catch the bus.
> 4 You're not old enough to drive./You're too young to drive.
> 5 It's raining too hard to go out./It's not dry/sunny enough to go out.
> 6 This is too difficult to do./This isn't easy enough to do.

Exercise 8

- Read out the pair of sentences in question 1. Draw Ss' attention to the comparative expressions *the same as* and *different from*.
- Ss complete the exercise working individually.
- Check Ss' answers by asking individuals to read out the pair of sentences for each item.

> **Answers**
> 2 sings brilliantly
> 3 dance worse than you
> 4 is more exciting than the book
> 5 isn't well enough to go to school
> 6 is too expensive to buy

Fun Time

- Read out the instructions to the class.
- Demonstrate the activity to the class by acting out a 'verb + adverb' yourself, e.g. *write very slowly* on the board or *read a book very quickly/quietly*.
- Ss may like to act out their 'verb + adverb' for their partner or small group before acting it for the class to guess.

▐▐▐➡ Check Yourself Units 29–32 – Activity Book page 80

▐▐▐➡ Check Units 29–32 – Teacher's Book page 118

▐▐▐➡ Language Tests A/B Units 29–32 – Test Book pages 34–37

Reading Corner

Lesson objectives

Skills

To practise reading and sequencing paragraphs in a
story
To talk about a film you have seen or a book you
have read
To practise matching visuals with a listening text
To complete a written review
To write about a famous book for your country
To make a display about a famous film

Key vocabulary

key, magical, robin, secret, wall

Background information

The Secret Garden was written by Frances Hodgson
Burnett (1849–1924). It was published in 1911. It
was made into a film in 1949 and then remade in
1993, this time starring Kate Maberly and Maggie
Smith.
The Lord of the Rings is a trilogy written by J.R.R.
Tolkien (1892–1973). *The Fellowship of the Ring* is
the first part of the trilogy (the other two are *The
Two Towers* and *The Return of the King*). The film,
released in 2001, was directed by Peter Jackson and
starred Elijah Wood, Sir Ian McKellen, Ian Holm
and Christopher Lee.

Before class

- Ss will need large pieces of paper and sellotape or
  glue to fix their pictures for the Project.

 Exercise 1

- Ask Ss to look at the picture. Find out how many
  in the class have either read the book or seen the
  film.
- Ss work in pairs, reading the text.
- Check comprehension by asking:
  'Does Mary live with her parents?' (No. They are
  dead.)
  'Why is she unhappy?' (because she doesn't have
  any friends)
  'What are the names of her two friends?' (Dickon
  and Colin)

Reading

 Exercise 2

- Read out paragraph (A) to the class.
- Advise Ss to read the first sentence of each
  paragraph quickly to see if it could follow on. If
  they think it is the next paragraph, Ss read the
  entire paragraph and check that they are correct.
- Ss work individually or in pairs, if you wish,
  reading the remaining paragraphs and putting
  them in the correct order.

- Play the recording once for Ss to check their
  answers.
- After checking Ss' answers, ask:
  'Where did Mary find the key?' (on the ground
  near the robin)
  'Where was the door to the garden?' (in the wall)
  'Were there any flowers in the garden?' (no)
  'Were there any trees?' (yes)
  'What colour was the grass?' (brown)
  'What did Mary do for the little green plants?'
  (She pulled up the grass round them.)

> **Answers**
> B 4   C 5   D 3   E 2

Speaking

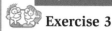 **Exercise 3**

- If possible, group Ss in pairs, with one S in each
  pair who has read the book or seen the film and
  the other S who hasn't.
- Read out the instructions and cues to the class.
- Ss work in pairs, talking about the story and how
  it continues. Go round and monitor the activity,
  helping with vocabulary if necessary and making
  a note of any general points to revise with the
  whole class later.
- Choose two or three Ss who have seen the film or
  read the book to tell the whole class what
  happens in the story.

Listening

 Exercise 4

- Ask Ss to look at the picture and describe what
  they can see.
- Play the recording twice for Ss to listen and
  identify Colin and Dickon.
- When checking Ss' answers, ask them to give
  reasons for their choice.

> **Tapescript**
> The children went to the garden nearly every day.
> Dickon often brought his animals and birds, and the
> children played with them. Colin grew stronger and
> happier. One day he took a spade and he started to
> dig. He only worked for five minutes. But each day he
> worked for a longer time. One afternoon he walked
> round the garden. Dickon and Mary walked next to
> him and the robin sang in the tree. 'The magic is
> making me strong!' Colin cried. 'I'm not going to tell
> the doctor,' he said. 'I'll only tell him when I can run
> really well. And when my father comes home, I'll walk
> into his room. I'll say, "Here I am. I'm very well and
> I'm going to be a strong, happy man."'

> **Answers**
> Colin: the dark-haired boy in the middle
> Dickon: the light-haired boy on the right

Reading

Exercise 5

- Ss work individually, reading the review and then choosing the missing sentence.
- If Ss disagree about the answer, ask them to support their choice by referring back to the review.

> **Answer**
> b

Writing

Exercise 6

- Read out the instructions and example text to the class. Point out that the review begins with the title of the book and the author.
- Elicit suggestions from Ss for completing the two sentences about *Harry Potter and the Philosopher's Stone*.
- Elicit suggestions from Ss for famous books from their own country.
- Elicit suggestions from Ss for expressions to use if they did not like a book, e.g.:
  'I did not like this book because the story was boring/the characters were silly/there were too many characters.'
- Ss write their reviews working individually. Go round and help with vocabulary where necessary and point out any errors to be corrected.
- Ss then form groups of four or five and read each other's reviews.

Project

- Read out the instructions to the class and ask Ss to complete the information about *The Lord of the Rings* (see Background information).
- Ss can work individually or in pairs, making a poster of a famous film. They will need time to find out information and pictures about their chosen film so allow them some homework time to do this.
- Ss then make a display of all their posters. If you wish, they can vote for the best poster.

III➡ Skills Corner 8 – Activity Book page 81

III➡ Skills Tests A/B Units 25–32 – Test Book pages 50–53

> **Activity Book Answers for Skills Corner 8**
> **Exercise 1**
> 2 b   3 c   4 c   5 a
> **Exercise 2**
> Students' own answers

Top Band

A play to act

Objectives

The play gives Ss the opportunity to enjoy speaking English in a communicative way, and to demonstrate to themselves and their audience what they can achieve.

Basic questions

The play can be used in a variety of ways to suit the abilities of the Ss and the time available for practising and performing it in your teaching situation. Here are some questions for you to think about:

1 When should I do the play with my class?

You can work on the play intensively at the end of the course or you can introduce it earlier and have regular practices leading up to the performance. The theme of bands ties in with 'The Streetboys' story beginning in Unit 28.

2 How many students are involved?

The whole class should take part in the play. The number of judges and fans can be changed to suit different class sizes. All Ss should have at least one line to say in the play: the weaker Ss can be judges and fans who have fewer lines. The fans need to be Ss who can sing and dance reasonably well.

3 What props do we need?

The illustration at the beginning of the play (*Students' Book* page 100) shows you how to arrange the room. If you have no stage, mark a section of floor as the stage. Ss who are band members and fans wear their normal casual clothes. The members of each band might like to wear something distinctive, e.g. the same colour shirt/blouse/socks. The judges need to be slightly smarter, perhaps wearing jackets.

The essential props are: a big poster ('Top Band Competition Tonight'), four chairs for the judges (arranged in a semi-circle at one side of the stage), autograph books for the fans, clipboards and paper for the judges, a small CD player, a recording of *Sad and Blue*. The play works well if Ss in the bands use imaginary musical instruments, e.g. guitar, keyboard, drums. However, if there are Ss in your class who want to bring in their own instruments to play, this may provide an additional motivating factor. However, they must play their instruments badly!

4 Do the students have to learn the play by heart?

This depends on the level of your class and how much time you can spend on rehearsing the play. The Ss should learn at least the songs by heart. If there isn't enough time, or your Ss can't memorise the play, they can keep their lines with them throughout the performance.

5 How should I use the recording of the play?

The recording can be used when presenting a section of the play to the class so that Ss listen and hear the correct pronunciation and intonation and stress patterns.

When practising the play later, Ss can listen and repeat their lines after the recording. The bands listen to the recording to hear how to sing 'badly'. When memorising their lines and songs, Ss can mime along to the recording. Ss will also find it helpful to compare a recording of themselves speaking the dialogue and singing the songs with the original recording.

6 Who will be in the audience?

It will be motivating for the Ss to perform their play to a 'real' audience of fellow Ss and Ts and/or parents. If there is time, Ss can produce posters and tickets for the performance.

7 Outline classroom procedure

The time and number of lessons available for practising the play will vary and so these suggested procedures may need amending to suit your own teaching situation.

- Present the play to the class, section by section, letting Ss read the script and listen to the recording. Check Ss' comprehension by asking them to look at the pictures and say who the people are and what is happening.
- Allocate roles and make sure every S has something to say in the play.
- Tell Ss to look at their lines at home and practise saying them to themselves. If Ss are going to memorise their lines, they can spend time in class testing each other on their lines.
- With each band and the fans, practise their songs, one at a time, using the recording until Ss know them by heart. It will help if each band and the fans can meet separately to work out their singing and dancing.
- Give Ss sufficient practice saying their dialogues and singing their songs before they stand up and start acting out the scenes.
- When Ss are ready to start acting the play, go through each scene slowly and carefully with them, ensuring that they know what they should be doing and when.
- Before Ss perform the play to their audience, have at least two 'dress rehearsals' so that Ss are comfortable with their clothes and their props.
- If you have video recording facilities, video the performance for Ss to watch later and assess their performance.

Check
Units 1 – 4

1 Put the words in the correct columns.

> ~~news~~ luggage postcard sightseeing
> film advertisement

TV programmes	Holidays
news	

`5`

2 Put the letters in the correct order.

0 My sister is a **daltenet** singer. talented..

1 *Oasis* is a **mosauf** band. ....

2 Kelly gave me an expensive present. She's very **sureegno**. ....

3 This TV programme is interesting – really **nisaftingac**. ....

4 It was a **catifsatn** party. ....

5 He tried but he wasn't **ulscfsecus**. ....

`5`

Grammar

3 Complete. Use the Present Continuous or the Present Simple.

Jan Come and meet my cousin Maria. She (live) 0 lives..... in Italy but she (stay) 1........... with us for a month.

Harry Hi, Maria. (you / have) 2........... a good time in Britain?

Maria Yes, I am. But life here is very different. In Italy we (often / eat) 3........... in restaurants or cafés, but in Britain you (usually / have) 4........... your meals at home. And it's cold! I (wear) 5........... two jumpers at the moment!

Harry But it (not / rain) 6........... – you're lucky!

`6`

4 Megan's class is going to see a play in London next Saturday. She's talking to her teacher. Complete the dialogue.

A Where are we meeting?

B 0 We're meeting. in the classroom.

A What time 1..................... ?

B The bus is leaving at quarter to eleven.

A Are we having lunch on the bus?

B No, we 2..................... lunch at the theatre.

A When 3..................... London?

B We're leaving London at five.

A When 4..................... back at school?

B We're arriving back at about half past seven.

`8`

5 Complete. Use the correct form of the words in the box. Use the Past Simple or the Past Continuous.

> telephone carry go hear lie move
> say ~~shine~~ ride

The sun 0 was shining. . Kathy and her friend Sophie 1................. their bikes to school when they 2.................. a noise. A little cat 3.................. in the road. It 4(not) ....

'It can't walk!' 5.................. Kathy. 'Oh, the poor little thing!'

They 6.................. it carefully to school and their teacher 7.................. the vet. After three weeks at the vet's, the cat was better, and it 8.................. to live with Kathy!

`16`

Vocabulary	`10`
Grammar	`30`
Total	`40`

Check
Units 5 - 8

Vocabulary

1 Complete. Use the words in the box.

> time race house lunch record rest
> ready line ride title ~~lost~~

0 'Why are you late?' 'Sorry, I got
lost ....'

1 Are you hungry? Would you like to have
.... now?

2 He crossed the .... first and
won.

3 I'd love to have a .... on your
new bike.

4 I'm sure we'll have a great ....
on the trip tomorrow.

5 Let's get .... and go out.

6 The .... has just finished. Sid
is the winner.

7 The runner broke the world
.... for 1000 metres.

8 We moved .... last year and
now we live in London.

9 We're all tired, so let's have a
....

10 Who won the .... 'World's
Strongest Man'?

> 10

Grammar

2 Complete. Use the Present Perfect or the
Past Simple.

A When (you / arrive) ⁰did you arrive ... ?

B We (get) ¹....................... here five
minutes ago.

A How (you / travel) ²....................... ?

B We (come) ³....................... by bus.

A (you / be) ⁴....................... here
before?

B No, we ⁵....................... .

> 10

3 Write sentences. Use the Present Perfect
and *for* or *since*.

0 I / live / here / last April
I've lived here since last April.

1 you / know / Jenny / a long time?
....

2 They / have / a dog / a month
....

3 She / not / phone / two weeks
....

4 I / not / see / her / her birthday
....

5 He / wear / glasses / last year
....

> 10

4 Complete. Use the words in the box.

> for since (x 2) yet just already

0 I've had piano lessons since.... last
summer.

1 'Why don't you want to watch this
programme?' 'I've .... seen it.'

2 He hasn't finished his breakfast
....

3 My hair is wet because I've .... had
a shower.

4 I haven't had a holiday .... ages.

5 I haven't seen you .... last summer.

> 5

5 Complete. Use the Present Perfect, the
Past Simple or the Past Continuous.

0 My mum (just / go) has just gone. out
to the shops.

1 Tom (sleep) .... at the back
of the class when the teacher (shout)
.... at him.

2 (you / ever / swim) .... in
the sea?

3 I (sunbathe) .... when it
(start) .... to rain.

> 5

Vocabulary	10
Grammar	30
Total	40

Check
Units 9 – 12

Vocabulary

1 Complete. Use the words in the box.

> bored careful cool interested lonely
> ~~messy~~ normal shy stupid terrified
> unlucky

0 Please tidy your room. It's too .....messy..... .

1 My friends are all on holiday. I'm
....

2 It was a great lesson. I was very
.... in it.

3 He wasn't nervous – he stayed very
....

4 Nothing special happened yesterday, it
was just a .... day.

5 The opposite of clever is ....

6 I've seen this programme three times –
I'm ....

7 We lost the match yesterday – we were
very ....

8 .... means very, very frightened.

9 Please be .... with that vase – it's
very old and valuable.

10 Ben is .... – he doesn't like talking
to people.

`10`

Grammar

2 Complete. Use *will, won't* or *may / might*.

0 He knows all the answers so he .will.......
pass the exam.

1 He's ill. He .... go to school
tomorrow.

2 I .... have a pizza for lunch,
but I'm not sure.

3 My brother is fifteen now. He ....
be sixteen next year.

4 'What are you doing tomorrow?'
'I don't know. I .... go shopping.'

5 I don't like this T-shirt. I .... buy it.

`5`

3 Complete. Use the First Conditional.
Circle *if* or *when*.

0 John (watch) .will.watch. TV *if* / (*when*)
he finishes his homework this evening.

1 *If* / *When* it (be) .... sunny
tomorrow, we'll have a picnic.

2 I'll have a rest *if* / *when* I (finish)
.... this exercise.

3 I'll be surprised *if* / *when* you (not win)
.... the race.

4 (you / phone) .... me *if* / *when*
you arrive?

5 *If* / *When* I miss the two o'clock train,
I (catch) .... the next one.

`10`

4 Complete. Use the Second Conditional.

0 What (you / do) .would.you.do. if you
(win) .won............. one million pounds?

1 If you (can) .... meet a
famous person, who (you / choose)
.... ?

2 If I (not / have) .... any
homework, I (watch) .... TV.

3 I (go) .... to the concert if I
(have) .... a ticket.

4 Where (you / travel) .... if
you (can) .... go anywhere
in the world?

5 If it (be / not) .... so hot, I
(play) .... football.

`10`

5 Complete.

0 .I'm.not.clever.. . I wish I was clever.
1 I don't speak French. ....
2 .... I wish I could sing.
3 I don't live near a park. ....
4 .... I wish I had a pet.
5 My baby brother cries all the time.
....

`5`

Vocabulary	10
Grammar	30
Total	40

Check
Units 13 – 16

Vocabulary

1 Put the words in the correct columns.

> ~~bus~~ court double-decker escalators
> ~~goal~~ net pitch racket trainers tram
> tube underground

sport	travelling
goal	bus

`10`

Grammar

2 Complete. Use the correct form of *used to*.

A Where (you / live) ⁰*did you use to live* before you came to live here?

B I (live) ¹............................ in London.

A (you / go) ²............................ to school in London?

B Yes, I (travel) ³............................ to school by underground.

A (your parents / have) ⁴............................ a car?

B Yes, they did, but they (not / like) ⁵............................ driving in London.

`5`

3 Circle the correct words.

0 They are in a library. They (*mustn't*) / *don't have to* make a noise.

1 We *mustn't / don't have to* use mobile phones in class.

2 Parents *mustn't / don't have to* go to school.

3 John *mustn't / doesn't have to* go to bed early because it's Sunday tomorrow.

4 I *mustn't / don't have to* tidy my room because my mum's done it for me!

5 I *mustn't / don't have to* forget my homework.

`5`

4 Complete. Use the correct forms of *make* or *let*.

0 (your parents / you) *Do your parents* *let you* .... choose your clothes?

1 (your dad / you) .... stay at home last night?

2 (Our teacher / us) .... work hard next week.

3 (My mum / me) .... do the shopping for her sometimes.

4 (your brother / you) .... ride his bike?

5 (My mum / not / me) .... go to the party tomorrow.

`10`

5 Answer the questions. Use the correct form of *have to* and the answers in the box.

> ~~pay for it~~ take an exam tomorrow
> get up early every day buy new shoes
> go to school walk

0 George has broken the neighbour's window and he's worried. Why?
   He'll have to pay for it............................

1 She doesn't like Mondays. Why?
   ....

2 My sister is always tired. Why?
   ....

3 I was late for school yesterday. Why?
   ....

4 Kate is nervous. Why?
   ....

5 I went shopping last week. Why?
   ....

`10`

Vocabulary	`10`
Grammar	`30`
Total	`40`

Check
Units 17 – 20

Vocabulary

1 Put the words in the correct columns.

> click   cotton   email   glass   ~~height~~   metal
> mouse   printer   size   weight   wood

measuring	computers	materials
height		

`10`

Grammar

2 Complete. Use the Passive Voice in the Present Simple.

0 Bread (buy) is bought.... at the baker's.

1 Cheese (not / sell) .... at the butcher's.

2 Tomatoes (often / grow) .... under glass.

3 These tables (make) .... of plastic.

4 (the computer / connect) .... to the Internet?

5 How often (this website / visit) .... ?

`5`

3 Write sentences or questions. Use the Passive Voice in the Past Simple.

0 The pyramids / discover / about two hundred years ago
The pyramids were discovered about two hundred years ago.

1 The letter / post / last week
....

2 When / the ancient city / discover
.... ?

3 That cartoon / make / last year
....

4 I / not / invite / to the party
....

5 The diamonds / steal / from the bank
....

`5`

4 Rewrite the sentences. Use *by* if you need to.

0 John won the prize.
The prize   was won by John............ .

1 Somebody ate the cake.
The cake   ....

2 My dad washes the car.
The car   ....

3 People don't grow coffee in England.
Coffee   ....

4 Did David record this music?
Was   .... ?

5 Somebody painted the wall.
The wall   ....

`10`

5 Complete. Use the correct form of the verbs in the box.

> go   ~~do~~   have   see   study   use

0 What do you want to do.... when you leave school?

1 Would you like .... lunch?

2 I want .... that new film.

3 He enjoys .... shopping.

4 I'm planning .... French.

5 My brother hates .... the phone.

`10`

Vocabulary	`10`
Grammar	`30`
Total	`40`

Check
Units 21 – 24

Vocabulary

1 Complete. Use the correct form of the words in CAPITALS.

0 Where's 'Flight Information'? INFORM
1 I'll meet you by the '.................' sign. ARRIVE
2 We need to look for the '................. Luggage' sign. LOSE
3 He was very .... ANGER
4 This film is full of .... TERRIFIED
5 I think the story is .... HORROR
6 The plane .... soon. DEPARTURE
7 Do you feel any .... ? PAINFUL
8 Don't worry, you're .... SAFETY
9 I was .... when I heard the news. AMAZEMENT
10 Well done! I'm .... of you! PRIDE

10

Grammar

2 Agree with these sentences. Use *so* or *neither*.

0 I get up at 7.00. So do I.
1 I've seen this before. ....
2 I can't cook. ....
3 I won't eat that. ....
4 I'm going home. ....
5 I had a great time. ....

10

3 Put the words in the correct order.

0 did Max what you give
What did Max give you?
1 card I sent her a
I ....
2 the John pass sugar
Pass ....
3 you the book lend to could me
Could .... ?
4 picture your to show Harry
Show ....
5 your did sell bike him you
Did .... ?

5

4 Join the sentences. Use *who* or *which*.

0 I like the CD. It's number 1.
I like the CD which is number 1.
1 I saw the girl. She was on TV.
....
2 Is that the dog? It bit you.
.... ?
3 These are the children. They helped us.
....
4 My brother's got a friend. He's met Steven Spielberg.
....
5 This is the bank. It was robbed last night.
....

5

5 Write questions. Use *who* or *what*.

0 What did you buy?
I bought **a CD**.
1 .... ?
Jane drew the picture.
2 .... ?
I'm doing **my homework**.
3 .... ?
The window is broken.
4 .... ?
I phoned **Rosie**.
5 .... ?
My parents paid.

10

Vocabulary	10
Grammar	30
Total	40

Check
Units 25 – 28

Vocabulary

1 Put the letters in the correct order to make adjectives. Then match them with words of opposite meaning.

> iraf   ynosi   hefssli   mmonco   eputs
> kitryc

0 not the same for everybody .....fair..........

1 unusual   ....

2 happy   ....

3 quiet   ....

4 generous   ....

5 easy   ....

`10`

Grammar

2 Write advice for each problem. Use the ideas in the box.

> get a job   tell your mum   learn to sing
> not run   send her a card   not buy it

0 My little sister is crying. (should)
You should tell your mum.

1 I need some money. (If I were you)
....

2 I want to be in a band. (should)
....

3 My foot hurts. (If I were you)
....

4 This CD is expensive. (should)
....

5 Ann has just passed an exam.
(If I were you)
....

`10`

3 Complete the questions and answers about Maystock School. Use the correct forms of *allow* and *let*.

> MAYSTOCK SCHOOL
> running ✗   jewellery ✓   mobile phones ✗
> shorts ✓   eat in class ✗   talk in class ✗

0 ..Are...... pupils .allowed. to run inside the building? .No, they aren't..

1 .... pupils .... to wear jewellery? ....

2 .... the teachers .... pupils use mobile phones in class?
....

3 .... they .... pupils wear shorts? ....

4 .... pupils .... to eat in the classroom? ....

5 .... the teachers .... pupils talk in class? ....

`10`

4 Circle the correct words.

0 Did your dad *allow* / *let* you go to the club?

1 Drivers *mustn't* / *shouldn't* drive when the light is red.

2 The baby has eaten all her food. She *must* / *can't* like it.

3 I'd *rather* / *prefer* to relax than work.

4 He's just failed the exam. He *must* / *can't* be happy.

5 My mum *let* / *allowed* us watch TV.

6 Are you *allowed* / *let* to go out?

7 She prefers rap *to* / *than* rock.

8 I *shouldn't* / *'m not allowed* to vote because I'm too young.

9 Congratulations! You *must* / *can't* be proud!

10 I'd *rather* / *prefer* dancing to swimming.

`10`

Vocabulary	10
Grammar	30
Total	40

Check

Units 29 – 32

Vocabulary

1 **Write the opposites.**

0 bored   i n t e r e s t e d
1 ill   _ _ _ _
2 rough   _ _ _ _ _ _
3 hard   _ _ _ _
4 disgusting   _ _ _ _ _ _ _ _ _
5 wrong   _ _ _ _ _

   5

2 **Circle the correct words.**

0 What a great lesson! It was really *interested* / *interesting.*
1 She's *excited* / *exciting* because it's her birthday.
2 I was *amazed* / *amazing* when I opened my present.
3 Do you think History is *bored* / *boring*?
4 I'm not *interested* / *interesting* in Art.
5 I'm going to bed. I've had a *tired* / *tiring* day.

   5

Grammar

3 **Complete. Use the correct form of the word in brackets.**

0 I like all those shops, but that one is *the best* . (good)
1 A bicycle is .... than a skateboard. (expensive)
2 An elephant is .... than a lion. (big)
3 Harry swims really .... (good)
4 I get up .... than you. (early)
5 I walk .... than you. (slow)
6 I worked very .... (hard)
7 Is History .... than Geography? (useful)
8 The Nile is .... river in the world. (long)
9 We're all bad cooks, but I'm .... ! (bad)
10 Who can run .... , John or Frank? (quick)

   10

4 **Circle the correct words.**

0 Sophie doesn't dance as well *as* / *like* you.
1 Do I look *as* / *like* my sister?
2 Does he dance as badly *as* / *than* you?
3 He worked very *careful* / *carefully*.
4 I can cook *better* / *well* than you.
5 I'm *too* / *enough* poor to buy that bike.
6 I'm *very* / *too* young to drive a car.
7 That was *a* / *the* most boring film in the world.
8 That is the *most* / *more* interesting book in the library.
9 The sweets taste *like* / *as* fruit.
10 The picture looks *nice* / *nicely*.

   10

5 **Rewrite the sentences. Use the words in brackets.**

0 His bike isn't the same as yours. (different)
His bike is different from yours.
1 Claire is clever and Sally is too. (are)
Both ....
....
2 Ken is as old as James. (age)
Ken is ....
....
3 I can't get a job because I'm too young. (enough)
I'm ....
....
4 You get up earlier than me. (early)
I ....
....
5 Dave is the same weight as Tom. (heavy)
Dave ....
....

   10

Vocabulary	10
Grammar	30
Total	40

Check tests answer key

Units 1–4
Exercise 1
TV programmes: film, advertisement
Holidays: luggage, postcard, sightseeing
Exercise 2
1 famous   2 generous   3 fascinating
4 fantastic   5 successful
Exercise 3
1 is staying   2 Are you having
3 often eat   4 usually have
5 'm/am wearing   6 isn't raining
Exercise 4
1 is the bus leaving?
2 're/are having
3 are we leaving
4 are we arriving
Exercise 5
1 were riding   2 heard   3 was lying
4 wasn't moving   5 said   6 carried
7 telephoned   8 went

Units 5–8
Exercise 1
1 lunch   2 line   3 ride   4 time
5 ready   6 race   7 record   8 house
9 rest   10 title
Exercise 2
1 got   2 did you travel   3 came
4 Have you been   5 haven't
Exercise 3
1 Have you known Jenny for a long
time?
2 They've/have had a dog for a month.
3 She hasn't phoned for two weeks.
4 I haven't seen her since her birthday.
5 He has worn glasses since last year.
Exercise 4
1 already   2 yet   3 just   4 for   5 since
Exercise 5
1 was sleeping, shouted
2 Have you ever swum
3 was sunbathing, started

Units 9–12
Exercise 1
1 lonely   2 interested   3 cool
4 normal   5 stupid   6 bored
7 unlucky   8 terrified   9 careful
10 shy
Exercise 2
1 won't   2 may/might   3 will
4 may/might   5 won't
Exercise 3
1 If/is
2 when/finish
3 if/don't win
4 Will you phone/when
5 If/'ll/will catch
Exercise 4
1 could/would you choose
2 didn't have/'d/would watch
3 'd/would go/had
4 would you travel/could
5 wasn't/would play
Exercise 5
1 I wish I spoke French.
2 I can't sing.
3 I wish I lived near a park.
4 I don't have a pet.
5 I wish my baby brother didn't cry all
the time.

Units 13–16
Exercise 1
Sport: court, net, pitch, racket, trainers
Travelling: double-decker, escalators,
tram, tube, underground
Exercise 2
1 used to live
2 Did you use to go
3 used to travel
4 Did your parents use to have
5 didn't use to like
Exercise 3
1 mustn't   2 don't have to
3 doesn't have to   4 don't have to
5 mustn't
Exercise 4
1 Did your dad make you
2 Our teacher will make us
3 My mum makes/lets me
4 Does your brother let you
5 My mum won't let me
Exercise 5
1 She has to go to school.
2 She has to get up early every day.
3 I had to walk.
4 She has to take an exam tomorrow.
5 I had to buy new shoes.

Units 17–20
Exercise 1
measuring: size, weight
computers: click, email, mouse, printer
materials: cotton, glass, metal, wood
Exercise 2
1 isn't sold
2 are often grown
3 are made
4 Is the computer connected
5 is this website visited
Exercise 3
1 The letter was posted last week.
2 When was the ancient city discovered?
3 That cartoon was made last year.
4 I wasn't invited to the party.
5 The diamonds were stolen from the
bank.
Exercise 4
1 The cake was eaten.
2 The car is washed by my dad.
3 Coffee isn't grown in England.
4 Was this music recorded by David?
5 The wall was painted.
Exercise 5
1 to have   2 to see   3 going
4 to study   5 using

Units 21–24
Exercise 1
1 Arrivals   2 Lost   3 angry   4 terror
5 horrible   6 departs   7 pain   8 safe
9 amazed   10 proud
Exercise 2
1 So have I.   2 Neither can I.
3 Neither will I.   4 So am I.
5 So did I.
Exercise 3
1 sent her a card
2 John the sugar
3 you lend the book to me
4 your picture to Harry
5 you sell him your bike

Exercise 4
1 I saw the girl who was on TV.
2 Is that the dog which bit you?
3 These are the children who helped us.
4 My brother's got a friend who has met
Steven Spielberg.
5 This is the bank which was robbed
last night.
Exercise 5
1 Who drew the picture?
2 What are you doing?
3 What is broken?
4 Who did you phone?
5 Who paid?

Units 25–28
Exercise 1
1 common   2 upset   3 noisy   4 selfish
5 tricky
Exercise 2
1 If I were you, I'd get a job.
2 You should learn to sing.
3 If I were you, I wouldn't run.
4 You shouldn't buy it.
5 If I were you, I'd send her a card.
Exercise 3
1 Are pupils allowed to wear jewellery?
Yes, they are.
2 Do the teachers let pupils use mobile
phones in class?   No, they don't.
3 Do they let pupils wear shorts?   Yes,
they do.
4 Are pupils allowed to eat in the
classroom?   No, they aren't.
5 Do the teachers let pupils talk in
class?   No, they don't.
Exercise 4
1 mustn't   2 must   3 'd rather   4 can't
5 let   6 allowed   7 to
8 'm not allowed   9 must   10 prefer

Units 29–32
Exercise 1
1 well   2 smooth   3 soft/easy
4 delicious   5 right
Exercise 2
1 excited   2 amazed   3 boring
4 interested   5 tiring
Exercise 3
1 more expensive   2 bigger   3 well
4 earlier   5 more slowly   6 hard
7 more useful   8 the longest
9 the worst   10 more quickly
Exercise 4
1 like   2 as   3 carefully   4 better
5 too   6 too   7 the   8 most   9 like
10 nice
Exercise 5
1 Both Claire and Sally are clever.
2 Ken is the same age as James.
3 I'm not old enough to get a job.
4 I don't get up as early as you.
5 Dave is as heavy as Tom.

Resource 1A

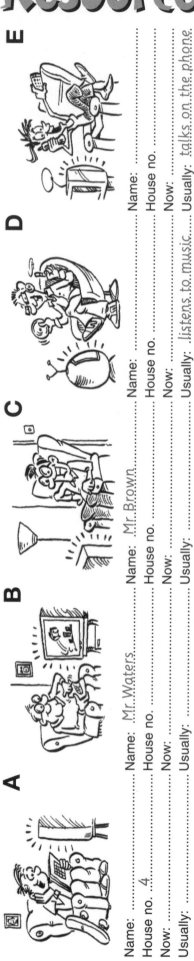

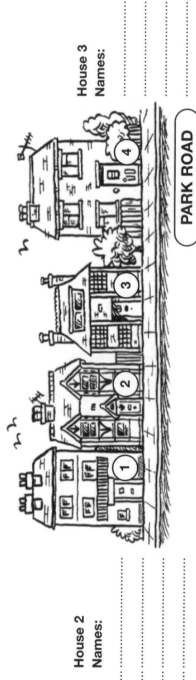

A

Name: ....
House no. ... 4 ....
Now: ....
Usually: ....

B

Name: ... Mr. Waters. ...
House no. ....
Now: ....
Usually: ....

C

Name: ... Mr. Brown. ...
House no. ....
Now: ....
Usually: ... listens. to. music. ...

D

Name: ....
House no. ....
Now: ....
Usually: ... talks. on. the. phone. ...

E

F

Name: ....
House no. ... cartoon. .....
Now: ....
Usually: ....

G

Name: ....
House no. ... documentary. ...
Now: ....
Usually: ....

H

Name: ....
House no. ....
Now: ....
Usually: ... cooks. dinner. ...

I

Name: ... Sally. ....
House no. ....
Now: ....
Usually: ....

J

Name: ....
House no. ....
Now: ... quiz. ....
Usually: ....

House 1
Names: ....

House 2
Names: ....

House 3
Names: ....

House 4
Names: ....

PARK ROAD

120

Photocopiable

© Pearson Education Limited 2003

Resource 1B

He usually plays basketball but now he is watching a cartoon with his wife Sally. They live at number 1.

Sally usually goes to the cinema but now she is watching a TV programme with her husband, John. They live at number 1.

Mrs Waters usually goes for a walk but now she is watching a documentary about the richest people in the world.

Mr Waters usually works in the garden but now he is watching a documentary about the richest people in the world.

Chris Waters usually listens to music but now he is watching a TV programme with his parents. He lives at number 2.

Emma lives at number 3. She usually talks on the phone but now she is watching a soap.

Mrs Brown usually cooks dinner in the evening but now she is watching a very interesting quiz.

Mr Brown usually reads newspapers in the evening but now the whole family are watching a quiz.

Tim Brown lives at number 4. He usually reads books but now he is watching a quiz with his parents and sister.

Sue Brown is a very good student. She usually does her homework every night but now she is watching a quiz with her family.

 © Pearson Education Limited 2003

Resource 2

Harry's Week

Monday	Basketball training.
Tuesday	
Wednesday	
Thursday	
Friday	
Saturday	
Sunday	

Harry's Week

Monday	
Tuesday	Meet Claire and write an article for 'Crazy Reporters'.
Wednesday	
Thursday	
Friday	
Saturday	
Sunday	

Harry's Week

Monday	
Tuesday	
Wednesday	No school! Trip to the Natural History Museum.
Thursday	
Friday	
Saturday	
Sunday	

Harry's Week

Monday	
Tuesday	
Wednesday	
Thursday	Visit grandparents.
Friday	
Saturday	
Sunday	

Harry's Week

Monday	
Tuesday	
Wednesday	
Thursday	
Friday	Cinema with Dan, film 'Billy Elliot'.
Saturday	
Sunday	

Harry's Week

Monday	
Tuesday	
Wednesday	
Thursday	
Friday	
Saturday	Help Mum with shopping / tidy up my room.
Sunday	

Harry's Week

Monday	
Tuesday	
Wednesday	
Thursday	
Friday	
Saturday	
Sunday	Dad's birthday – big garden party at home.

Resource 3

Name: Leonardo Da Vinci (1452–1519)
Nationality: Italian
Clue: He was a famous painter, scientist and inventor. He painted the 'Mona Lisa' and 'The Last Supper'. He also designed and invented many machines, for example a prototype of a helicopter.

Name: Albert Einstein (1879–1955)
Nationality: German and American
Clue: He was one of the most intelligent people in the world. He was a genius, scientist and mathematician. He didn't learn to speak until he was eight.

Name: Marie Skłodowska-Curie (1867–1934)
Nationality: Polish
Clue: She was a famous scientist. She discovered radioactivity and radium. Her husband was French and he was also a famous scientist. She was the first woman to win the Nobel Prize twice.

Name: Christopher Columbus (1451–1506)
Nationality: Italian
Clue: He was a sailor and explorer. He discovered America in 1492. One of the South American countries is named after him.

Name: Mother Teresa (1910–1997)
Nationality: Albanian
Clue: She lived in India, and helped the sick and the poor there. She won the Nobel Peace Prize in 1979.

Name: Elvis Presley (1935–1977)
Nationality: American
Clue: He was called 'The King of Rock and Roll'. People from all over the world still listen to his songs and his beautiful voice. He lived in Memphis. There is a museum there now.

Name: Wolfgang Amadeus Mozart (1756–1791)
Nationality: Austrian
Clue: He was one of the most talented classical composers. He wrote famous operas, e.g. *Don Giovanni* and *The Magic Flute*. He could play the piano when he was three and started composing when he was five.

Name: Frederic Chopin (1810–1849)
Nationality: Polish
Clue: He was a famous pianist. He composed a lot of piano pieces based on Polish traditional music. He composed his first piece of music when he was seven.

Name: William Shakespeare (1564–1616)
Nationality: English
Clue: He was the best English writer in history. He lived in Stratford-upon-Avon. He wrote thirty-seven plays, including *Romeo and Juliet*, *Hamlet* and *Macbeth*.

Name: Princess Diana (1961–1997)
Nationality: British
Clue: She was Princess of Wales, wife of Prince Charles. She had two children, William and Harry. She was a kindergarten teacher before she married Prince Charles.

Name: ....
Nationality: ....
Clue: ....

Name: ....
Nationality: ....
Clue: ....

Name: ....
Nationality: ....
Clue: ....

Name: ....
Nationality: ....
Clue: ....

Resource 4

It happened yesterday morning. I got up very late.

I was eating breakfast in a hurry when I heard a knock at my door.

I opened the door but there was nobody there.

Suddenly I saw a nice box next to my door.

I wanted to see what was inside.

When I was opening the box a little kitten jumped out of it.

I hate cats and I was already late for work.

I caught the kitten and put it back into the box.

I put the box next to my neighbour's door,

knocked at the door and escaped.

While I was working in the office, Sally rang.

She was talking about her cats. She has hundreds of them!

I lied to her as usual and told her that I love cats too.

When I came back home from work my neighbour came to see me.

He said: 'We found this box at our door today.

It must be for you, look there is a note inside.'

Dear Harry,
Your dreams came true!
Love, Sally

I know what you are going to say now: 'Honesty is the best policy.'

Resource 5

Use the verb forms, A or B, to make pairs of correct sentences below.
Underline the words or phrases which helped you to make the right choice.

1   I .... a lot of photos.
2   I .... a lot of photos yesterday.
   A   took
   B   have taken

3   When .... your friend Carl?
4   .... my friend Carl before?
   A   did you meet
   B   have you met

5   .... your aunt last week?
6   .... your aunt?
   A   Did you visit
   B   Have you ever visited

7   This is the most fantastic place we ....
8   This is the most fantastic place we .... last year.
   A   went to
   B   have ever been to

9   My daughter was with me and she .... a minute ago!
10 My daughter .... ! Where is she?
   A   disappeared
   B   has disappeared

11 I .... Leeds Castle before.
12 I .... Leeds Castle on our last school trip.
   A   didn't see
   B   have never seen

13 We .... a nice restaurant and had lunch there.
14 We .... a nice restaurant. Let's have lunch there.
   A   found
   B   've found

15 Oh dear! I .... my bag!
16 It was a terrible day yesterday. I.................. my bag.
   A   lost
   B   've lost

17 *Harry Potter and the Philosopher's Stone* was on TV last night.
   .... it?
18 .... *Harry Potter and the Philosopher's Stone*?
   A   Did you see
   B   Have you seen

Resource 6

DO HOMEWORK

SEND A POSTCARD

WRITE A BOOK

TIDY UP

HAVE A SHOWER

WAKE UP

WAKE UP

FIND A MUSEUM

DO THE SHOPPING

FIND

FALL OFF

WIN

READ

HAVE LUNCH

HAVE LUNCH

MEET A FAMOUS PERSON

PASS AN EXAM

DRINK TEA

Resource 7

1 Read the sentences about Emma. Write sentences which will link her past and present. Use the Present Prefect tense and *since* or *for*.

PAST		PRESENT
PAST SIMPLE	**PRESENT PERFECT**	**PRESENT SIMPLE**
1 Emma was born in Cambridge in 1992.	She has lived in Cambridge since 1992.	She lives in Cambridge.
2 Emma started violin lessons in 1997.		She loves playing the violin.
3 Emma started school in 1998.		She goes to school.
4 Emma last watched television last month.		She doesn't like watching television.
5 In 2001 Emma started summer classes in dancing.		She attends summer classes in dancing.
6 Emma met Jo in her first year of school in 1998.		She has a very good friend. Her name is Jo.
7 Her mum bought her a cat in 1999 and a dog in 2000.		She has a dog and a cat. They are very good friends.

2 Write similar sentences about yourself.

 © Pearson Education Limited 2003

Resource 8

just	never	yesterday	in 2000
already	for	last week	when I was five
yet	since	an hour ago	on Sunday
ever	while	ages ago	last year
last Tuesday	at twelve o'clock yesterday	when you rang	when I saw you
two days ago	last month	in 1984	when

Resource 9A

Questionnaire A

	I			My partner		
	will	may/might	won't	will	may/might	won't
1 go to university						
2 speak English fluently						
3 learn to drive						
4 fall in love						
5 get married						
6 have children						

Questionnaire B

	I			My partner		
	will	may/might	won't	will	may/might	won't
7 write a book						
8 be on TV						
9 travel abroad						
10 play a sport for my country						
11 live abroad						
12 become a millionaire						

Resource 9B

Students A and B

	We will	We won't	We may/might
1 go to university			
2 speak English fluently			
3 learn to drive			
4 fall in love			
5 get married			
6 have children			
7 write a book			
8 be on TV			
9 travel abroad			
10 play a sport for my country			
11 live abroad			
12 become a millionaire			

Resource 10

I'll tell her.	If you get the next question right,	I'll tell her.	If you get the next question right,
you'll win.	If you don't hurry,	you'll win.	If you don't hurry,
you'll be late.	If you pass the exam,	you'll be late.	If you pass the exam,
you'll get a certificate.	If you don't want this magazine,	you'll get a certificate.	If you don't want this magazine,
I'll throw it away.	If you give me your address,	I'll throw it away.	If you give me your address,
I'll write to you.	If there is a fire,	I'll write to you.	If there is a fire,
an alarm will ring.	If I don't see you tomorrow morning,	an alarm will ring.	If I don't see you tomorrow morning,
I'll ring you in the afternoon.	If they invite me,	I'll ring you in the afternoon.	If they invite me,
I'll go to the party.	If I have a lot of money next year,	I'll go to the party.	If I have a lot of money next year,
I'll travel around the world.	If the weather is nice,	I'll travel around the world.	If the weather is nice,
we'll go for a walk.	If we walk,	we'll go for a walk.	If we walk,
it will be cheaper.	If I see her tomorrow,	it will be cheaper.	If I see her tomorrow,

Photocopiable   © Pearson Education Limited 2003

Resource 11

Questionnaire A

	You	Why?	Your friend	Why?
1 If you were an animal, what would you like to be?				
2 If you could travel anywhere in the world, where would you go?				
3 If you could be a famous film star, who would you like to be?				
4 If you could speak three foreign languages fluently, which would you choose?				
5 If it was your birthday today, what present would you like to get?				

✂

Questionnaire B

	You	Why?	Your friend	Why?
1 If you were a colour, what colour would you like to be?				
2 If you could live anywhere in the world, where would you like to live?				
3 If you went on a trip to the desert, what three things would you take with you?				
4 If you could see the future, what would you like to know?				
5 If you had more time, what would you do?				

© Pearson Education Limited 2003

Resource 12

Start

like

can

Good Luck! Go forward two spaces.

call

remember

be

Bad Luck! Go to the beginning.

live

go

dance

Good Luck! Make your own sentence!

speak

do

come

can

Bad Luck! Go back five spaces.

laugh

show

paint

Good Luck! Make your own sentence!

have

know

Good Luck! Go forward four spaces.

see

run

win

hurt

rain

Bad Luck! Miss a turn.

sing

Finish

Resource 13A

STUDENT A

1 When Tina was four, she used to walk in her sleep and wake up other people.
2 Tina has a friend, Francis, but they meet only once a week.
3 When Tina was five, she used to have long hair.
4 Tina always comes to classes on time.
5 When Tina was six, she used to be sad and lonely.
6 Jim is good at sport, and he often wins school sports competitions.
7 When Jim was a child, he used to collect model cars.
8 Jim doesn't like eating too much.
9 When Jim was seven, he used to take pictures of people with his toy camera.
10 Jim doesn't have time to read a lot because he has to study hard.

STUDENT B

1 Tina's got a lot of friends and they spend their free time together.
2 When Tina was four, she used to meet her friend Francis every day.
3 Tina doesn't walk in her sleep and she doesn't wake up other people.
4 When Tina started school, she used to be punctual.
5 Tina's got long hair.
6 When Jim was five, he used to be hungry all the time and he ate a lot.
7 Jim likes photography. He enjoys taking pictures of people.
8 When Jim learnt to read, he used to read four children's books every month.
9 Jim has got a big collection of model cars, and he is hoping to get two new ones for his birthday.
10 When Jim was ten, he used to win many sports competitions at school.

Resource 13B

	Name	Does he/she still do this?
Who used to ...		
... be hungry all the time?		
... meet his/her friend every day?		
... read a lot?		
... walk in his/her sleep?		
... have long hair?		
... be punctual?		
... win a lot of sports competitions?		
... take a lot of photos?		
... be lonely?		
... collect model cars?		

	Name	Does he/she still do this?
Who used to ...		
... be hungry all the time?		
... meet his/her friend every day?		
... read a lot?		
... walk in his/her sleep?		
... have long hair?		
... be punctual?		
... win a lot of sports competitions?		
... take a lot of photos?		
... be lonely?		
... collect model cars?		

Resource 15
People in my life

1

I really like him. We spend a lot of time together. He makes me laugh at his funny stories and he lets me use his bike. I tell him about all my problems and I have one problem with him too! He is a bit lazy and sometimes makes me do his homework!

2

I can't imagine my life without her but she is very strict with me. She makes me tidy my room and wash the dishes. She doesn't let me stay up late and I can't even chew gum at home! She makes me eat things that I really hate. Yesterday she made me eat spinach! But I forgive her because she lets me invite friends home whenever I want.

3

I like him but I'm also afraid of him a bit. He makes me study very hard and gives me a lot of homework. He understands that I am good at some subjects and that I am not so good at the others. He lets me sit with Bruce because we promised to behave well.

4

I argue a lot with him. He sometimes makes me do his housework and even tidy his room. But he is not always bad. He sometimes lets me wear his clothes and use his mobile phone. Once he even let me go to the cinema with him and his friends!

5

She is my favourite woman! She is always very elegant. She lets me use her computer and sometimes teaches me how to drive her car. When my parents are out she lets me stay up late and watch films. There is only one problem, she makes me listen to stories from her youth and I know them all by now!

6

I love him a lot but he is rather strict. He doesn't let me use the phone for too long and he doesn't let me watch too much television. Fortunately, there are good things too. He lets me earn my own money by delivering newspapers. He made me play tennis with him and now it is my favourite sport.

7

I don't complain about her. We argue sometimes but she lets me use her walkman, and sometimes I let her play my guitar. I sometimes make her iron my clothes and she makes me wash the dishes when it is her turn. She sometimes says that I am very silly but that is because I make her laugh at my jokes.

Resource 16

21 December, Saturday

1. buy ...
2. write Christmas cards
3. clean ...
4. decorate Christmas tree in the evening

31 December, Tuesday

1. prepare for the party
2. call ...
3. call a taxi to pick me up at 10 p.m.
4. make ...

1 January, Wednesday

My New Year's Resolutions!
1. study French much harder
2. learn to drive because I'm taking my test in the summer
3. help ... with cooking
4. ... in the morning

STUDENT A

---

21 December, Saturday

1. buy Christmas gifts
2. write ...
3. clean the house
4. ... in the evening

31 December, Tuesday

1. prepare for ...
2. call Mary & Mark
3. call a taxi to pick me up at ... p.m.
4. make a list of New Year's resolutions

1 January, Wednesday

My New Year's Resolutions!
1. study ... much harder
2. learn to drive because ...
3. help Mum with cooking
4. exercise in the morning

STUDENT B

Resource 17

Circle the correct answer.

1 **… is spoken as the first language by the largest number of people in the world.**
   a) English   **b)** Mandarin Chinese **c)** Spanish

2 **… are not eaten by vegans.**
   a) Vegetables   **b)** Eggs   **c)** Nuts

3 **Kilts are worn by …**
   a) Scottish people. **b)** Welsh people.   **c)** Irish people.

4 **Most films are produced in …**
   a) the USA.   **b)** Brazil.   **c)** India.

5 **Seventy percent of the Earth's surface is covered by …**
   a) ice.   **b)** forest.   **c)** water.

6 **In the USA, teachers are given … at the end of the school year.**
   a) sweets   **b)** apples   **c)** flowers

7 **Most rice is grown in …**
   a) China.   **b)** India.   **c)** Korea.

8 **… of Greenland is covered by ice.**
   a) Eighty-five percent **b)** Thirty-five percent **c)** Sixty-five percent

9 **Thanksgiving is celebrated in …**
   a) the UK.   **b)** the USA.   **c)** Canada.

10 **Nokia mobile phones are produced in …**
   a) the USA.   **b)** Japan.   **c)** Finland.

11 **Most tea is produced in …**
   a) China.   **b)** India.   **c)** Russia.

12 **… different alphabets are used in the world.**
   a) Forty-six   **b)** Twenty-three   **c)** Sixty-five

13 **… is measured on the Richter scale.**
   a) A volcano   **b)** An earthquake   **c)** A tornado

14 **Gaelic is spoken in …**
   a) England.   **b)** New Zealand.   **c)** Scotland.

15 **Sushi is made of …**
   a) raw fish.   **b)** raw meat.   **c)** raw vegetables.

16 **Most coffee is produced in …**
   a) Brazil.   **b)** Turkey.   **c)** Kenya.

17 **Hogmanay is celebrated in …**
   a) Ireland.   **b)** Scotland.   **c)** Wales.

18 **… is not eaten by vegetarians.**
   a) Meat   **b)** Cheese   **c)** Butter

19 **Most rock music is recorded in …**
   a) English.   **b)** Russian.   **c)** German.

20 **Rolls-Royce cars are made in …**
   a) Italy.   **b)** the UK.   **c)** Spain.

Resource 18A

1 Who are cars and machines designed by? ....

2 Who are taxis driven by? ....

3 Who are books written by? ....

4 Who are students taught by? ....

5 Who are fruit and vegetables sold by? ....

6 Who are photographs taken by? ....

7 Who are planes flown by? ....

8 Who are eyes tested by? ....

journalist

mechanic

nurse

painter

watch repairer

vet

politician

carpenter

Resource 18B

1 Who are articles written by? ....

2 Who are cars repaired by? ....

3 Who are injections given by? ....

4 Who are walls painted by? ....

5 Who are watches repaired by? ....

6 Who are animals looked after by? ....

7 Who are speeches made by? ....

8 Who is furniture made by? ....

engineer

pilot

greengrocer

teacher

writer

photographer

taxi driver

optician

Resource 19

invented in 1926.	*Jurassic Park* was …	sung by the Beatles.	Rock and Roll music was …
created in the fifties.	The theory of evolution was …	developed by Darwin.	The Statue of Liberty was …
given to the Americans by the French.	President J. F. Kennedy was …	shot in the sixties.	The telephone was …
invented by Alexander G. Bell.	*Hamlet* was …	written by William Shakespeare.	The first hamburgers were …
sold in 1895 in America.	*Harry Potter* was …	written by J. K. Rowling.	The theory of Relativity was …
discovered by Albert Einstein.	Bikes were …	invented in France in 1865.	Radium was …
discovered by Marie Curie.	Books about Sherlock Holmes were …	written by Conan Doyle.	*Shrek* was …
created by DreamWorks.	The opera *Don Giovanni* was …	composed by Wolfgang Amadeus Mozart.	Sandwiches were …
invented by Lord Sandwich.	*Star Wars* was …	directed by George Lucas.	Television was …
directed by Steven Spielberg.	The first jeans were …	made by Levi Strauss in 1873.	*Yellow Submarine* was …

NAME: Tom
AGE:
I REALLY ENJOY:

I HATE:

I'D LIKE MY PARTNER TO BE:

I PLAN:

NAME: Chris
AGE:
I REALLY ENJOY:

I HATE:

I'D LIKE MY PARTNER TO BE:

I PLAN:

NAME: Stephen
AGE:
I REALLY ENJOY:

I HATE:

I'D LIKE MY PARTNER TO BE:

I PLAN:

NAME: Mike
AGE:
I REALLY ENJOY:

I HATE:

I'D LIKE MY PARTNER TO BE:

I PLAN:

NAME: Carl
AGE:
I REALLY ENJOY:

I HATE:

I'D LIKE MY PARTNER TO BE:

I PLAN:

NAME: Peter
AGE:
I REALLY ENJOY:

I HATE:

I'D LIKE MY PARTNER TO BE:

I PLAN:

NAME: Andrew
AGE:
I REALLY ENJOY:

I HATE:

I'D LIKE MY PARTNER TO BE:

I PLAN:

NAME: Mark
AGE:
I REALLY ENJOY:

I HATE:

I'D LIKE MY PARTNER TO BE:

I PLAN:

Photocopiable © Pearson Education Limited 2003

Resource 20B

NAME: *Jenny*
AGE:
I REALLY ENJOY:

I HATE:

I'D LIKE MY PARTNER TO BE:

I PLAN:

NAME: *Mary*
AGE:
I REALLY ENJOY:

I HATE:

I'D LIKE MY PARTNER TO BE:

I PLAN:

NAME: *Lisa*
AGE:
I REALLY ENJOY:

I HATE:

I'D LIKE MY PARTNER TO BE:

I PLAN:

NAME: *Kate*
AGE:
I REALLY ENJOY:

I HATE:

I'D LIKE MY PARTNER TO BE:

I PLAN:

NAME: *Emma*
AGE:
I REALLY ENJOY:

I HATE:

I'D LIKE MY PARTNER TO BE:

I PLAN:

NAME: *Clare*
AGE:
I REALLY ENJOY:

I HATE:

I'D LIKE MY PARTNER TO BE:

I PLAN:

NAME: *Sarah*
AGE:
I REALLY ENJOY:

I HATE:

I'D LIKE MY PARTNER TO BE:

I PLAN:

NAME: *Christine*
AGE:
I REALLY ENJOY:

I HATE:

I'D LIKE MY PARTNER TO BE:

I PLAN:

So do I.	So do I.	Neither do I.	Neither do I.
So did I.	So was I.	Neither did I.	Neither did I.
So can I.	So can I.	Neither can I.	Neither can I.
So have I.	So have I.	Neither have I.	Neither have I.
So will I.	So will I.	Neither will I.	Neither will I.
So am I.	So am I.	Neither am I.	Neither am I.
So would I.	So would I.	Neither would I.	Neither would I.

I like bananas.	I love chocolate.	I don't watch television very often.	I don't like school.
I went to the cinema yesterday.	I was at the cinema yesterday.	I didn't have breakfast today.	I didn't go on the last school trip.
I can swim.	I can play the guitar.	I can't speak Japanese.	I can't drive.
I've done my homework already.	I've been abroad many times.	I haven't read this book yet.	I have never been to Paris.
I will go for a walk tomorrow.	I'll be famous one day.	I won't go skiing with you.	I won't tell you my secret.
I am very tired.	I'm listening to music now.	I'm not hungry.	I'm not sure.
I would like to have something to drink.	I'd like to talk to him.	I wouldn't like to be late.	I wouldn't like to fail the exam.

Resource 22

AUCTION SHEET: Your budget is £5000.00

SENTENCES TO BUY	BOUGHT FOR	BUDGET LEFT
1		
2		
3		
4		
5		
6		
7		
8		
9		
10		
11		
12		
13		
14		
15		

Teacher's sentences

1 The rain alarm will beep if it rains.
2 What are you going to demonstrate to us?
3 She showed her photos to us.
4 If you will press this button, it'll be lovely and warm.
5 Could you pass me the watering can, please?
6 I wouldn't like to buy any of these inventions.
7 Claire likes the shoes with springs.
8 I borrowed him my book.
9 Claris Hunter's invented some amazing things last year.
10 Harry and Claire write reports for *Crazy Reporters*.
11 I think I'll buy these shoes for your birthday.
12 Could you send to me a catalogue?
13 My favourite inventions is musical T-shirt and Fluffy Legs Lamp.
14 Claris is showing her inventions to Harry and Claire.
15 You can check your temperature with a thermometer.

Resource 23

© Pearson Education Limited 2003

Resource 24A

Ask your partner questions to complete the text. Use *who* and *what*.

STOP THIEF!

Last week a thief stole ¹..................... from a shop in the High Street. When he left the shop, ²..................... rang and ³..................... chased him. The thief ran round a corner and hid in some bushes. Unfortunately for him, he ⁴..................... . Then ⁵..................... spoke! 'We looked everywhere,' said policeman Tim Powell, 'but we couldn't find him. We were going back to the shop when I heard a voice. It was saying ⁶".....................".'

Read the text. Answer your partner's questions.

TAKEN FOR A RIDE!

Martin Parsons is a ten-year-old schoolboy. Last week he and his guinea pig, Nibbles, went to town by bus. When the bus conductor asked for 10p for Nibbles' bus fare, Martin was very surprised and upset. Later, the manager of the bus company said 'Sorry', and Martin and his pet had a free ride round town on a special bus. A sign on the bus said 'The Guinea Pig Special'. The bus company also gave Nibbles a free bus ticket for life. Later, Martin said 'Our presents are very nice, but really Nibbles wanted a new wheel.'

Resource 24B

Ask your partner questions to complete the text. Use *who* and *what*.

TAKEN FOR A RIDE!

Martin Parsons is a ten-year-old schoolboy. Last week [1]...................... , went to town by bus. When the bus conductor asked for [2]...................... , Martin was very surprised and upset. Later, [3]...................... said 'Sorry', and Martin and his pet had a free ride round town on a special bus. A sign on the bus said [4]"......................'. The bus company also gave Nibbles [5]...................... . Later, Martin said 'Our presents are very nice, but really Nibbles wanted [6]...................... '

Read the text. Answer your partner's questions.

STOP THIEF!

Last week a thief stole an electronic toy robot from a shop in the High Street. When he left the shop, the alarm bell rang and two policemen chased him. The thief ran round a corner and hid in some bushes. Unfortunately for him, he pressed one of the buttons on the toy. Then the robot spoke! 'We looked everywhere,' said policeman Tim Powell, 'but we couldn't find him. We were going back to the shop when I heard a voice. It was saying "I come from Galaxy Beta".'

Resource 25

NAME: Nancy
AGE: ....
PROFESSION: ....
FAMILY RELATIONSHIP: ....
....

NAME: Jo
AGE: ....
PROFESSION: ....
FAMILY RELATIONSHIP: ....
....

NAME: Dorothy
AGE: ....
PROFESSION: ....
FAMILY RELATIONSHIP: ....
....

NAME: Bruce
AGE: ....
PROFESSION: ....
FAMILY RELATIONSHIP: ....
....

NAME: Helen
AGE: ....
PROFESSION: ....
FAMILY RELATIONSHIP: ....
....

NAME: John
AGE: ....
PROFESSION: ....
FAMILY RELATIONSHIP: ....
....

NAME: Charles
AGE: ....
PROFESION: ....
FAMILY RELATIONSHIP: ....
....

NAME: Kate
AGE: ....
PROFESSION: ....
FAMILY RELATIONSHIP: ....
....

NAME: Mark
AGE: ....
PROFESSION: ....
FAMILY RELATIONSHIP: ....
....

Resource 26

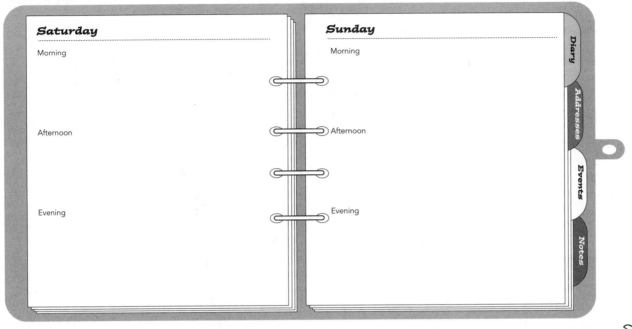

Saturday		Sunday
Morning		Morning
Afternoon		Afternoon
Evening		Evening

Diary · Addresses · Events · Notes

A

You would like to:

- play cards
- go cycling
- go to the cinema
- play football
- go to the disco
- listen to music
- go for a picnic
- sleep late and read in bed
- go to the museum
- play tennis

You don't want to:

- visit Emily
- play computer games
- build a tree house
- make pizza

B

You would like to:

- go cycling
- go to the cinema
- visit Emily
- go to the disco
- visit the castle
- make pizza
- go for a picnic
- sleep late and read in bed
- play tennis
- watch TV

You don't want to:

- go to the museum
- go to the zoo
- go fishing
- visit Mark and Rob

C

You would like to:

- play computer games
- go cycling
- go to the zoo
- visit Mark and Rob
- go to the cinema
- go to the disco
- go for a picnic
- play chess
- sleep late and read in bed
- play tennis

You don't want to:

- play cards
- watch TV
- sunbathe at the seaside
- go riding

D

You would like to:

- sunbathe at the seaside
- go cycling
- go riding
- go to the cinema
- build a tree house
- go for a picnic
- sleep late and read in bed
- go fishing
- play tennis
- go to the disco

You don't want to:

- listen to music
- visit the castle
- play chess
- play football

You have problems with English grammar, especially with present tenses. You can't remember when to use them and you confuse the Present Simple with the Present Continuous.

You have problems with writing in English. You make a lot of spelling mistakes.

You have problems with speaking in English. You usually don't say anything during the lessons and when you were on a holiday abroad last year you couldn't say a word.

You have problems with English grammar, especially with tenses. You can't remember when to use them and you confuse the Present Perfect with the Past Simple.

You have problems with listening tasks. You think that the speakers talk too fast. You usually take notes when you are listening to the recording but later you can't answer the questions about the listening task.

You have problems with writing in English. Your teacher says your essays are very difficult to read and that they are just one big text. You also have problems with using linking words.

You have problems with reading exercises. It takes you a long time to do them, especially if there are a lot of new words in these texts.

You have problems with speaking in English. Your teacher says that you sound rude. You usually give very short answers – 'Yes/No' – to all questions and when you don't understand something you just say 'Repeat'.

You have problems with remembering new words. You understand them when your teacher explains them during the lesson but then you forget them very quickly and you never use new words in your homework.

You have problems with understanding idiomatic expressions. You don't know how to find them in a dictionary.

Resource 28

Are your parents very strict?

	YOU	YOUR FRIEND	YOUR FRIEND
1 Are you allowed to watch as much TV as you like? (Yes – 10 points; No – 0 points)			
2 Are you made to do your homework every night? (Yes – 0 points; No – 10 points)			
3 Do your parents let you wear what you want? (Yes – 10 points; No – 0 points)			
4 Are you allowed to go out as often as you want? (Yes – 10 points; No – 0 points)			
5 Do your parents let you have parties at home? (Yes – 10 points; No – 0 points)			
6 Are you made to get home early? (Yes – 0 points; No – 10 points)			
7 Are you allowed to have lots of pocket money? (Yes – 10 points; No – 0 points)			
8 Are you allowed to spend your free time the way you want? (Yes – 10 points; No – 0 points)			
9 Do your parents let you use a mobile phone? (Yes – 10 points; No – 0 points)			
10 Are you made to help with the housework? (Yes – 0 points; No – 10 points)			
TOTAL	/100	/100	/100

 © Pearson Education Limited 2003

Resource 29

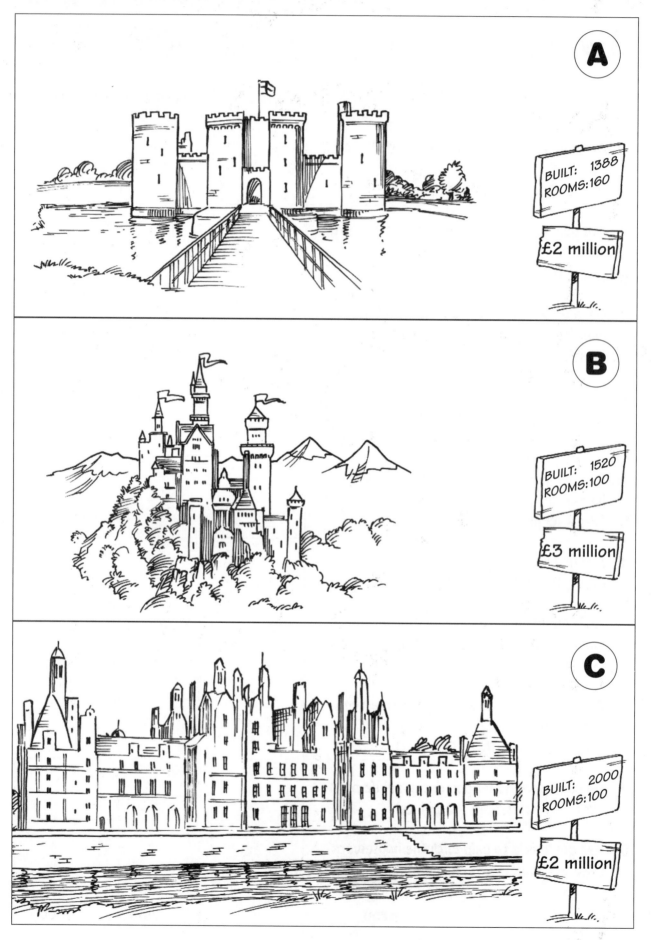

© Pearson Education Limited 2003

Resource 30A

1	2	3	4
5	6	7	8
9	10	11	12
13	14	15	16

Resource 31

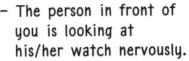

- You are the first person in the queue.
- You are talking on your mobile happily.
- The person behind you is studying hard.

- The person in front of you is talking on his/her mobile happily.
- You are studying hard.
- The person behind you is looking at his/her watch nervously.

- The person in front of you is studying hard.
- You are looking at your watch nervously.
- The person behind you is playing the guitar nicely.

- The person in front of you is looking at his/her watch nervously.
- You are playing the guitar nicely.
- The person behind you is very sad and is waiting quietly.

- The person in front of you is playing the guitar nicely.
- You are sad and you are waiting quietly.
- The person behind you is drinking cola very quickly.

- The person in front of you is waiting quietly.
- You are drinking cola very quickly.
- The two people behind you are playing tennis.

- The person in front of you is drinking cola very quickly.
- You are playing tennis well with the person behind you.

- You are playing tennis badly with the person in front of you.
- The person behind you is eating a hamburger carefully.

- The person in front of you is playing tennis badly with the person in front of them.
- You are eating a hamburger carefully.
- The person behind you is reading a book very slowly.

- The person in front of you is eating a hamburger carefully.
- You are reading a book very slowly.
- The person behind you is dancing brilliantly.

- The person in front of you is reading a book very slowly.
- You are dancing brilliantly.
- The person behind you is eating an ice cream very fast.

- The person in front of you is dancing brilliantly.
- You are eating an ice cream very fast.
- The person behind you is singing a song loudly.

- The person in front of you is eating an ice cream very fast.
- You are singing a song loudly with the person who is standing behind you.

- You are singing a song awfully with the person in front of you.
- The person behind you is looking at everybody angrily.

- The person in front of you is singing a song awfully.
- You are looking at everybody angrily. You are the last person in the queue.

1

You have a very big family (four children) and you are looking for a house which has **four bedrooms**, a **kitchen**, a **living room**, a **bathroom** and a **toilet** and a **small garden**. The house mustn't be too expensive. It can't cost more than **£180,000**.

2

You have a very big family (four children and a dog) and you are looking for a house which has **four bedrooms**, a **kitchen**, a **living room**, a **bathroom** and a **toilet**. It is very important for you that the house has a **big garden**. You can pay up to **£200,000** for the house.

3

You have a very big family (three children) and you are looking for a house which has **three bedrooms**, a **kitchen**, a **living room**, a **bathroom** and a **toilet** and a **small garden**. The house mustn't be too expensive. It can't cost more than **£130,000**.

4

You have a very big family (three children and a dog) and you are looking for a house which has **three bedrooms**, a **kitchen**, a **living room**, a **bathroom** and a **toilet**. It is very important for you that the house has a **big garden**. You can pay up to **£150,000** for the house.

5

You have a very big family (five children and their grandmother) and you are looking for a house which has **five bedrooms**, a **kitchen**, a **living room**, **two bathrooms** and a **toilet**. You don't like gardening and the house doesn't have to have a garden. You are quite rich but the house shouldn't be over **£300,000**.

6

You have a very big family (five children and their grandmother) and you are looking for a house which has **five bedrooms**, a **kitchen**, a **living room**, **two bathrooms**, a **toilet** and a **very big garden**. The house can't cost more than **£310,000**.

7

You have just got married and you are looking for a small flat which has **two bedrooms**, a **living room**, a **bathroom** and a **kitchen**. The flat has to be as cheap as possible and shouldn't cost more than **£80,000**.

8

You have just got married and you are looking for a small flat which has **one bedroom**, a **living room**, a **bathroom** and a **kitchen**. The flat has to be as cheap as possible and shouldn't cost more than **£60,000**.

Resource 32B

four bedrooms, kitchen, living room, bathroom, toilet, small garden: **£180,000**

four bedrooms, kitchen, living room, bathroom, toilet, big garden: **£200,000**

three bedrooms, kitchen, living room, bathroom, toilet, small garden: **£130,000**

three bedrooms, kitchen, living room, bathroom, toilet, big garden: **£150,000**

five bedrooms, kitchen, living room, two bathrooms, toilet, no garden: **£300,000**

five bedrooms, kitchen, living room, two bathrooms, toilet, very big garden: **£310,000**

two-bedroom flat, living room, bathroom, kitchen: **£80,000**

one-bedroom flat, big living room, bathroom, kitchen: **£60,000**

© Pearson Education Limited 2003

Pearson Education Limited
Edinburgh Gate, Harlow,
Essex CM20 2JE, England
and Associated Companies throughout the world.

www.longman.com/friends

The rights of Patricia Mugglestone, Liz Kilbey, Carol Skinner, Elżbieta Leśnikowska and Katarzyna Niedźwiecka to be identified as authors of this work have been asserted by them in accordance with the Copyright, Designs and Patents Act 1988.

ISBN 0 582 81683 1

First published 2003
Second impression 2003

Set in Slimbach 9.5/11pt

Printed in Spain by Mateu Cromo S.A. Pinto (Madrid)

Prepared for publication by Stenton Associates

Illustratiions by Mark Davis

Cover photograph: © Pearson Education/by Peter Lake